A ROSE BY ANY NAME

Also by Douglas Brenner:

Real Art: The Paint-by-Number Book & Kit
Gardening 101 (coeditor)
Gardening from Seed (coeditor)
The Garden Design Book (coeditor)

Also by Stephen Scanniello:

A Year of Roses
Rose Companions
Easy Care Roses (guest editor)
Roses of America (with Tania Bayard)
Climbing Roses (with Tania Bayard)

A ROSE BY ANY NAME

BY DOUGLAS BRENNER
AND STEPHEN SCANNIELLO

ALGONQUIN BOOKS OF CHAPEL HILL 2009

Published by
ALGONQUIN BOOKS OF CHAPEL HILL
Post Office Box 2225
Chapel Hill, North Carolina 27515-2225

a division of
WORKMAN PUBLISHING
225 Varick Street
New York, New York 10014

DESIGN / LAYOUT: ANNE WINSLOW AND JACKY WOOLSEY

Library of Congress Cataloging-in-Publication Data
Brenner, Douglas, and Stephen Scanniello.
A rose by any name / Douglas Brenner and Stephen Scanniello. — 1st ed.
    p. cm.
ISBN-13: 978-1-56512-518-6
1. Roses — Varieties.   2. Roses — Miscellanea.   I. Scanniello,
Stephen.   II. Title.
SB411.6.B74 2009
635.9'33734 — dc22

                                                      2008038292

10 9 8 7 6 5 4 3 2 1
First Edition

To Irene and Richard Brenner
with love and admiration —D. B.

For Dana, always —S. S.

CONTENTS

INTRODUCTION

WHY DOES 'BARBRA STREISAND' share a bed with 'Queen Elizabeth'? And why is 'Sexy Rexy' with them? Because all three are rosebushes. Sooner or later, anyone who orders a florist's dozen stems, plants a bush in the backyard, visits a botanical garden, or just loves flowers—the colors, the scents, the shapes, the textures—is bound to ask how roses got their often quite-peculiar names. Today there are more than fifteen thousand different rose species and cultivars in commerce worldwide. (Thousands more have become extinct, and yet they live on in the texts and illustrations of old nursery catalogs, books, and journals.) Each of these plants has its own distinct name—given, perhaps, by the person who first picked it for a sweetheart, by a botanist who dissected it long ago, by a horticulturist who nurtured it through laborious hybridizing, or by the innumerable others (famous, infamous, or forgotten) who felt a special kinship to a particular flower.

We first planned to tell the stories of only four dozen roses with intriguing histories (they're still the title flowers of our forty-eight chapters), but by the time we'd finished writing, our list had stretched to include more than twelve hundred names. Together, the tales of these names spin a larger narrative about the ways individual people, communities, and cultures identify the living things that matter to them. In the beginning, of course—long before horticultural wizards started tinkering with nature's species—a rose was simply a rose. The Greek *rhodon*; the Latin, Italian, French, and Spanish *rosa*; the German *Rose*; the Dutch *roos*; the Swedish *ros*; and the English *rose* all probably sprang from one primal Indo-European root, *wrdho*, meaning "thorn" or "bramble."

Although the Greek poet Sappho dubbed the rose "queen of flowers" nearly twenty-five hundred years ago, it took centuries for the plant to acquire many other names. Before the late eighteenth century, most roses were raised for medicinal or culinary purposes, not floral beauty, and their names prosaically identified them by use (*Rosa canina*, Latin for "dog rose," because its root supposedly cured rabies; 'Tidbit Rose', because cooks prepared its petals as sweets), anatomy ('Hundred-petaled Rose'), or geographical origin ('Provence Rose'). Other names reflect the flower's long reign as a solemn icon in religion (*R. sancta*), and politics ('The Jacobite Rose'). The fanciful sensuality that has always lurked in gardens had come to the fore by 1824. That's when labels like 'Rosier d'Amour' ("rosebush of love") appeared in Pierre-Joseph Redouté's epic *Les roses,* an illustrated compendium of 169 different plants in the garden created by the godmother of modern rosomaniacs, Empress Joséphine.

A consummate trendsetter, Joséphine swept aside stuffy botanical nomenclature and championed rose names that were fun, chic, flirtatious, romantic, and endearingly personal. Throughout Europe and North America, it became ultrafashionable to have one's name bestowed upon a charming new hybrid. Of course, the nineteenth century also nurtured the flowering of science, technology, and commerce, and rosarians did their part by attempting to systemize plant breeding, naming, and marketing.

Only during the twentieth century, however, did copyrights and patents impose legal restraints on rose names in the United States. Since 1930 the American Rose Society has issued a master checklist called *Modern Roses*, which is updated every ten years or so. And because a catchy name can be the key to successful sales (imagine, for example, if the present-day best seller, 'Knockout', had been given the label initially proposed, 'Razzleberry'), naming rights are fiercely guarded. The perceived need for global control led to the founding in 1955 of the International Cultivar Registration Authority (ICRA) for Roses, a clearinghouse for new names whose regulations are widely observed but not legally enforceable. One ICRA rule sets a maximum of ten syllables and thirty letters or characters, a backlash against earlier long-winded names such as 'Souvenir de la Princesse Alexis Swiatopolk-Czetwertinski' and 'Mevrouw G. de Jonge van Zwynsbergen'. Name duplications are verboten, although a previously registered name can be reassigned if the new rose's grower proves that the original plant is extinct—no simple matter. Throughout this book we have followed the convention of putting registered cultivar names between single quotation marks (e.g., 'American Beauty'). Double quotation marks (e.g., "Corner, Church and Main") indicate a "found" variety—a rose discovered in a garden or cemetery that has yet to be identified by its original name.

As with vanity license plates, anybody can have his or her name officially conferred upon a rose. All it takes is a phone call and a big check (see "A Rose of One's Own," page 154). Major rose wholesalers keep unnamed seedlings in reserve for just that purpose. Other anonymous hybrids stand ready to commemorate—and gain free publicity from—current events and people in the news. Of the yellow hybrid tea 'Mrs. Franklin D. Roosevelt', which made its debut in 1933 after FDR's inauguration, legend has it that the First Lady later remarked, "I once had a rose named after me and I was very flattered. But I was not pleased to read the description in the catalogue: no good in a bed, but fine up against a wall." Although these words are cited on Internet quotation sites as historical fact, we've found no documentary evidence to verify that Eleanor Roosevelt ever said or wrote them.

Apocrypha and faux pas thrive wherever rose names are discussed. In his career as a rosarian, Stephen has committed a few bloopers of his own. He had been working at the Brooklyn Botanic Garden's Cranford Rose Garden for several years before he realized that the rose 'Triomphe de la Guillotine' was really a 'Triomphe de la Guillotière' (a reference to the native region of the plant's French breeder) purchased from a dyslexic nurseryman. Stephen singlehandedly mislabeled a hybrid perpetual 'Earl of Bufferin', when it in fact honors the Irish nobleman Lord Dufferin. During a visit to the home of the English actor and enthusiastic gardener Nigel Hawthorne, Stephen offered to help identify and label his roses. When Hawthorne said of one, "Oh, it's 'Frau Dagmar's Jockstrap' or some such thing," that's exactly what Stephen scribbled on a plastic tag. He didn't get a chance to correctly relabel the plant 'Fru

Dagmar Hartopp' before the jaunty malaprop was read by hundreds of visitors on a National Trust garden tour.

The idea for a book like this one sprouted in Stephen's mind at the Cranford Rose Garden, when he happened to overhear a conversation between a little boy and his father. Only a few roses were then in bloom, and the boy entertained himself by reading each rose label aloud. "Look, Daddy, this one says 'Dolly Parton'! And here's 'Rosie O'Donnell'. Wow! 'Babe Ruth' *and* 'Santa Claus'! How come their names are on these signs?" The man answered with fatherly conviction, "It's because they all gave money to this garden."

If you want to learn how to prune a large-flowered hybrid tea rose like 'Dolly Parton' or quell an infestation of aphids on a miniature like 'Santa Claus', put this book down. But if you want to discover how such plants—along with 'Gourmet Popcorn', 'Tipsy Imperial Concubine', and 'The Stinkbug'—really got their names, read on. You'll soon understand why there isn't a 'Gertude Stein': once you know it by name, a rose definitely isn't a rose isn't a rose.

AMERICAN BEAUTY

T HE STATUE OF LIBERTY first shone her lamp over New York Harbor in 1886, the same year that another national icon, the **'American Beauty'** rose, made a well-publicized debut at a nursery in Washington, D.C. "No flower, except perhaps the tulip during that period of memorable madness in Holland, has ever so seized the popular imagination," an American rose breeder recalled during the 1920s. This glamorous hybrid perpetual had ample charms: dramatically long, sturdy stems; intense fragrance; and large, fragrant blooms in a mauve-tinged pink perfectly keyed to Victorian and Edwardian taste. But it faced stiff competition. By the late nineteenth century, roses had replaced camellias as high society's favorite cut flowers, and growers on both sides of the Atlantic offered a profusion of gorgeous new varieties every season. Many a well-bred 'Madame This' or 'Duchesse de That' could rival the physical allure of 'American Beauty'. What really lifted this

'AMERICAN BEAUTY' IN AN 1896 PAINTING
BY BOTANICAL ARTIST PAUL DE LONGPRÉ

rose above the crowd was a simple yet resonant name that instantly established it as an emblem of republican pride and a byword for feminine grace.

Prominent clubmen toasted 'American Beauty', artists painted it, deb-
utantes carried it to cotillions, stage-door johnnies tossed it at the feet of
chorines, and manufacturers applied its name and image to everything from
corsets to silverware to bicycles. Cashing in on the phenomenon, a string of
nurseries have pushed wannabes into the spotlight. **'Climbing American
Beauty'** and **'White American Beauty'** appeared early in the twentieth
century; **'Red American Beauty'** and **'Miss All-American Beauty'** made
their respective curtseys in 1959 and 1965. The lasting fame of 'American
Beauty' made it the fail-safe cut flower for generations of nervous hostesses,
bashful beaux, and penitent spouses—and an easy target for satire. By the
time a rose and the words *American Beauty* appeared on a 1970 Grateful Dead
record album and in a 1999 Hollywood film with the same title, the flower
had wilted into a byword for disillusionment.

The charisma of 'American Beauty' has turned out to be a lot hardier than
the rose itself—a plant so notoriously finicky (and expensive to cultivate in
the greenhouse conditions it prefers) that by the mid-1930s commercial breeders had largely abandoned it in favor of less demanding blooms. Frustrated
home gardeners gave up on this weakling decades earlier. Hardly anyone
grows 'American Beauty' now, except for rosarians with inexhaustible patience
and a passion for rare antiques.

Nevertheless, people still walk into florists' shops and request American
Beauties (minus the horticulturally correct single quotation marks) by the
dozen. The average consumer regards the name as a brand so familiar that

it's virtually generic, like Band-Aid, Jell-O, or Xerox. Unlike products bearing those trademarks, however, the flowers purchased as American Beauties today are almost always impostors. Those in the florist's cooler are probably scentless hybrid teas harvested on a farm in Ecuador or Colombia; the potted bush tagged 'American Beauty' at the garden center may actually be **'Ulrich Brunner fils'**, a pretty good stand-in because it, too, is a fragrant pink hybrid perpetual dating to the late nineteenth century.

Well before they labeled the plant, however, the term *American beauty* had become a popular phrase with social commentators. During the French Revolution, *La belle américaine* ("the beautiful American") was the affectionate nickname bestowed on Elizabeth Monroe, wife of the U.S. minister to Paris and future president, James Monroe, after she personally intervened to save the marquise de Lafayette from the guillotine. Early nineteenth-century visitors to the United States wrote home about the unique breed of female that had flowered in the young republic. In 1837 Daniel Boll, a Swiss nurseryman who settled in New York City, echoed a conventional theme when he named a miniature rose **'Belle Américaine'**. American men put in their two cents, as well. The New York journalist Junius Henri Browne observed, in "Types of American Beauty," an article published in 1871: "We declare nothing more frequently than that our women are lovely beyond those of any other nation . . . *Les belles Américaines* are famous all over [Europe], and the opinion that every woman here is lovely is almost as common there as that every citizen of this country is uncomfortably rich." In Henry James's *Roderick Hudson*, published the year of the centennial, an Ohioan traveling through Rome refers to a Yankee expatriate as "our great American beauty!" He goes on to say, "I observed her the other evening at a large party, where some of the proudest members of the European aristocracy were present—duchesses, princesses, countesses, and others distinguished by similar titles. But for beauty, grace, and elegance my fair countrywoman left them all nowhere . . . You see more beautiful girls in an hour on Broadway than in the whole tour of Europe."

Sure enough, it was on New York's Great White Way, during the 1880s, that theater playbills proclaimed the vaudeville and comic-opera star Lillian Russell (née Helen Louise Leonard of Clinton, Iowa) "the American Beauty"—an hourglass figure and china-doll features played as big a part in her success as her crystalline voice. In the title role of *An American Beauty*, an 1896 operetta, she was wooed by an English earl disguised as a gardener. Offstage, Russell enjoyed notoriety for her devotion to corn on the cob and poker, and a fondness for jewels that she shared with her frequent companion, the financier James Buchanan "Diamond Jim" Brady. While indulging Russell's appetite for gems, Brady supplied her with enough freshly cut 'American Beauty' roses to pack a theater. Presenting even one 'American Beauty' was always an extravagant gesture. During the winter holiday season of 1898, New York florists sold a single stem for $3.75 (about a dollar more than a carpenter earned in a day). Nicknamed "the Million-Dollar Rose," its per-

GILDED AGE SINGER AND
ACTRESS LILLIAN RUSSELL,
DUBBED "THE AMERICAN
BEAUTY," WITH HER
NAMESAKE ROSES

fume lingers in the Lillian Russell cocktail: one part crème de rose, one part crème de violette, and one part cream.

The next generation of stars might have turned down this rich concoction to preserve the slimmer physique that came into vogue during the early twentieth century, but the flower's attraction certainly had not faded. Florenz Ziegfeld extolled the "long-stemmed American beauties" who sang and danced in his 1910 *Follies*. The painter Ralph Albert Blakelock's drawing of 'American Beauty' appeared seven years later in the *American Art Student*, along with this commentary: "[T]he American Beauty rose stands for America and its beauty . . . [Blakelock] finds something patriotic as well as beautiful in the name of the flower."

When, however, the garden writer Georgia Torrey Drennan proclaimed in 1912 that this bloom was "the rose of roses of American origin," few of her readers could have been aware that Drennan unwittingly perpetuated a myth. In reality, like the Statue of Liberty, 'American Beauty' was created in France, a fact that growers and florists either didn't know or chose to forget. The rose was bred in 1875 by Henri Lédéchaux, who christened it **'Madame Ferdinand Jamin'** after the wife of a fellow nurseryman. Alas for madame, French and English connoisseurs were unimpressed by her namesake flower and largely ignored it. Because meager documentation survives for this early chapter of the plant's life, or its transatlantic crossing, the largely anecdotal history we have is a brambly tangle.

One story holds that in the spring of 1875 President Grant's gardener, James Brady, was amazed to see a strange, lovely pink rose emerge from a mixed bunch of European cuttings he had planted in the White House garden. But

Brady's foreman, George Field, cheated him out of a fortune by quickly propagating the plant on the sly, for mass production at a nursery Field ran with his brother. Other versions contend that the Fields were introduced to the rose by George Bancroft, a historian, statesman, and amateur rosarian, who had either received it in a shipment from his English supplier, Henry Bennett, in 1882 or discovered it amid the inventory of Anthony Cook, a Baltimore nurseryman. Cook later told Georgia Torrey Drennan that the rose wasn't an import at all but a foundling he had raised from a seed of unknown parentage.

In any case, Bancroft came up with the name 'American Beauty', although nobody knows exactly where or when. His credentials were ideal. Descended from a long line of Yankee bluebloods, he wrote the classic ten-volume *History of the United States*, served as secretary of the navy under President Polk, delivered the eulogy at Abraham Lincoln's funeral, and represented the United States on diplomatic missions to Europe. Bancroft honored his best-known maxim — "Beauty is but the sensible image of the Infinite" — by establishing magnificent gardens at his residence in Washington, D.C., and his estate in Newport, Rhode Island. Prominent among the beds was the hybrid tea **'Hon. George Bancroft'**, a tribute to a loyal customer from Henry Bennett.

In their gardens, as in every aspect of life, nineteenth-century Americans strove to measure their accomplishments against Old World standards and, wherever possible, surpass them. The cannily timed release of 'American Beauty' during the tenth anniversary of the U.S. centennial, a festival of national self-congratulation, made every purchase of the rose seem like a pledge of allegiance. The story of the flower's origin came full circle in the late 1880s with an ironic flourish. The prestigious French *Journal des Roses* decreed that in spite of the identical flower colors of 'Madame Ferdinand Jamin' and 'American Beauty', a trained eye could discern differences between the habits of their stems and foliage, indicating that *la française* and *l'américaine* truly were distinct varieties. Modern rosarians shake their heads and smile. For them this is simply one more case of a rose that happens to have multiple names—and the power to represent whatever the beholder wishes to see.

HORTICULTURAL HOAXES

The notorious affair of the "Blue Rose Men" made headlines in New York City in 1869 when a firm of French self-styled horticulturists at a Broadway address advertised imported moss roses of purest azure, a color that hybridizers only dreamed of achieving. Gawkers and covetous gardeners flocked to the store where these marvels were on display in the form of vivid lithographs. The bushes whose flowers they depicted had not yet come into bloom, making purchases of seeds or bushes an act of faith. The scandalous truth emerged after Peter Henderson, the proprietor of a rose nursery in Jersey City and a seed store in Manhattan, purchased several of the blue wonders, only to discover that they were actually a pink-flowered North American species, *Rosa setigera*. Henderson alerted the *New York Times*, which published an exposé, but the French con artists managed to abscond all the same.

"Just a swindle! Why cannot people deal square?" fumed the Bridgeton, New Jersey, hybridizer Richard Bagg in a 1928 letter to the American Rose Society. Bagg had just got wind that his pink tea rose **'William R. Smith'**—which he had named after the president of the United States Botanic Garden twenty years earlier—was currently being sold under a handful of different names. Not only had he failed to get credit or royalties for any of these impostors, the entire scam arose from a personal betrayal. Over the years, unbeknownst to Bagg, a trusted friend had repeatedly sold the "nameless" rose for $500 a pop to four unsuspecting rosarians, none of whom knew about the others. Bagg tracked down the resulting aliases: **'Jeannette Heller'** (for the daughter of a nurseryman in New Castle, Indiana); **'Charles Dingee'** (for the Pennsylvanian founder of Conard-Dingee Roses); **'Blush Maman Cochet'** (adapted from a well-known French variety's name); and **'Maiden's Blush'** (already attached to a much older rose). Bagg's only reward was the satisfaction of exposing this unfortunate ruse.

In 1937 the rosarian Jean Henri Nicolas revealed another "example of intentional fraud that should not be tolerated." This case involved **'Henry Ford'**, a seemingly respectable yellow hybrid tea. Nicolas explained: "The Henry Ford for which this rose was named is not the Detroit automobile man but a mediocrity somewhere in New Jersey who permitted the use of his name, probably for a consideration."

A modern instance of confused identity centers on a hardy climbing rose named **'Sombreuil'** (not to be confused with the cold-sensitive tea rose **'Mademoiselle de Sombreuil'**). In 1959 a "rose specialist" in Mentor, Ohio, began selling plants of 'Sombreuil'—which had been in commerce since at least the late 1940s—as his own new cultivar, **'Colonial White'**, complete with a bogus genealogy. By the 1980s perplexed gardeners had begun to ask why their 'Colonial White' looked and behaved exactly like 'Sombreuil'. An investigation by the Heritage Rose Foundation finally pinpointed the source of this mixup but not the Ohioan's motives. Speculation about that enigma continues to spin long threads of postings, and even hate e-mail, on rose Web sites. Fortunately, though, thanks to greater vigilance throughout the rose world, such scams are increasingly rare.

APOTHECARY'S ROSE

GES BEFORE CHICKEN SOUP attained cure-all status, nature's wonder drug was a rose: *Rosa gallica* **'Officinalis'**. The species name *gallica* reflects its association with France, where Crusaders are said to have brought it from the Middle East; *officinalis* comes from the Latin for "shop" or "pharmacy." Gardeners call it **'Apothecary's Rose'**, because its bud, crimson pink flower, and oval red hip, or fruit, once supplied ingredients for remedies dispensed by apothecaries throughout the Western world.

For the herb gardener in a medieval monastery no less than the clerk in a nineteenth-century drugstore, *R. gallica* 'Officinalis' offered the cure for many a malady. Do you have have a bellyache, sir? A rose cordial should do the trick. Congested sinuses? Fill a cloth bag with powdered rose petals, and hang it around the neck. Premarital jitters? Strew fresh rose petals among your bedsheets. A pallid complexion? Prick a finger with a thorn of the rose, leave a drop of blood under the bush, and a lovely blush will color your cheeks. A troublesome neighbor? Grind rose petals and mustard seed with green woodpecker fat; spread some of this mixture on the rascal's apple tree, and its branches will never again bear fruit.

What English speakers know as 'Apothecary's Rose' goes by **'Rosier de Provins'** in France, after Provins, a town southeast of Paris, where farmers

cultivated this plant as a cash crop from the Middle Ages into the nineteenth century. Louis XIV's royal apothecary, Pierre Pomet, wrote that Provins roses "are most esteemed of any flowers in the whole world, because they are astringent and cordial, strengthen the nerves, and other weak parts of the body." Pomet stressed the potency of fresh petals and cautioned readers to avoid cheaper, less effective rose varieties and products tinted with red dye to disguise a weak solution.

Rose remedies traveled westward to America, too. Colonial governor John Winthrop, writing from Massachusetts in 1631 to his son, about to embark from the mother country, advised: "Bring no provision with you but meale and pease, and some otemeale and Sugar, fruit, figges and pepper, and good store of saltpeeter, and Conserve of redd roses." The last item was the Dramamine of its day.

American druggists, like their European counterparts, pulverized rose petals in mortars, distilled them, and added other substances to yield a panoply of nostrums, elixirs, and potions. Many pharmacies sold rose honey to soothe inflamed tonsils, and rose vinegar to alleviate headaches. Rose poultices were prescribed to stanch wounds; rosewater compresses on the forehead supposedly allayed female hysteria. A potent-sounding "eye water for weak eyes" called for one teaspoon of laudanum (a tincture of opium), two teaspoonfuls of Madeira, and twelve teaspoonfuls of rose water. In his popular book *Dr. Chase's Receipts* of 1865, Detroit apothecary William Chase touted a rose-based cure for male baldness. The formula called for equal parts vinegar of

'APOTHECARY'S ROSE', IN AN 1873 PRINT FROM FRANCE,

WHERE IT WENT BY 'ROSE DE PROVINS ORDINAIRE'

cantharides (a preparation of dried beetles, better known as Spanish fly), cologne water, and rose water. Chase suggested rubbing this solution into the
head twice daily "until the scalp smarts."

Apothecaries, who conventionally labeled storage jars in Latin, didn't need
to translate *R. gallica* 'Officinalis', but gardeners knew the plant by other
names — as they do to this day. Vermonters call it the **'English Rose'**, because bushes survived beside cellar holes in early English settlements, long

after the houses had vanished. Generations of southern Marylanders have handed the flower from yard to
yard as the **'Tulip Rose'**. And Virginians cherish it as
the **'Offley Rose'**, a name with its own tale to tell. During the Revolutionary War, Lucy Grymes Nelson — wife
of Thomas Nelson Jr., signer of the Declaration of Independence and a brigadier general under George
Washington — prepared to evacuate as British troops
advanced on Yorktown. She wouldn't budge, however,
until specimens of her beloved 'Apothecary's Rose' could
be dug up and sent to Offley Hoo, the family estate near
Richmond. The bushes Lucy transplanted there bloomed
faithfully year after year, long after the house burned
down. Those roses eventually disappeared, but slips cut
from them took root at the homesteads of Nelson kin,
and descendants continue to share cuttings with friends.

A VICTORIAN PHARMACY STAPLE, EASTMAN'S EXTRACT
WAS FORMULATED WITH 'APOTHECARY'S ROSE' PETALS.

HOW TO MAKE
ROSE WATER

t's easy to prepare this gentle astringent and skin toner, which can also be used in cooking. The essential ingredient is fresh petals, preferably picked early in the morning when the flowers are just opening, before the sun's heat causes fragrant oils to evaporate. You will need four cups of petals, loosely packed, from 'Apothecary's Rose' or other full-scented varieties, such as **'Yolande d'Aragon'** (a pink hybrid perpetual), **'Autumn Bouquet'** (a pink shrub), or **'Oklahoma'** (a deep red hybrid tea). Among old garden roses, those with red and deep pink flowers tend to have the strongest perfume. The most fragrant modern roses are usually dark crimson or mauve. In any case, do not use flowers that have been sprayed with pesticide.

- Place 2 cups of petals in a 3-quart saucepan.
  Reserve remaining 2 cups petals in a large heatproof bowl.

- Boil approximately 2 quarts water. Pour enough over petals
  in saucepan to cover.

- Cover pan tightly with lid or aluminum foil, and let steep
  for 15 minutes. Do not heat.

- Place a strainer over the bowl of reserved fresh petals.
  Pour liquid from saucepan through a fine-mesh strainer onto
  fresh petals. Cover bowl. Discard first batch of steeped petals.

- After contents of bowl have cooled, pour liquid through strainer
  into a glass jar. Use this rose water immediately or refrigerate
  for up to 2 weeks.

BALTIMORE BELLE

AS THE STAGECOACH BOUNCED along a Massachusetts road one wintry day in 1841, a well-dressed passenger turned to the girl beside him and pointed out the window. "Hannah, look there my child," he said, "see that poor hut? I suppose some miserable drunkard lives there who like your once poor unfortunate father is giving himself up to the intoxicating cup." The man in the carriage was John Hawkins, a forty-four-year-old Baltimore hatter; Hannah, age thirteen, was his daughter. They were headed for Boston, where an eager throng would assemble to hear John speak.

Acclaimed from Louisiana to Maine as a "silver-tongued" orator, John never mounted a podium without Hannah on his arm. Together, they were the public face of the Washingtonian Total Abstinence Society, the most powerful temperance organization in the United States. Hannah left speechifying to her eloquent parent, but crowds cheered her as the little girl who had helped him wrestle the demon in the bottle. John told spellbound audiences how Hannah had come to his rescue during the summer of 1840, when binge drinking had nearly destroyed him. "I hated the darkness of the night," he recalled, "and when morning came I hated the light, I hated myself, hated existence . . . Then my daughter, Hannah, came up—my only friend, I always loved her the most—and she said, 'Father, don't send me after whisky to-day!'"

This and other edifying episodes inspired *Hannah Hawkins; or, the Reformed Drunkard's Daughter,* a best seller published by the Washingtonians in 1843. The Reverend W. H. Daniels, a historian of temperence reform, praised it as "a book over which many tears have been shed and many good resolutions made." Well in advance of the book, its heroine had already won fame through her father's speeches as the Belle of Baltimore. And in 1842, friends of abstinence could express devotion to the cause by planting **'Baltimore Belle'**, a rose introduced that year. This pale-pink-to-white climber was bred by Samuel Feast, a Baltimore nurseryman and pillar of the Baptist church. It's

tempting to think that Feast had Hannah in mind when he named his rose, but no one knows for sure whether he did or not.

America's female legions battling "King Alcohol" gained new prominence after the Civil War under leaders such as Frances E. Willard. This redoubtable midwesterner was a founder of the Women's Christian Temperance Union in 1874, a WCTU president,

'BALTIMORE BELLE' IN A LITHOGRAPH FROM A NINETEENTH-CENTURY NURSERY CATALOG

a pioneering suffragist, and an early advocate of cycling, a sport she took up at age fifty-three. Her 1895 book *A Wheel within a Wheel; How I Learned to Ride the Bicycle* rallies women to shorten their long skirts (by a sensible three inches), grip the handlebars, and conquer the world. Unaffected and generous, she was, a contemporary said, "the fairest rose in the garden." Willard invariably wore the WCTU emblem of purity, a white ribbon bow, pinned to her bodice. In 1901, three years after her death, a Pennsylvania nursery marketed the **'Frances E. Willard'** tea rose as part of a seven-variety, all-white collection "[that] appeals very strongly to white ribbon people everywhere." But Willard's ghost must have arched an eyebrow above her signature pince-nez, because someone, somewhere, goofed. Other growers, it transpired, were selling the same rose as **'President Cleveland'**, hardly a tribute to self-restraint or feminism. Grover Cleveland had made headlines for fathering an illegitimate child during his bachelor days. In the White House he vigorously opposed women's rights. And though married to a teetotaler, he drank stronger stuff than lemonade.

Teetotalers faced a quandary when cooking with roses, a standard ingredient of nineteenth-century cuisine, because several basic preparations required alcohol. For example, the doyenne of Yankee domesticity, Catharine Beecher—a daughter of the Reverend Lyman Beecher, founder of the American Temperance Society—published a rose-water recipe calling for fresh petals soaked in brandy. She assured abstainers that they could virtuously keep brandy in the larder for culinary and medicinal purposes. Beecher's contemporary Samuel Parsons wasn't so sure about this. The New York nurseryman lamented the growing abuse of "spirit of roses," an alcohol-based rose water often used as a flavoring agent in bitter physics, but he tactfully avoided the subject of stimulating cookery.

THE OTHER BALTIMORE BELLE

In turn-of-the nineteenth-century Baltimore, a city renowned for its beautiful women, all eyes focused on Elizabeth Patterson (1785–1879). The daughter of William Patterson, a rich merchant, Betsy was known in her youth as the Belle of Baltimore. It is improbable, however, that the climbing rose with that name was intended to honor her. Aside from the unlikeliness of any nurseryman celebrating a belle in her sixties—a ripe old age in those days—at the time the rose appeared, there was a bigger obstacle: Betsy loathed Baltimore and made no bones about it.

At age nineteen, she wed Jérôme Bonaparte, Napoléon's younger brother, jubilant that she would never again be trapped in a provincial backwater. This dream ended when Napoléon persuaded Jerome to have his marriage to "the young person" from America annulled so that he could make an Austrian princess his wife. Betsy and her newborn son, Jérôme Jr., were henceforth forbidden to set foot in Europe. As she put it, "The emperor hurled me back on what I most hated on earth—my Baltimore obscurity." Betsy never remarried, and she refused to relinquish her imperial surname. Cut off without a cent or a sou, she held court in a Baltimore boardinghouse. Dressed in black, brandishing a red umbrella like a scepter, and attended by a French poodle, Bibi Bonaparte, she reminisced fondly about her triumphs as a princess, conveniently overlooking the fact that Jérôme did not become a prince until after their marriage had been dissolved. On bad days, she dished the invidious "Malapartes."

BARBRA STREISAND

A CASTING CALL FOR THE role of **'Barbra Streisand'** set the rialto abuzz in the winter of 1997. Even the greenest rose seedling was aware that a light pink miniature had received good critical reviews during a fourteen-year run as **'Funny Girl'**. But that might as well have been summer stock, compared with an unlimited engagement as Barbra herself. Three hybrid teas were up for the big part: a ravishing pink-tinted white, a sultry red whose petals reversed to yellow, and a glamorous lavender blushed with purple. Streisand announced that she would personally view every audition in her own California garden, growing sample bushes among the twelve hundred roses she already owned, and that the tryouts would last two whole years—enough to give any budding talent a case of the butterflies.

Normally, a PR-conscious nursery invites a celebrity to stop by its growing fields, select an as-yet-anonymous flower, sign a release form granting permission to use his or her name, and pose with the plant for a publicity photo, all in a few hours. But Weeks Roses, the firm approached by Streisand's gardener, realized that a quick once-over would not do for a famed perfectionist.

Having observed the trial plants in every season, from every angle, and in every light, Streisand chose the lavender variety. It had everything she wanted: large flowers with high centers surrounded by a swirl of petals, superb color, and a powerfully sweet fragrance. Tom Carruth, who hybridized 'Barbra Streisand' for Weeks, couldn't have been happier if his plant had won an Oscar. (Carruth is also the creator of **'Della Reese'**, **'Julie Newmar'**, **'Marilyn Monroe'**, and **'Phyllis Diller'**.) Streisand has displayed pictures of the rose on her album covers and often sets an arrangement onstage at concerts.

Incidentally, Weeks's two runners-up didn't fade into obscurity. The white-pink number became **'Moonstone'**, while the red-yellow ended up taking a bow as **'Rosie O'Donnell'**.

Rosarians have been dedicating plants to entertainers for more than a century. **'Jenny Lind'**, a pink moss rose bred in 1845 (and now extinct), honored the soprano known as the Swedish Nightingale, whose portraits depict her wearing a similar blossom in her hair and on her dress. Thanks to brilliant celebrity merchandising by showman P. T. Barnum, the singer's fans could also acquire a Jenny Lind cap, a Jenny Lind cradle, Jenny Lind–pattern china, or a Jenny Lind locomotive. *A Lady's Morals*, a 1931 movie based on Lind's life,

starred the American operatic star Grace Moore. Known as the Tennessee Nightingale, Moore often performed wearing a red rose, her favorite flower, in her hair. The red hybrid tea **'Grace Moore'** was introduced in 1948, at the request of the Chattanooga Rose Society, after her death in a plane crash.

'BARBRA STREISAND'

Nursery catalogs from the 1840s list **'Kean'**, named for the English thespian Edmund Kean, whose melodramatic death scenes and fits of rage brought audiences to their feet. Perhaps the crimson-purple of this gallica seemed appropriately florid. A Sarah Bernhardt devotee whose father was the French hybridizer Francis Dubreuil persuaded Papa to send the tragedienne his highest compliment. "Madame," he wrote, "permit a rose grower from Lyon, a sincere admirer of your talent who has had the good fortune to obtain a certain number of new roses which have made their way, to give one of those creations the name that you have represented so well." La Divine Sarah (born Rosine Bernard) graciously agreed to accept **'Sarah Bernhardt'**, a violet-scented scarlet climber.

Like the French actress, who made her first movie in 1900, rose growers took to the silver screen. Film studios welcomed the release of hybrid teas like **'Lillian Gish'**, **'Mary Pickford'**, **'Clara Bow'**, **'Shirley Temple'**, and **'Greer Garson'**, which helped to keep stars in the public eye, even those whose only notion of working the soil involved pressing handprints into wet cement outside Grauman's Chinese Theater. Garson, however, gardened in real life and held a still-unbroken record in Hollywood as the only actress to have three roses honor her. The 1942 tearjerker *Mrs. Miniver*, set in an English village during World War II, features a comic subplot about a bossy dowager's scheme to prevent the local stationmaster from naming his prize-winning rose after the vivacious Kay Miniver, played by Garson. Her performance as a devoted wife and mother whose mettle withstands the test of Nazi bombing won an Academy Award. The rose **'Mrs. Miniver'**, a carmine hybrid tea, didn't enter retail catalogs until 1944, when its U.S. distributer breathlessly recounted the narrow escape of the French-bred rose (né **'Souvenir de Louis Simon'**) from Europe in 1939, to find "sanctuary in the free soil of appreciative America," and a better box-office name. Pink 'Greer Garson' and yellow **'Madame Marie Curie'** (Garson portrayed the chemist in a blockbuster biopic) both came out in 1943. Around the end of the war, Garson confided to the *American Rose Annual*, "Probably there are some rose varieties missing from the gardens surrounding my Bel-Air home but if so, it is not an intentional oversight . . . Two or three of the Greer Garson roses suddenly went wild last summer, a development which I trust does not portend a similar happening to their namesake!"

Meanwhile, on the East Coast, actress Helen Hayes—the First Lady of the American Theater—claimed to have inherited a horticultural crazy streak. As a child, she would hide in her grandfather's garden to eavesdrop on his conversations with rosebushes. "Now look at that one over there," he would admonish an underachieving plant. "You've had just as much to eat and drink as that one . . . and look at you. You're so small. You're not really trying." Hayes acquired a hand-me-down rosebush along

GREER GARSON PLANTS 'MRS. MINIVER' IN HOLLYWOOD, 1944.

with Pretty Penny, the Victorian house in Nyack, New York, that she and her husband, playwright Charles MacArthur, bought during the 1930s. The stubborn old plant refused to bloom, but Hayes pruned, fertilized, and lectured it for years until it finally flowered. "[This] is a good rose," she told MacArthur, "and no Brooks Atkinson or any other drama critic can tell me otherwise."

Her garden expanded until it held more than 350 roses, including, of course, **'Helen Hayes'**, a hybrid tea introduced in 1956. Yellow with hints of red and pink reminiscent of grease paint, the flower became as popular as the star. Hayes preferred to tend her plants on her own. "I didn't have a whole nail on my fingers," she wrote of one season, "because I can't bear to wear gloves. I have to work with my bare hands." Elizabeth Scholtz, director emeritus of the Brooklyn Botanic Garden, tells of the day, some years ago, when she led a tour of Hayes's estate. The actress, then eighty-five, was supposed to be out of town. "But as we walked among the rose beds," Scholtz recalled, "we heard a voice from the direction of the house. Standing on the balcony, in a very Juliet moment, was Helen Hayes, welcoming us to her garden."

Roses named after female performers far outnumber those honoring male ones, and a disproportionate number of the guy flowers have received their names only after the men have died. Perhaps this is because the image of a man clasping his very own bloom might cause gossip columnists to titter and press agents to get ulcers. Still, nobody questioned John Wayne's masculinity when **'The Duke'**, a red, mildly scented, large-flowered hybrid tea named for him, moseyed into garden centers in 1956, or when a posthumous tribute, **'The Big Duke'**, was said to give off a "fruity" fragrance.

The suave British actor James Mason, a master spy in Alfred Hitchcock's

1959 thriller *North by Northwest*, made no bones about his horticultural incli-
nations. An aficionado of old garden roses, he especially loved gallicas. His
wife, actress Clarissa Kaye, worked closely with the English old-rose specialist
Peter Beales to create the ideal present for Mason. Doing what no grower had
attempted since the late nineteenth century, Beales hybridized a new gallica:
crimson eight-petaled **'James Mason'**, which made its debut in 1982. Mason
took particular pleasure in the Victorian aura of his specially commissioned
period piece.

Another English thespian-gardener, the late Nigel Hawthorne, prided himself on having succeeded by dint of talent, not matinee-idol looks. Shortly
before his sixtieth birthday, he challenged his friend Peter Harkness, a distinguished hybridizer, to develop a **'Nigel Hawthorne'** rose that "won't look
like most people's idea of a rose." The singular result, a scruffy, finicky bush
with five-petaled salmon pink flowers satisfied Hawthorne's zestful contrari-
ness: no one would ever mistake it for a mass-market hybrid tea. Harkness
gave his creation its distinctive character by crossing a hybrid *Rosa rugosa* with
a plant that has been classified for centuries as another rose species, *R. persica*. And therein lies a controversy in which Hawthorne would revel. Many
distinguished rosarians now assert that *R. persica* is in fact not a rose at all but
a separate genus of shrub, *Hulthemia persica*, which convincingly mimics the
traits of a rose. If true, this would make 'Nigel Hawthorne' the first rose variety ever produced by "intergeneral" breeding—that is, by crossing a member
of the genus *Rosa* with a plant from a different genus. Definitely a breakthrough role.

ENCORE

Starstruck gardeners who wish to mingle with great performers have plenty of celebrity roses to choose among. Deadheads take note: a red and white **'Jerry Garcia'** hybrid tea is rumored to be waiting in the wings.

'Alice Faye': Miniature. The U.S. distributor of the Irish rose calls it "a buxom blend of bright yellow and lipstick red . . . as bright as the early Technicolor films that made the lady famous."

'Andie MacDowell': Orange-red miniature. Born Rosalie Anderson MacDowell, Andie is "Rose" to family and friends.

'Angela Lansbury': Pink and cream hybrid tea. The actress tends her own rose beds.

'Audrey Hepburn': Light pink hybrid tea. Hepburn narrated the TV series *Gardens of the World.*

'Barbara Mandrell': Apricot miniature. The five-foot-two-inch country singer grows this at home.

'Bing Crosby': Persimmon orange hybrid tea. "Mexicali Rose" was a big hit for the heartthrob crooner.

'Bob Hope': Cherry red hybrid tea. Hope twice served as grand marshall of the Tournament of Roses Parade, once noting, "I would have been Rose Bowl queen, but my wig fell off during semifinals"; his wife's rose, **'Delores Hope'**, is a deep pink hybrid tea.

'Brenda Lee': Red-edged yellow miniature. At the rose's debut in Nashville, during an American Rose Society convention, the petite singer held a private concert at Opryland for ARS members.

'Buffy Sainte-Marie': Orange-pink hybrid tea. A British Columbian breeder and his wife went backstage at one of the Canadian folk singer's concerts to ask her permission to name a rose for her.

'Cary Grant': Orange hybrid tea. Grant's fifth wife ordered it as a Valentine's present in 1986. The couple planted the rose alongside their driveway.

'**Catherine Deneuve**': Coral-to-pink French hybrid tea. The actress also has a pink-flowered astilbe named for her.

'**Céline Dion**': Crimson-orange shrub. This flower was originally sold in Canada to benefit the singer's favorite charity.

'**Claudia Cardinale**': Yellow and orange shrub. Cardinale played Rosa in the 1967 Italian film *Una rosa per tutti* (*A Rose for Everyone*).

'**Dolly Parton**': Bright orange-red hybrid tea. Wary of breaking a fingernail, the singer and actress does not garden, but staff grow the rose both at her home and at Dollywood.

'**Elizabeth Taylor**': Deep pink hybrid tea. An amateur rose breeder wrote a fan letter to Taylor requesting her permission to name the flower—and got it.

'**Elvis**': Orange-pink hybrid tea. Presley's song "Mama Liked the Roses" eulogizes filial love. '**Graceland**': Yellow hybrid tea. This plant refers to the King's Memphis home, where he and his mother are buried in the Meditation Garden.

'**George Burns**': Yellow-, red-, and cream-striped floribunda. Its introduction honored the comedian's hundredth birthday. '**Gracie Allen**': Pink and white floribunda. Burns selected this rose for his late wife.

'**Helen Traubel**': Pinkish apricot hybrid tea. Its alias, 'Hell 'n' Trouble', refers not to the opera singer's temperament but to the rose's horticultural failings.

'**Henry Fonda**': Golden hybrid tea. His role in *On Golden Pond* gained the actor an Oscar.

'**Hoagy Carmichael**': Medium red hybrid tea. The musician and songwriter was buried in Rose Hill cemetery in his native Bloomington, Indiana.

'**Ingrid Bergman**': Dark red hybrid tea. A Dane bred this tribute to the sometimes controversial Swedish actress.

'**James Galway**': Pink shrub. The Irish flutist with a green thumb played "The Last Rose of Summer" when his namesake was introduced at London's Chelsea Flower Show in 2000.

'José Carreras': Creamy white hybrid tea. It is one of the rose garden's Three Tenors, along with **'Pavarotti'**, a bright pink hybrid tea, and **'Placido Domingo'**, a red hybrid tea. All are suitable for flinging onto opera-house stages.

'Judy Garland': Yellow and red floribunda. Garland fans commissioned the plant after her death, and bushes grow outside her birthplace in Minnesota and her mausoleum in New York.

'Julie Andrews': Orange-pink floribunda. A keen gardener, the actress and singer was disappointed by the plant's performance in her California garden. "The Julie Andrews rose is a tiny little bright thing that seems to be fairly hardy," she said, "but it needs the kind of dampness not found in Los Angeles."

'Laurence Olivier': Red floribunda. The actor interpreted many of Shakespeare's lines about roses.

'Lily Pons': Pale yellow hybrid tea. This French-born soprano's 1946 recording of Gabriel Fauré's "Les roses d'Ispahan" ("The Roses of Ispahan") is legendary.

'Lucille Ball': Apricot hybrid tea. Oddly, the flower color doesn't come close to the vivid hue of Lucy's hair.

'Lynn Anderson': Pink-edged cream hybrid tea. The country singer's hit "(I Never Promised You a) Rose Garden" won her a Grammy in 1970. Because Anderson's water-conserving Xeriscape garden in New Mexico is too dry for roses, she donated her namesake to irrigated sites at public institutions.

'Maria Callas': Pink hybrid tea. This large-flowered beauty was introduced in France in 1965, the year of the diva's farewell performance onstage.

'The McCartney Rose': Pink hybrid tea. It was bred by Alain Meilland, who presented the flower to its namesake, Paul McCartney, on his fiftieth birthday. Meilland had planned to call it 'Paul McCartney' but changed the name at the composer-singer's request, to celebrate his entire family. A suitable backup group for this rose might include **'Marmalade Skies'**, an orange floribunda; **'Oh Darlin''**, an apricot miniature; **'Penny**

Lane', a honey-colored climber; and **'Yesterday'**, a pink polyantha.

'Minnie Pearl': Pink miniature. Hybridizer Harmon Saville presented the comedienne with a bouquet of these at the Grand Ole Opry.

'Patsy Cline': Pink and white hybrid tea. In a classic ballad, the country singer spurned "A Rich Man's Gold" for "A Poor Man's Roses."

'Pearlie Mae': Apricot grandiflora. Vocalist Pearl Bailey, baptized "Pearlie Mae," was a June baby, making her birthstone the pearl and her flower the rose.

'Peggy Lee': Peachy pink hybrid tea. The singer grew four dozen of these plants in her rose garden. She said, "These roses are like living friends. There's a bush outside my window and when I watch it the roses turn toward me and bend, like a bow. They do, they do!"

'Red Skelton': Orange-red hybrid tea. The comic's nickname was inspired by his orange-red hair.

'Satchmo': Fiery orange floribunda. Jazz master Louis "Satchmo" Armstrong grew this flower at his home in Queens, New York. An offspring of the rose, **'Trumpeter'**, is an orange-red floribunda.

'Victor Borge': Soft orange hybrid tea. This toast to the urbane comedian and pianist was bred in his native Denmark.

'Will Rogers': Dark red hybrid tea. It came on the market in 1936, a year after the humorist's death in a plane crash.

'Whoopi!': Red and white miniature. Entertainer Whoopi Goldberg told HGTV, "I love to garden and love roses, so it was amazing to me that the rose people wanted to name such a beautiful, delicate miniature after me."

BLAZE

A CATCHY NAME COMBINED WITH a shrewd marketing scheme can transform a mediocre rose into a best seller. That's exactly what followed the publication of this notice in the December 1931 *American Rose Quarterly*: "Jackson & Perkins Company, wholesale growers of roses, will disseminate, in the fall of 1932, a climbing rose which they expect to prove tremendously popular. For the best name suggested for this rose they will pay $100 . . . The name should be impersonal (one or two words), preferably descriptive; it may denote brightness, the ever-blooming or climbing feature, and, above all, it should be adaptable for publicity purposes." By the deadline, December 31, Jackson & Perkins had received twenty-five thousand entries, and three months later the firm announced the winning name: **'Blaze'**.

As anticipated, the rose's launch sparked much hoopla. Retail nurseries distributed full-color images of the "Blaze of Glory" enveloping porches, smothering arbors, spilling over fences, and raising what one catalog called "a vigorous pillar of rich scarlet [that] kindles the warmth of welcome your home extends as guests approach." Adding fuel to the promotional fire, 'Blaze' won the highest award for a climbing rose in the 1933 International New Rose Contest at Bagatelle, in Paris. But even as sales skyrocketed in the United States and Europe, serious rosarians muttered that the climber's garden performance fell far short of its billing. The American Rose Society's annual "Proof of the Pudding," a compilation of members' remarks about new roses, began to publish comments such as these: "A flicker maybe, but surely no blaze yet" (from Oregon, 1935); "[It] does not even 'glow', much less 'blaze'" (Washington, D.C, 1937). In many gardens, apparently, the "everblooming" plant never did rebloom. Some British rosarians called the fuss over 'Blaze' a false alarm, alleging—wrongly—that the "new" rose was in fact a twenty-year-old English variety, **'Paul's Scarlet Climber'** (which Jackson & Perkins had listed as a parent of 'Blaze'), reissued under a bogus American trademark.

Rather than acknowledge the complaints of rose cognoscenti, J&P sharpened its pitch to the masses. Patriotism played especially well during the forties. One catalog compared the color of 'Blaze' petals to "the Red of the Flag, in all its flaming glory—symbol of courage and devotion to country in every American heart . . . Blaze is a flower for America!" And America had to have it. Demand was so great that by 1949, when the patent for 'Blaze' expired, its original hybridizer had collected

'BLAZE' IN A 1932 NURSERY CATALOG

more than $600,000 in royalties, a phenomenal sum at the time. Other nurseries attempted to cash in on the success of 'Blaze' but couldn't compete with J&P's commercial clout. In 1935 **'Blaze Superior'**—imported from Czechoslovakia where it went by **'Demokracie'**—quickly fizzled. A few years later, **'Flash'** ("As spectacular as the Fourth of July celebration is a plant of Flash in bloom") was a flash in the pan. **'Torch'**, depicted against a drawing of the Statue of Liberty ("This new climbing rose will flame gloriously in your garden") also burned out fast.

J&P gradually, and discreetly, cut back on propagating 'Blaze' once it had introduced "An entirely New Improved Strain of Blaze" in 1954. Without specifying the first plant's shortcomings, advertisements accentuated the newcomer's most positive trait: "Absolutely Guaranteed to Bloom in June-July-August-September!" J&P spokesmen maintained that the "improved" variety was simply a sport of 'Blaze' that staff discovered growing in the nursery fields. Because the firm never patented this plant, its exact parentage remains a mystery. Most shoppers probably assumed that this was the same brand-name 'Blaze' they'd admired for years, only revitalized with the horticultural equivalent of vitamins or wonder drugs—just as they must have figured that the in fact unrelated **'Baby Blaze'**, a compact J&P offering in 1954, was its inevitable offspring. Now and then, a rose labeled **'Blaze Improved'** or confusingly 'Blaze Superior' turns up at a garden center today. It invariably turns out to be the 1954 model of 'Blaze', the name under which the plant is still registered with the American Rose Society. In 1957 Charlie Perkins, the owner of J&P, gave this candid assessment: "There have been better red climbers since ['Blaze'], but that rose still outsells them all and, as far as I can figure, all because of that name." His company has kept the faith, releasing **'Blaze of Glory'**, a coral orange climber, in 2005.

WHEN J&P, ALREADY THE NATION's largest wholesaler, started mail-order and retail nursery operations in 1939, its hot new rose was **'World's Fair'**. The velvety red-flowered shrub was the fair's official "theme rose," as iconic as the Trylon and Perisphere that dominated the skyline. 'World's Fair' commanded its own bed at the center of an eight-thousand-plant "Parade of Modern Roses." J&P also took this opportunity to introduce a new class of clustered-flowered hybrid rose, the floribunda. Not coincidentally, 'World's Fair' happened to be one of numerous floribundas in the firm's inventory. One year later, a group of leading commercial rose growers, including J&P, inaugurated All-America Rose Selections, an annual awards program honoring the best new hybrids—and 'World's Fair' made the list. Almost immediately, the AARS seal of approval became one of the rose industry's most effective marketing tools, which it remains to this day.

J&P didn't always hit the bull's-eye. Take **'Siren'**, a shrill orange-red floribunda that captured the Gold Medal at Britain's Royal National Rose Society trials of 1952. Anticipating a sellout, J&P dug up and prepared to ship a huge crop of 'Siren' for the 1953 retail season. But at summer's end, seventy-five thousand unsold plants had to be destroyed. Charlie Perkins blamed this fiasco on an ill-chosen name: "The public didn't want a rose to look like a fire engine." No one at J&P headquarters seems to have queried whether any customers recoiled from the nasty reputation of the Sirens in Greek mythology, or whether the plant was just a dud.

Hype-wary consumers doubted the credibility of a rose called **'Carefree Beauty'**, bred in 1977 by Iowa State University horticulture professor Griffith Buck and distributed by Conard-Pyle. But, to widespread amazement, the plant fulfilled the promise of its name: the large, lush, deeply fragrant pink flowers really are beautiful, and the shrub that produces them in abundance is formidably resistant to powdery mildew, rust, and blackspot. Thanks to word of mouth over back fences, Buck had a nationwide hit on his hands. Although International plant registration law prohibits the reuse of a patented name unless the original variety is proven to be extinct, Conard-Pyle could not legally prevent other growers from piggybacking on Buck's success by substituting different nouns for "Beauty"—as Conard-Pyle itself has, from the 1990s on, with **'Carefree Wonder'**, **'Carefree Delight'**, and **'Carefree Marvel'**, none of which has Buck's rose in its family tree.

So far, no one has adapted 'Carefree Beauty' by means of another well-tried ploy: adding a number. The historic numerals of the 1974 floribunda **'Independence '76'**, for example, simultaneously differentiated it from another grower's **'Independence'** and got a head start on America's bicentennial. **'Eden 88'**, a French climber introduced in the United States in 1988 carefully sidestepped any mixup with the preexisting **'Eden'**. Ironically, 'Eden' (sans '88) has since disappeared.

Associating a rose with a familiar household product can boost profits, too. In 1957, for instance, a creamy pink hybrid tea received the name **'Gail Borden'**—as in Gail Borden Jr. (1801–1874), the Texan inventor, publisher, and dairy tycoon—to celebrate the centennial of Elsie the cow's parent company. The naming of **'Silent Night'**, a soft yellow hybrid tea, occurred in

1969, after a British bedding firm called Silentnight Beds paid breeder Sam McGredy £2,000 for the privilege. McGredy described the bush as an "ideal bedder." The maker of Fisherman's Friend cough drops won naming rights to a David Austin shrub in a 1987 benefit auction for the charity Children in Need. **'Fisherman's Friend'** has garnet red flowers and a strong scent.

Tupperware vice president Brownie Wise, who cooked up the plastics company's home-party marketing program in 1948, sponsored the creation of **'Tupperware Rose'**. By design, this thornless pink hybrid tea has never been sold; Wise conceived it as an incentive for her sales force. Those enterprising women caught their first glimpse of the flower on the cover of the 1953 July–August issue of *Tupperware Sparks*. An inscription read: "Both [are] symbolic of enduring perfection—the exquisite artistry of Tupperware . . . and the matchless and delicate beauty of the regal rose." The color of the rose became the signature tone for Tupperware and for Wise. Her wardrobe, her car, her pet canary (dyed), and her office decor were all "Tupperware Rose Pink." Women who emulated her could set their tables with Tupperware Rose flatware, intro-

duced by International Silver in 1955. But the days of Wise and roses came to a bitter end in 1958, when management handed the executive a pink slip. She and her flower fell into obscurity.

FROM THE MID-NINETEENTH CENTURY ON, ROSES ADORNED ADVERTISEMENTS FOR HOUSEHOLD PRODUCTS LIKE CONDENSED MILK.

In 1981 Tupperware commissioned a new pink hybrid tea, named simply **'Tupperware'**, for corporate use as an award to employees. Besides receiving blooms of the flower, they can look forward to earning wristwatches and other tokens of esteem that display its image. Mary Kay cosmetics also uses a pink rose as its emblem, though the firm's presentation blossoms were made from silk until 1984 when rosarian Ernest Williams—based in Dallas, Mary Kay's hometown—bred the miniature **'Mary Kay'**. Unlike 'Tupperware', 'Mary Kay' is available for retail distribution.

Even a well-orchestrated promotional campaign can strike a sour note, as J&P's David Stump learned in 1978, when he presided over a staff meeting to announce the name of an important new rose. Its sweetly fragrant flowers in a striking mauve-pink-tinged ivory were sure to cause a sensation. But Stump hadn't anticipated the nervous giggles that broke out among the women in the room when he read its label: **'Pristine'**. Someone had to break the news to him that his rose happened to have the same name as a popular feminine deodorant. Nevertheless, 'Pristine' the plant remained, and sales have surpassed Stump's brightest forecast. Peaudouce (meaning "soft skin"), France's leading disposable-diaper manufacturer, confidently pinned its marketing hopes to a silky-smooth rose called, of course, **'Peaudouce'**. When the hybrid tea—in shades of pale yellow—won top honors from Britain's Royal National Rose Society, company representatives traveled to the Gardens of the Rose in St. Albans, England, to accept the award at a grand ceremony. Taking advantage of the spotlight, they diligently worked the crowd, handing out free nappies to one and all, including members of the royal family.

ON THE AIR

n the 1930s, radio became an important channel for rose marketing. When J. Horace McFarland, president of the American Rose Society, took the microphone to talk about each year's new rose varieties, listeners tuned in from coast to coast. Rose growers vied to name plants after radio personalities, in hopes of an on-the-air plug. When the pink hybrid tea **'Mary Margaret McBride'**, a Jackson & Perkins tribute to the talk-show host, won the 1943 All-America Rose Selection Award, McBride broadcast her daily one o'clock program live from the J&P display gardens. Six years later, on the show's fifteenth anniversary, fans cheered as she mounted a platform in Yankee Stadium, surrounded by hundreds of 'Mary Margaret McBride' bushes.

The shell pink J&P floribunda **'Ma Perkins'** was introduced on the CBS soap opera of the same name. During a 1952 episode, broadcast from a J&P garden, Ma's tribulations momentarily came to a halt so that she (played by Virginia Payne) could receive her very own bloom. Listeners heard Ma exclaim, "I am really proud to think that such a lovely rose has been named after me."

In character as Mirandy of Persimmons Holler on the *National Farm and Home Hour*, writer-actress Marjorie Edith O'Neill Bauersfeld took a down-home approach to horticulture. In 1944 hybridizer Walter Lammerts honored her with **'Mirandy'**, one of the most beautiful red-velvet roses ever created.

MARY MARGARET MCBRIDE WITH A BOUQUET OF HER NAMESAKE ROSE

CABBAGE ROSE

THE LATIN BINOMIAL *Rosa* x *centifolia* means "hundred-petaled rose," a forgivable exaggeration because the plant's pink, globe-shaped flowers are exceedingly full, making them resemble cabbages. The first **'Cabbage Rose'**, sometimes called **'Holland Rose'** in England, was probably bred in the Netherlands during the sixteenth century. This valuable plant soon reached France where extracts from its fragrant flowers became an essential ingredient for perfumers. Provençal farmers cultivated it in fields, as they still do; hence the common name that Shakespeare used, **'Provence Rose'**.

When growers look to other garden plants for flower-naming ideas, most prefer ornamentals to edibles. The large petals of single-

'CABBAGE ROSE', 1801

petaled **'Anemone Rose'** recall its fluttering namesake. **'Clematis'**, like the vine of the same name, is a climber. **'Oeillet'**, French for "carnation" or "dianthus," has small flowers with fringed petals like carnations and, to some noses, smells like them, too. Anyone can see why the rose we know as **'Austrian Copper'**, a large orange single flower with yellow stamens and a dark eye, became **'Corn Poppy Rose'** in nineteenth-century France. The list of color-matched look-alikes continues with white **'Edelweiss'**, yellow **'Primrose'**, pink **'Cyclamen'**, and scarlet **'Poinsettia'**. The 1951 floribunda **'Geranium'** was the first of many modern roses to derive an orange-red hue from pelargonadin, the natural pigment responsible for the tone of the annual geranium, properly known as *Pelargonium*. Americans often assume that the contemporary English rose breeder David Austin had perky spring bulbs in mind when he registered his **'Crocus Rose'**. In fact, it honors the Crocus Trust, a cancer charity.

References to woody plants abound. Take **'Magnolia Rose'**, the first tea rose bred in England. Also known as **'Devoniensis'** (a Devonshire nursery introduced this variety in 1841), it has large, lush creamy white blossoms like those of the tree. **'Lilas'**, French for "lilac," not only produces lilac-colored flowers but also canes, prickles, and leaves tinged with the same hue. **'Blackberry Rose'** (*R. rubus*) honors the wild bramble's sweet-smelling clustered white blooms. A striking similarity to the foliage of other plants accounts for **'Bamboo Rose'** (*R. multiflora* **'Watsoniana'**) **'Barberry-leaved Rose'** (*R. berberifolia*); **'Hemp-leaved Rose'** (*R. canabifolia*, as in cannabis); and **'Lettuce-leaved Rose'** (*R. centifolia bullata*). Different viewers, of course, make out different likenesses. For example, **'Celery-leaved Rose'** (*R. x centifolia* **'Bipinnata'**) also goes by **'Gooseberry-leaved Rose'** and **'Parsley-leaved Rose'**.

Names referring to hips, or fruits, which are most noticeable in the fall, contradict the misconception that rosebushes offer nothing after summer's flowers fade. This late-season cornucopia includes **'Pumpkin'**, a florist's hybrid valued for its orange hips; red-fruited **'Apple Rose'** (*R. pomifera*); and spiny auburn-fruited **'Gooseberry Rose'** (*R. stellata mirifica*), a North American species. China gave us the bizarrely appealing **'Chestnut Rose'** or **'Burr Rose'** (*R. roxburghii* — William Roxburgh, a Scots botanist, discovered it in Canton), with bristly hips reminiscent of chestnut burrs. Southerners call it **'Chinquapin Rose'**, because the hips also resemble those of the chinquapin, *Castanea pumila*. This American chestnut takes its name from the Algonkian word *chechinkamin*, meaning "great berry."

LOOK-ALIKES

R oses have reminded people of just about everything under the sun, not to mention everything to do with the sun itself (e.g., **'The Sun'**, **'Sun Umbrella'**, and **'Sunburn'**—ouch).

'Church Mouse': Tannish brown with a lavender tinge.

'Fire Chief': Flame red.

'Freckles': Light red with deep red spots.

'Goldfinch': A yellow rambler. In their book *Roses*, Roger Phillips and Martyn Rix say it is "good trained into old apple trees."

'Hat Pin': Introduced by Tiny Petals Miniature Rose Nursery.

'Lady Godiva': Often described in rose literature as "flesh pink."

'Leaping Salmon': Pink climber.

'New Penny': Coppery miniature.

'Piñata': Sprays of yellow and scarlet flowers.

'Sealing Wax': Hips are sealing-wax red.

CHEROKEE ROSE

GAZING AT THE PRISTINE, pure white petals of '**Cherokee Rose**', you wouldn't know that its history is stained with blood, sweat, and tears. Cherokee Indian legends tell of a long-ago tribal massacre during which immortal Spirit People protected the maiden Dowansa by transforming her into a rosebush. Its blossoms had snowy petals as chaste as her heart and golden centers as lovely as her breasts. Unfortunately, though, her beauty remained vulnerable. Heedless passersby—among them Dowansa's bereaved lover, who had been off hunting when she turned into a plant—trod on her stems. The Spirit People rescued Dowansa again by arming her canes and fruit with sharp hooked prickles. These kept humans at bay but not, alas, smaller creatures. The rose's Cherokee name is *tsist-unigisti*, "the rabbits eat it"—"it" being the succulent seed-bearing hip.

In northern Georgia early in the nineteenth century, on land passed down through generations, prosperous Cherokee farmers built houses, schools, and churches (many tribe members converted to Christianity). They wrote a constitution proclaiming a sovereign Cherokee Nation and argued their rights before the United States Supreme Court—a futile effort. The discovery of gold on Cherokee soil in 1828 added greedy prospectors to the steady influx of non-Indian homesteaders who regarded the taking of this fertile territory as manifest destiny. Federal authorities shared their vision. Ten years after the gold rush, the U.S. Army rounded up Cherokee of all ages, about seventeen thousand all told, for a brutal forced march to Oklahoma. At least four thousand died from hunger and disease during their journey. Decades later, one of the troops in charge, a white Georgian, wrote: "I fought through the civil war and have seen men shot to pieces and slaughtered by thousands, but the Cherokee removal was the cruelest work I ever knew."

Anyone who now retraces the route of that thousand-mile trek, which the Cherokee call *Nunahi dunoklo hilui*, the "Trail Where They Wept" or "Trail of Tears," can spot clumps of 'Cherokee Rose' growing wild along the way. Tribal storytellers say that during the exodus from Georgia, the Great Spirit gave his despairing people a hopeful sign: Wherever a mother's teardrop moistened the soil, a rose grew. Its waxy white petals symbolized those tears; its golden center, the treasure of the lost Georgia homeland; the seven (usually five to seven) leaflets on its stem, the seven Cherokee clans driven westward.

Meanwhile, back east, 'Cherokee Rose' flourished. The vigor, density, and prickliness of this rambler's canes, which can rapidly extend twenty feet, recommended it for hedges. On April 29, 1804, Thomas Jefferson wrote in his garden notebook: "Planted seeds of the Cherokee rose . . . near the N. E. corner of the Nursery." The 1847 edition of *Norman's Southern Agricultural Almanac* reported that plantation owners and managers valued the rose as a cheaper, more effective alternative to wooden fences (barbed wire wasn't invented until the 1870s). Besides enclosing livestock and protecting them from wolves and thieves, the almanac said, a 'Cherokee Rose' barrier would keep foxhunters out of crop fields and discourage runaway slaves.

CHEROKEE ROSES ON A PURPLE VELVET CLOTH, PAINTED BY MARTIN JOHNSON HEADE IN 1894

After the Civil War, nostalgic Southerners reminisced about 'Cherokee Rose' as a picturesque vestige of antebellum glory. In 1916 the Georgia State Assembly resolved, "Whereas, The Cherokee Rose, having its origin among the aborigines of the northern portion of the State of Georgia, is indigenous to its soil, and grows with equal luxuriance in every county of the State, Be it therefore . . . resolved, That, at the suggestion and request of the Georgia Federation of Women's Clubs, the Cherokee Rose be . . . declared to be the floral emblem of the State of Georgia."

Proud Georgians would cite the French botanical explorer André Michaux, who identified the plant in 1802 as a North American species he had discovered among the Cherokee. He named the wilding *Rosa laevigata*, from the Latin for "smoothed," a reference to its glossy leaves. The Latin name stuck, but Michaux misidentified the plant's geographical origin. *R. laevigata* is in fact native to China and Southeast Asia. Before 1759 seeds or seedlings somehow reached London, where the plant was initially labeled *R. sinica*, or "Chinese rose." No one knows how it arrived in America, although rose historian Leonie Bell surmised in the 1980s that seeds got mixed up with Chinese rice shipped to the Carolinas.

Like many other naturalized Americans, *R. laevigata* eventually reinvented itself on the West Coast. A California grower introduced the red 'Cherokee Rose' hybrid **'Ramona'** in 1913, three years after the release of D. W. Griffith's silent film *Ramona*, an adaptation of Helen Hunt Jackson's 1884 novel of the same title. Set in Spanish colonial California, Jackson's tale about the doomed love of the part–American Indian, part-Scottish heroine for an Indian sheepherder was meant to stir popular sympathy for oppressed Native Americans. Despite Jackson's noble intentions, it was the roses and romance, not the social message, that thrilled her fans. For moviegoers who saw the Ramona portrayed by Mary Pickford (or Loretta Young in the 1936 talkie), the Trail of Tears led only to a Hollywood tearjerker.

GEORGIA CHEROKEE HEAD WESTWARD
ON THE TRAIL OF TEARS.

O, CANADA!

The Canadian maple leaf has long been a giant red flag for rose growers. Unlike bone-hardy native Americans, such as *Rosa acicularis* ('Arctic Rose') and *R. nutkana* ('Nootka Rose'), many delicate European and Asian garden roses imported into Canada have succumbed to deep freezes. Early in the twentieth century, Canada's first professional plant hybridizer, Isabella Preston, pioneered the development of rosebushes tough enough to endure harsh winters without extraordinary protection. She named many of her creations after American Indian tribes. **'Algonquin'**, for example, was a 1928 hybrid rugosa; **'Mohawk'**, a 1930 shrub; and **'Ojibway'**, a 1946 climber. Sadly, all have vanished.

The plant geneticist Felicitas Svejda carried on Preston's mission at the Canadian Department of Agriculture by creating the Explorer series, hybrids primarily derived from varieties of *R. rugosa* or *R. x kordesii*. These roses have not, however, proved consistently reliable. Red-flowered **'Champlain'** (named after Samuel de Champlain, founding father of Quebec) blooms abundantly but is prone to mildew and severe winter dieback. The dark green leaves of **'John Franklin'** (a nineteenth-century navigator) have a weakness for blackspot. Blush pink **'Martin Frobisher'** (a seeker of the Northwest Passage in the 1570s) resists most diseases, though the upright shrub can look gawky. Justly acclaimed as one of the best-all-around Explorers, bright pink **'William Baffin'** (an early nautical astronomer in Arctic waters) grows vigorously, flowers profusely, and withstands fierce chills. Hardy to -31°F, soft-pink **'John Davis'** (the Elizabethan discoverer of Davis Strait, west of Greenland) gives off a delicate fragrance. Also dependable in a frigid climate, **'Marie-Victorin'** stands alone among the Explorer series in commemorating a plant expert: Frère Marie-Victorin, a twentieth-century botany professor in Montreal and a founder of that city's botanical garden.

CHINA ROSE

I N THE EIGHTEENTH CENTURY, from St. Petersburg to Paris and London, and Boston to Philadelphia and Charleston, civilized existence for stylish households revolved around China tea, Chinese silk, and Chinese porcelain. In the early 1800s, another Asian luxury became a must: China roses. For status-conscious shoppers, *China* was merely an impressive label, implying that a plant's owner had the discernment and the means to obtain exotic rarities. For rosarians, however, this one word signaled a horticultural revolution.

Before English and French growers hybridized the class of roses they called

AN EVERBLOOMING CHINA LABELED "EVER-BLOWING ROSE" IN LONDON'S *BOTANICAL MAGAZINE*, 1794

"China"—initially using "stud" plants bought at the Fa Tee ("Flowery Land") nurseries in Guangdong (Canton) during the 1790s—almost all Western roses flowered in one short spring or early-summer burst, after which their show was over for the year. The revelation that China's *Yuejihua* ("monthly roses") flower continually throughout the growing season astonished European visitors. Some of those venerable roses date at least to the Han Dynasty, around 140 BC, when an emperor supposedly remarked that one "monthly" blossom outshone the smile of his favorite concubine. The first studs transported to Europe, **'Pink Monthly Rose'** and **'Red Monthly Rose'**, became the ancestors of all future repeat-blooming, or remontant, roses.

By crossing original Chinese stock with Western roses, European hybridizers produced offspring so diverse, and so different from their parents, that they were assigned to new categories, such as hybrid perpetual. Even those officially classed as Chinas tended to acquire typical Western names, with only the word *China* acknowledging Asian ancestry. 'Pink Monthly Rose' and 'Red Monthly Rose', for instance, became **'Old Blush China'** and **'Slater's Crimson China'**, for the English plantsman Gilbert Slater. But soon, allusions to the Orient faded in early nineteenth-century rose catalogs — perhaps because of the waning fashion for chinoiserie decor — and nurserymen and gardeners preferred to ennoble European-bred Chinas with titles like **'Archduke Charles'** and **'Louis Philippe'**.

THE CONCEPT OF NAMING plants after well-known individuals mystified the Chinese, who customarily identified roses by notable physical traits (such as petal color or bloom time), by analogies to similar flowers or to animals (mythic or real), or by images that convey an emotion, sensation, or state of mind. Their green-flowered rose — *Rosa chinensis* **'Viridiflora'** in the West — was simply **'Lü E'** ("green calyx"; the calyx is a flower's outer whorl of sepals), while pink **'Yu Ling Long'** ("exquisite jade") reminds us that the gemstone comes in colors other than green. The blossoming of **'Saosihua'** ("silk-reeling flower," or *R. roxburghii*), coincides with the season for winding thread. *R. multiflora* **'Carnea'** was known as **'Hehua Qiangwei'** ("lotus rose"), because its flesh pink double blossom recalls that of the aquatic plant.

The eighteenth-century *Treatise on the Monthly Rose*, by the pseudonymous Ping Hua Guan Gu ("Master of Flower Reviewer"), mentions a cool greenish yellow variety, **'Jin Niao Fan Lu'** ("golden bird splashing in water"), and says of another: "Petals edged with a tint of red surround a grayish-white rose named **'Xiao Feng Chan Yue'** to convey a picturesque scene of dawning day, with a cool, gentle breeze as the moon pales in the sky." Poetic **'Yuguo tianqing'** ("after rain — clear shining") refers to a buff white, sweet-scented climber. The cherry red petals and white-flecked eye of **'Chi Long Han Zhu'** ("white pearl in crimson dragon's mouth") summon up a traditional motif in Chinese art: a dragon guarding a pearl, a Taoist symbol of wisdom and creative energy. Perhaps the similarity of another rose's saffron petals to the color of a bonze's robe and a perfume redolent of sandalwood incense inspired the naming of **'Chan Yi Xiang'** ("Buddhist clothing fragrance"). What we call *R. x fortuniana* is **'Dahuabai Muxiang'** ("big white flower with woody fragrance"), as self-explanatory a name as you'll find anywhere.

Chinese gardeners cast an indulgent eye on ruddy pink or red roses like **'Three Drunks of Yaoyang'** and **'Drunk Green Lotus'**, probably because the flowers' florid faces radiate a convivial mood. While teetotalers in China imbibe summer coolers perfumed with an extract called "rose dew," wine drinkers occasionally flavor their beverage with roses. **'Tipsy Imperial**

Concubine'—pink tinged with yellow and red—was introduced to the West by English garden historian Hazel Le Rougetel, who had traveled in China and grew this plant from a cutting brought to her in 1982 by a member of the Beijing Rose Society. More recently, the Scottish novelist and historian Jane Stevenson speculated that the rose name commemorates Yang Guifei, the "precious consort" of an eighth-century T'ang emperor whose fatal obsession with her beauty plunged him into a life of debauchery. The couple's notorious all-night revels — they both performed the Rainbow and Feather Garments dance!—may well have involved some tippling.

DURING THE EARLY TWENTIETH century, the rose trade wind reversed direction. Young Chinese reformers and cosmopolites began looking westward for modern roses, as well as political ideas, music, and modes of dress. Rather like the Jazz Age sophisticates in Shanghai and Nanjing who wore Parisian high-heeled pumps but

'BENGAL ROSE', ONE OF THE FIRST CHINESE REPEAT-BLOOMING ROSES IN WESTERN GARDENS, ARRIVED VIA INDIA.

clung to a traditional cheongsam, fashionable nurserymen devised old-style names for novel imports. Hybrid perpetuals were assimilated as "tree peony roses"—a profound compliment from the Chinese, who had always ranked roses, both aesthetically and symbolically, far beneath peonies and chrysanthemums. **'Ulrich Brunner Fils'** became **'Red Peony Rose'**; **'Maréchal Niel'** was **'Shandong Yellow'**; and **'Frau Karl Druschki'**, **'Big White'**.

A Western-educated Beijing resident, Shohtsu G. King, wrote in the 1924 *American Rose Annual*: "I am very keen in interesting more [Chinese] people with gardens to take up these modernized roses, as they are infinitely more beautiful, floriferous, with more colors and bigger blossoms than the native sorts which may have been their forefathers'." That season, she reported that **'Hoosier Beauty'**, **'American Pillar'**, **'Ophelia'**, and **'Columbia'** enjoyed great popularity in Beijing. Despite intervening shifts in the social and cultural climate, imports such as **'Chicago Peace'** and **'Tropicana'** were best sellers in Beijing when Hazel Le Rogetel visited in 1981, and the Chinese now grow more European and American roses than ever. Horticulturists in charge of collections like that of the Beijing Botanical Garden, which displays approximately seven hundred cultivars, systematically distinguish among hybrid teas, floribundas, and other repeat-flowering descendants of the original China studs. But many Chinese gardeners call all of these plants—native or foreign, old or young—by one ancestral name: *Yuejihua*, Monthly Roses.

AN INTERNATIONAL SNAFU

The ever-popular **'Macartney Rose'** (not to be confused with the hybrid tea **'The McCartney Rose'**, honoring Paul, the former Beatle; see page 32) pays tribute to Lord Macartney, Britain's first ambassador to China, who carried this Asian species home to London in 1793. *Rosa bracteata*, as botanists know it, has conspicuous leafy bracts, or leaves, ringing its strong-scented single flowers. The rose was actually discovered by Macartney's embassy secretary, George Staunton, a horticulturist whose English estate became a landmark of Anglo-Chinese gardening. Macartney himself proved less adept at cross-cultural ventures, right from the start of his dealings with Emperor Qianlong. The Chinese sovereign granted the British envoy a rare personal audience, which included a ritual exchange of gifts. Macartney presented an elaborate gem-studded casket on behalf of King George III, and Qianlong reciprocated with a jade scepter. Unaware that this ostensibly simple offering symbolized peace and prosperity to the Chinese, Macartney misinterpreted it as a diplomatic slight — and made no secret of his displeasure. In the journal he published after returning to England, he scoffed that the scepter did not "appear in itself to be of any great value." British gardeners, though, accepted *R. bracteata* with unalloyed enthusiasm.

CHRYSLER IMPERIAL

HAD THERE BEEN A way to graft tailfins and chrome onto a rosebush, some American grower would have given it a shot during the 1950s. Postwar faith in progress through science and technology fueled a desire for flowers as up-to-date as any modern gizmo. "Roses for the Television Age," an article by E. A. Piester in the 1951 *American Rose Annual*, prophesied: "Television, like autos and income taxes, will have a definite impact on gardening, even though a completely synthetic television garden does seem impossible . . . It is perfectly certain that there will be something new in garden roses with each decade, keeping pace with television and space ships."

Throughout the United States, people expected innovations in outdoor living—still a fresh concept in the 1950s—to originate on the West Coast, seedbed of the patio, the backyard swimming pool, and the barbecue pit. So it made perfect sense that in 1952 a Californian with a Ph.D. in genetics, Walter E. Lammerts, should create the snazziest hybrid tea on the block—and that it should be named for a luxury automobile, the Chrysler Imperial. It's difficult to pinpoint the exact moment when the flower first got hitched to the car, or what sort of deal may have been struck, but it is clear that Lammerts approved the link. Rose breeder Sam McGredy IV later wrote that in addition to gaining valuable publicity, Lammerts received the gift of a Chrysler.

Whether shopping for a sedan to cruise the freeway or a bush to plant beside the carport, America's conspicuous consumers believed that bigger was better. And as Lammerts's business rival Gene Boerner commented, "It was more difficult to build obsolescence into a rose than an automobile, but nurserymen came out with annual model changes, just like Detroit." The rose **'Chrysler Imperial'** couldn't offer the latest V-8 engine, Hydraglide power steering, or Fluid-Torque transmission, as its four-wheeled counterpart did, but it exceeded industry standards all the same. In 1953 All-America Rose Selections gave Lammerts's creation a coveted award for which breeders around the world compete every year. Entrants are planted in public trial gardens throughout the United States, and over a two-year period, experts rate each rose for disease-resistance, hardiness, flower quality, form, and viability in all North American climates. The annual award winners usually represent a mere 4 percent of all plants tested. AARS praised 'Chrysler Imperial' for the large, exceptionally

THE 1953 ALL AMERICA WINNER

The
Chrysler
Imperial
Rose

The All America Rose winner for 1953 by Germain's of California has been named The Chrysler Imperial Rose. Like its Imperial namesake the new rose is unique in quality—it is America's first truly red rose. In its perfection—attained through 6 patient years of the hybridizer's art—you will discover the reason why it was named after the Chrysler Imperial car.

The Finest Car
America Has Yet Produced!

'CHRYSLER IMPERIAL', A 1953 HYBRID
TEA, WITH THE CAR IT HONORED

fragrant blooms and elegant long stems that make it an "ideal red exhibition rose." Little did the judges know that this flower would soon dominate an exhibition avidly followed by nonrosarians.

Spectators at the 1954 Tournament of Roses Parade, in Pasadena, California—as well as millions of viewers watching the event on television's first coast-to-coast color broadcast—saw a float bedecked with twenty-five thousand 'Chrysler Imperial' blooms, each set in its own water vial. Representing the theme "Life of an American Workman," the title of Motor City pioneer Walter P. Chrysler's autobiography, the float carried "a heroic figure of an American workman striding out of the pages of the book and striking an anvil with a heavy hammer. Out from the anvil flow floral 'sparks' and at the end of each of these was some product of Detroit's great workshop—an automobile, a truck, a plane, a tank, a boat."

TOUTING THE LATEST HYBRID as an emblem of progress was in fact old news in the rose world. From the early nineteenth century on, rosarians have likened the introduction of "improved" varieties to contemporary advances in science and technology. State-of-the-art bouquets have been tossed at chemists (**'Dr. Pasteur'**, 1887; **'Madame Marie Curie'**, 1943; and **'Radium'**, 1913), biologists (**'Charles Darwin'**, 1879; **'Evolution'**, 1995; and **'Genius Mendel'**, 1935), and inventors (**'Thomas A. Edison'**, 1931; **'Guglielmo Marconi'**, 1934; and **'Radio'**, 1937). New York nurseryman Samuel Parsons wrote in 1847: "After the invention of the Daguerreotype and the Magnetic Telegraph, nothing can be deemed impossible or incredible, respecting the natural agents which have been placed by Supreme Wisdom in the hands of man." He predicted that a hitherto elusive goal, the breeding of a blue rose, might soon lie within the grasp of horticultural expertise.

The eminent French hybridizer Jean Laffay named his 1840 hybrid Bourbon **'Great Western'** after the first transatlantic steamship, which had made its maiden voyage from England to America three years earlier. Similarly, the 1893 hybrid perpetual **'Captain Hayward'** honored the skipper of the first steamer to carry train passengers on a return trip from London to Boulogne in one day; the 1922 rambler **'Ile de France'** paid tribute to the first ocean liner constructed after World War I; and **'Nautilus'** came out in 1960, when the nuclear submarine U.S.S. *Nautilus* became the first underwater vessel to circumnavigate the globe.

The 1910 rambler **'Aviateur Blériot'** hailed French pilot Louis Blériot, who made the first international flight, a thirty-seven-minute trip from Calais to Dover; the 1927 polyantha **'Lindbergh'** quickly followed Charles Lindbergh's epic nonstop New York to Paris solo crossing, another first, in the *Spirit of St. Louis*; the 1930 hybrid rugosa **'Dr. Eckener'** saluted Hugo Eckener, the German aeronautical engineer who

INCANDESCENT 'THOMAS A. EDISON',
INTRODUCED IN 1931

piloted the dirigible *Graf Zeppelin*, the largest aircraft to date when it was built and the first to circle the globe; and the hybrid tea **'Amelia Earhart'**, which was yellow like its namesake's beloved biplane, *Canary*, landed in nursery catalogs in 1932, the year Earhart became the first woman to fly solo across the Atlantic.

When outer-space travel was only a Buck Rogers fantasy, **'Rocket'**, a 1935 red hybrid tea hinted at future wonders. And once science fiction turned into reality, starry-eyed roses reflected the glow: **'Satellite'** in 1957, **'Sputnik'** in 1958, **'Apollo'** in 1971, **'Space Invader'** in 1990, **'Blastoff'** in 1993. When it accompanied seventy-seven-year-old astronaut John Glenn on the space shuttle *Discovery* in 1998, **'Overnight Scentsation'** made history as the first rose in space. Compact and perfumed, this cheery pink miniature made the perfect cabin mate.

Each generation of rosarians scans the horizon for vehicles to fame and fortune. In 1971, Sam McGredy wrote, "Of one thing I am sure, twenty years from now the rose will be as different from today's model as the Concorde is from the Sopwith Camel. My one ambition in life is to be part of that development." The last Concorde G-BOAA has been grounded in Scotland since 2000, but a fragrant yellow **'Concorde'** hybrid tea is ready for takeoff in a florist's shop near you.

SURPRISE

While rose growers strive to perfect the science of hybridizing, nature insists on springing genetic surprises. These "sports," as botanists call them, often take the form of a spontaneous change in flower color or a shift in growth pattern from shrubby to climbing. The following names perpetuate accidental success stories.

'Happenstance': Often grown as a ground cover, this miniature is a petite sport of the giant climber **'Mermaid'**. Both the parent and its offspring, which first appeared around 1950, have pale yellow single blooms.

'Keepit': The Australian two-tone pink hybrid tea resulted from an unplanned cross between unknown parents in 1988. Its grower was ready to throw this orphan out when a friend intervened, saying "Keep it!" Good advice. 'Keepit' has since become a favorite at flower shows Down Under.

'Surprise Surprise': This miniature, a 1998 sport of the red mini **'Cherry Magic'**, keeps gardeners guessing. Its mauve-lavender flowers can unpredictably display red stripes or even an occasional solid-red petal. Another mini, orange-pink **'What a Surprize'**, popped up as a 2004 sport of **'Hot Tamale'**.

'Vick's Caprice': The pink hybrid perpetual **'Archiduchesse Elisabeth d'Autriche'**, created in France in 1881, unexpectedly gave birth to this pink-striped sport sixteen years later, in the Rochester, New York, garden of James Vick. The American ran a successful seed business that purportedly mailed catalogs to more than two hundred thousand customers. Vick also sold the catalogs' color lithographs as wall decorations.

CONSTANCE SPRY

WELL-BRED ENGLISHWOMEN OF THE early twentieth century shunned the vulgarity of combining different cut flowers. Mixed arrangements, especially multicolor displays, betrayed a want of taste—or the lack of a proper cutting garden and hothouse to supply bunches of matching blooms. This Edwardian standard prevailed until the late 1920s, when floral designer Constance Spry flung decorum onto the compost heap. Over the next three decades, Spry championed self-expression and experimentation at her chic London and New York shops, in the thirteen books she wrote for do-it-yourselfers, and at the Domestic Science School where she taught the applied arts of decorating, cookery, and entertaining. In place of comme-il-faut long-stemmed roses, lilies, and carnations primly segregated in silver or crystal vases, she mingled wildflowers and weeds, artichokes and cabbage leaves, cannas and gourds inside containers that struck her contemporaries as daringly outré: a tureen lid, a birdcage, a straw hat, a baking tin. When she did take the route of a one-variety arrangement, the plant material might as easily be kale as magnolia blossoms. And when she opted for roses, she assigned them unexpected partners: wild strawberries, say, or horse-chestnut leaves. The panache of this approach thrilled upper-crust patrons, and its resourcefulness emboldened ordinary homemakers.

After she'd decked out Westminster Abbey and the royal parade route for Queen Elizabeth's coronation, Spry went on to publish *Simple Flowers: A Millionaire for a Few Pence*. Despite being caricatured as a drawing-room bohemian who treated vegetation as nature's craft kit, she truly did love flowers and respected their natural beauty. She just preferred varieties whose allure lay in strength of character, not a modish name or a fancy price tag.

Casual visitors expecting eccentric novelty must have found Spry's own garden a letdown, because rosebushes—a mainstay of conventional horticulture—dominated the scene. Keen-eyed observers, on the other hand, marveled at her originality. Paradoxically, this trendsetting designer's roses stood out because they *weren't* modern; rather, they represented the shock of the old. Spry eschewed the new and improved hybrid teas and floribundas one met in every mid-twentieth-century flower bed from London to Los Angeles. Her roses were the flora of folklore, history, and romance that many contemporary gardeners had never seen except in vintage botanical illustrations—plants out of fashion so long that nurseries hadn't stocked them within living memory: damasks and gallicas, musks and mosses, Bourbons and Chinas. Even rose enthusiasts took it for granted that some of Spry's archaic curiosities had gone the way of the dodo.

Shoppers today have become so accustomed to specialty catalogs

'CONSTANCE SPRY'

crammed with "heirloom," "antique," or "heritage" roses—all known to rosarians as "old garden roses"—that it's hard to comprehend the pioneering spirit of Spry's dedication to keeping such relics alive. Technically, an old garden rose antedates the introduction in 1867 of the first hybrid tea, **'La France'**. All hybrid teas and newer types of roses created after 1867, like the floribundas and grandifloras, are "modern." Fortunately, because Spry and like-minded antiquarians refused to accept that modern is invariably better than old-fashioned, many venerable roses escaped extinction. Spry couldn't have asked for a more suitable memorial than the magnificent hybrid that British rosarian David Austin created and named after her in 1961. **'Constance Spry'** was a landmark: the first in Austin's series of "English Roses," shrubs that merge the disease resistance of modern varieties with the full flower shapes and heady fragrance of species and old garden cultivars. Unlike most later Austin shrubs, however, it does not bloom repeatedly throughout the summer.

THE BUXOM, MYRRH-SCENTED PINK blossoms of 'Constance Spry' captivated the British plantsman, writer, and botanical artist Graham Stuart Thomas, who was the first to market this shrub at the nursery where he worked. Two decades later, acknowledging Thomas's stature as *the* international expert on heirloom varieties, Austin invited him to pick out a new English Rose to bear his name. The shrub he chose, **'Graham Thomas'**, stands out for the vibrant yellow of its large fragrant flowers. Their color recalls one of the numerous plant rescue missions in which Thomas partook: the deliverance of **'Hidcote Yellow'**, aka **'Lawrence Johnston'**. Major Lawrence Johnston, a wealthy American expatriate straight out of a Henry James novel, established the quintessential English Arts and Crafts garden of the early twentieth century at Hidcote Manor, his Cotswolds estate. The interlocking outdoor "rooms" he laid out have influenced landscape design ever since. On a jaunt to France during the 1920s, this energetic gentleman of leisure bought the only extant specimen of a yellow hybrid foetida bred by Joseph Pernet-Ducher, who had inexplicably set it aside as a failure. Johnston gave his purchase a good home at Hidcote. The few slips from the French climber that he bestowed upon fellow gardeners were informally called 'Hidcote Yellow', the name under which Graham Thomas made the plant's acquaintance after World War II. A consummate diplomat, he persuaded the squire of Hidcote to let him exhibit and sell this rose, labeling it 'Lawrence Johnston' into the bargain.

We have Thomas to thank for making other once-hidden gems accessible to the world at large, too. His discovery of the white-flowered species now called **"Graham Thomas Musk"** helped rosarians identify the elusive musk rose, a strain previously believed lost. None of his antique finds possesses a lineage more intriguing than that of **"La Mortola"**—a redolent white climber so vigorous it can easily top forty feet—which he named and brought to market in 1954. This rose's provenance leads to Sir Thomas Hanbury, an English Quaker who, after making his fortune in the Chinese silk and tea trades, purchased a ruined palazzo in the Italian village of La Mortola in 1867. The Mediterranean climate and Hanbury's ample means enabled him to indulge the passion for exotic plants he had developed in the Orient. (Recently restored, the botanical garden now comprises an outstanding collection of flora from around the world.) His son, Cecil, spotted "La Mortola" growing wild on the grounds. The plant's Italian label is deceptive, however, because botanists have concluded that "La Mortola" is a form of the Himalayan species *Rosa brunonii* collected in Szechuan around the turn of the twentieth century by the explorer E. H. Wilson.

Any roll call of English rose champions at home and abroad must number Gertrude Jekyll among Albion's finest. Through her designs, writings, and photographs, Jekyll did yeoman work to preserve the art of the cottage garden and to save old-fashioned plants from oblivion. She was no slouch at flower arranging, either. "Bumps," as the architect Edwin Lutyens fondly nicknamed this doyenne of Edwardian gardeners, endures in the roses **'Miss Jekyll'**, a white rambler, and **'Gertrude Jekyll'**, a David Austin shrub with intensely perfumed deep pink flowers.

Crimson purple **"Sissinghurst Castle"** alludes to novelist, poet, and gardening columnist Vita Sackville-West. The indefatigable aristocrat almost literally stumbled across this gallica among nettles and brambles at Sissinghurst, the rundown estate she acquired in 1930 after her love affair with Virginia Woolf. Scores of rose varieties, old and modern, pack the luxuriant yet firmly structured landscape that Sackville-West and her husband, Harold Nicolson, carved out of their overgrown domain. Constance Spry often visited, and Graham Thomas was always welcome. In Sackville-West's foreword to Thomas's *The Old Shrub Roses* (published in 1955), she warmed to his subject: "Rich they were, rich as a fig broken open, soft as a ripened peach, freckled as an apricot, coral as a pomegranate, bloomy as a bunch of grapes. It is of these that the old roses remind me . . . how right is Mr Thomas when he implies that they have 'all the attraction that sentiment, history, botany, or association can lend them.'"

Among the few hybrid teas that Sackville-West permitted to hobnob with their elders at Sissinghurst is creamy yellow-to-pink **'Ellen Willmott'**. Introduced in 1936, two years after its namesake's death, the British plant commemorates a woman born in 1858, back when hybrid teas were just a gleam in rose breeders' eyes. Family money gave Willmott the wherewithal to garden lavishly in the intricate landscapes she designed at her English country house, her French château, and her Italian villa. Willmott may not have pulled the weeds (eighty or more gardeners tended her grounds), but she took her horticulture seriously. The Royal Horticultural Society awarded her its Victoria Medal of Honour in 1897; she wrote *Genus Rosa*, originally published on the eve of the First World War and still the classic book about species roses, although unfortunately out of print; and she sponsored major botanical expeditions out of her own purse. E. H. Wilson named a mauve-flowered Chinese species *R. willmottiae* as a thank-you for her support of his plant hunting.

Still, Miss Willmott, as everyone called her, was an odd duck, generous one moment, cantankerous the next. She grew some one hundred thousand species in her prime but heartily disliked sharing plants with visitors. The exception were invasive species that would haunt the recipient for years to come. When paying calls, she slyly

THE ENGLISH FLORAL DESIGNER CONSTANCE SPRY BROUGHT MODERN FLAIR TO AN ANCIENT ART.

sprinkled seeds of *Eryngium giganteum*, a prickly gray-green biennial, onto her hosts' garden beds. That robust plant, now more widely known than her namesake roses, goes by 'Miss Willmott's Ghost'.

PARSONS' POSIES

When not delivering sermons or presiding over weddings, funerals, and village fêtes, English clergymen have spent their time taking rose culture to a higher plane. A litany of names acknowledges the clerical contribution to the breeding and nurture of earthly delights.

'Pemberton's White Rambler': As a little boy in Essex, Joseph Hardwick Pemberton helped his father tend the family rosebushes and cut a rose for his own his buttonhole every Sunday. By his twelfth birthday, in 1864, he had mastered the propagation technique of budding. Hybridizing, growing, and exhibiting roses became a lifelong passion, continuing throughout Pemberton's tenure as vicar of Romford. He and his sister (honored by **'Florence Pemberton'**, a white hybrid tea bred in Ireland in 1903) owned a nursery in the aptly named Havering-atte-Bower where, their catalog announced, 'We appreciate a visit from the lovers of roses, whether purchasers or not . . . it is a pleasure to have a talk." Unlike his namesake white rambler, a multiflora introduced in 1914, Pemberton's best-known varieties, such as **'Clytemnestra'** and **'Cornelia'**, are the small-flowered everblooming shrubs he originated as "hybrid musks."

'Rambling Rector': No one knows whether a peripatetic man of the cloth inspired this engaging name, first recorded before the First World War. Sweetly fragrant, creamy white flowers dapple the plant as it climbs or spreads, masking a multitude of landscape sins.

'Reverend Alan Cheales': The petals of this 1898 hybrid perpetual are deep pink on top, white below. Although the Reverend Cheales, vicar of Brockham, Surrey, did not create this variety (it came from a Hertfordshire nursery), he tended a noteworthy rose garden on the plot where the village school now stands.

'Rev. H. D'Ombrain': His surname looks French, and his rose is an 1863 pink Bourbon, but the Reverend H. Honywood D'Ombrain was a Kentish vicar who epitomized English respectability. The first secretary of the National Rose Society, D'Ombrain impressed the Society's president, S. Reynolds Hole, as "a true Rosarian, a trusty, genial writer, [and] an accomplished florist." Among Victorian gentlefolk, "florist" signified anyone who cultivated flowers.

'Reynolds Hole': The Reverend Samuel Reynolds Hole wrote some of the nineteenth century's most absorbing rose literature. The first edition of his masterpiece, *A Book about Roses: How to Grow and Show Them*, was published in 1869, seven years before Hole became the first president of the National Rose Society, a position he held until his death in 1904. Alfred, Lord Tennyson dubbed him the Rose King; Charles Dickens and Gertrude Jekyll both enjoyed his company; and worshippers flocked to hear him preach, as a vicar in Nottinghamshire and as dean of Rochester Cathedral. Two rose cultivars have borne the name **'Reynolds Hole'**. The earlier, an 1862 Bourbon, is extinct, but an 1874 red hybrid perpetual was recently rediscovered in the garden of a house where Hole once lived. Sadly, **'Dean Hole'**, a pink hybrid tea released the year of his death, seems to have vanished.

'Wolley-Dod's Rose': The free-flowering pink-petaled shrub may be a cross between the species *Rosa pomifera* and an unidentified hybrid, bred in France by Jean-Pierre Vibert, during the early nineteenth century. Decades later, it turned up in the garden of the Reverend Charles Wolley-Dod, an amateur horticulturist who resided at Edge Hall, in Cheshire. We'll take **'Wolley-Dod's Rose'** any day over its clinical-sounding alias, *R. pomifera* **'Duplex'**.

DAMASK ROSE

LUSTROUS THOUGH THEY ARE, the flowers known as damask roses do not take their name from heirloom linens, but from the belief that a common ancestor, *Rosa x damascena*, traveled from Damascus to Europe amid the booty of returning Crusaders. Medieval Englishmen called the Syrian capital Damaske, although the earliest-known linkages of that city name to the plant were written three centuries later: a prescription for "fyne pouldre of redde dammaske rosys" by Henry VIII's surgeon, Thomas Vicary; and a reference by the Spanish physician Nicolas Monardes to roses "which [the Italians, French, and Germans] call *Damascenae*." The most fragrant of old garden roses, damasks appear to be naturally produced hybrids with a good deal of *R. gallica* in their parentage; the "x" in *R. x damascena* denotes that this is not a true species but the result of a genetic cross.

From a Middle Eastern vantage point, the association of these native hybrids with Crusaders centers on the Christians' defeat by the Syrian army under Saladin's command in 1187. It is said that the Muslim leader had five hundred camels lug rose water from Damascus to Jerusalem, in order that the Mosque of Omar, which the invaders had converted into a church, could be ritually cleansed of this defilement. Rose water was customarily made from *R. x damascena*, rather than from the other species and hybrids grown throughout the region, although all roses held an exalted place in the Islamic world. Ancient lore relates that wherever drops of Muhammad's perspiration fell upon the earth, during the night of his miraculous flight to heaven, roses sprouted. The Persian painter Kamaleddin Behzad, a contemporary of Leonardo da Vinci, depicted Muhammad gazing at one of these flowers. One corner of the Ka'bah, the holiest shrine in Mecca, is periodically anointed with attar (the Arabic *'itr* means "perfume" or "essence") from R. x *damascena* **'Trigintipetala'** ("thirty-petaled"). In Muslim homes, finely wrought metal

and glass dispensers hold rose water, to be sprinkled on the hands of wedding guests as well as on loved ones' graves. The aromatic liquid also sweetens delicacies served to break the fasts of Ramadan. At everyday meals, rose extracts flavor many foods and beverages; our "julep" derives from *julāb*, the Arabic version of the Persian *gulāb*, *gul* means "rose," and *lab*, "water."

The sight, taste, and scent of damasks and other Middle Eastern roses have inspired contemplation, celebration, and passion throughout the

DAMASK ROSES PAINTED BY SWISS BOTANICAL ARTIST ANNE-MARIE TRECHSLIN, 1962 history of Persian poetry. Americans generally know only snippets from the *Rubáiyát*, a collection of verses written by the astronomer and mathematician Omar Khayyám in the early 1100s, and translated by the English poet Edward FitzGerald in 1859. Victorian readers swooned over lines like this:

> And David's lips are lockt; but in divine
> > High-piping Péhlevi, with "Wine! Wine! Wine!
> > > Red Wine!"—the Nightingale cries to the Rose
> That sallow cheek of hers t'incarnadine.

In Khayyám's homeland, the nightingale and the rose are inseparable. Sir Robert Ker Porter, an English artist and diplomat who traveled through Persia (present-day Iran) in 1817, wrote of visiting a garden where "the ear is enchanted by the wild and beautiful notes of multitudes of nightingales, whose warblings seem to increase in melody and softness, with the unfolding of their favorite flowers." Persian poets tell of the bird's infatuation with the flower and of other plants' complaints to Allah that incessant nocturnal twittering disturbs their sleep. In one legend, a lovesick nightingale pricks himself on the thorns of a white rose and stains its petals red.

For most scholars of Persian literature, this floral tradition reached its zenith in *Gulistan*, (*The Rose Garden*), a series of moral and philosophical tales written by Muslih al-Din (commonly known as Sa'di) in 1258. It's surprising that no one has named a damask rose after Sa'di or *Gulistan*. So far, the appropriate garden library shelf pretty much belongs to **'Omar Khayyám'** and **'Rubaiyat'**. Bushes of Khayyám's namesake, a light pink damask, were growing at the poet's tomb in Nishapur (now in northern Iran) when William

Simpson, an English artist, paid his respects in 1884. Simpson carefully gathered seeds from these plants and sent them to the Royal Botanic Gardens at Kew, where a bush was propagated. Members of the Omar Khayyám Club planted a cutting from this scion on Edward FitzGerald's grave in 1893, ten years after the translator's death. Even though it is a hybrid tea bred in Northern Ireland in 1946, deep pink 'Rubaiyat' gives off a fragrance reminiscent of the original Middle Eastern damask rose.

NINETEENTH- AND TWENTIETH-CENTURY EUROPEAN rose lovers indulged in lush Orientalist reveries. A romantic haze still envelopes **"Rose de Rescht,"** a purplish pink damask named after the Iranian city of Rasht (or Resht), in a region where the roses used to make attar are cultivated. When the dashing English plantswoman Nancy Lindsay — a close friend of novelist and fellow rose connoisseur Vita Sackville-West — gave "Rose de Rescht" its European debut in the 1940s, she claimed to have encountered it on a prewar expedition in Gilan. Horticultural doubting Thomases, who discerned traces of gallica in this plant's leaf and flower, murmured that Lindsay

THE SEDUCTIVE FRAGRANCE OF DAMASKS
WON ADMIRERS IN THE MIDDLE EAST AND EUROPE.

might actually have discovered the plant in France and then spun a fable à la Scheherazade. Neither confirming nor denying this persistent rumor, British garden writers Roger Phillips and Martyn Rix quote Lindsay's own account: "Happened on it in an old Persian garden in ancient Resht, tribute of the tea caravans plodding Persia-wards from China over the Central Asian steppes; it is a sturdy, yard-high bush of glazed lizard-green, perpetually emblazoned with full camellia flowers of pigeon's blood ruby, irised with royal-purple, haloed with dragon sepals like the painted blooms on oriental faience."

The pink damask **'Ispahan'** commemorates another Persian city whose roses stirred imaginations abroad—above all in France, where this damask has been grown as **'Rose d'Ispahan'** since 1832. Like migratory nightingales, Frenchmen have drunk deep of the old imperial capital and its famous flowers—poet Charles-Marie Leconte de Lisle, in the poem "Les roses d'Ispahan" ("The Roses of Ispahan"), which Gabriel Fauré set to music; artist Lucien Lévy-Dhurmer, who painted an image inspired by the Fauré song; novelist Pierre Loti, in a travel diary, *Vers Ispahan* (*Toward Ispahan*); and poet Guillaume Apollinaire, whose "Ispahan" distills the mystique that lured them all:

> Ispahan with the sounds of the morning
> Awakens the fragrance of the roses in its gardens
>
> I have perfumed my soul
> With the rose
> For all of my life.

LOCAL COLOR

"I believe that in no country in the world does the rose grow in such perfection as in Persia," wrote Ker Porter, "in no country is it so cultivated and prized by the natives. Their gardens and courts are crowded by its plants, their rooms ornamented with roses, filled with its gathered branches, and every bath strewed with the full-grown flowers, plucked with the ever replenished stems." Nevertheless, the Western rose name most conspicuously tied to that culture, **'Persian Yellow'**, refers not to a variety of sweet-scented *Rosa* x *damascena* but to unpleasant-smelling *R. foetida persiana*. Indigenous to Iran, the latter is an ancestor of most modern yellow hybrid teas and still supplies yellow pigmentation for plant-breeding programs and genetic experiments. Regrettably, 'Persian Yellow' also probably handed down black spot, a disease that plagues the foliage on roses of every color.

PERSIAN YELLOW' IS THE ANCESTOR OF ALL MODERN YELLOW ROSES.

DR. HUEY

DR. HUEY' REALLY GETS AROUND. In Brooklyn, New York, for instance, this local denizen is often seen lounging against stoops, crowding doorways, and leaning over concrete grottos that house statues of the Virgin Mary. Ninety miles east of there, upscale Hamptons nurseries sometimes tag the same plant **"Long Island Red,"** claiming to have found it on old estates, and price it at $350 a pop. From the rush of buyers, you'd have thought they were hawking heirloom Tiffany sterling. Sure, this rose is beautiful — but only for a day or two. Then heat and humidity leave the velvety flowers hanging like rags, their limp petals the color of dried blood. This is 'Dr. Huey', undercover agent of the rose world. Though a flop in the bloom department, the basic plant is so tough that many nurseries use it as the rootstock onto which they graft less hardy yet better-looking cultivars. Only the fancy cultivar up top gets an ID on the label a customer sees. Most of the time, 'Dr. Huey' is the rootstock that dares not speak its name, though the truth may emerge willy-nilly. That's what happened to one Brooklyn garden owner: after negligent pruning or a rough winter did in her pink **'Royal Highness'**, stubborn 'Dr. Huey' sent up suckers from below and flowered in its place. "Why have my roses turned red?" she asked a rosarian. He gently explained that her roots were showing.

Robert Huey, the gent behind the rose, had nothing to be ashamed of. After serving in the Union Army during the Civil War, he became a Philadelphia dentist, commuting from his home on the city's then semirural southwestern fringe, where he planted a two-acre garden in 1877. This was a time when having just hosted the nation's centennial festivities, Philadelphians proudly reflected on their rich horticultural heritage. Along the Schuylkill River, a few blocks east of Huey's property, America's pioneering plant collectors, botanists, and nurserymen, the Quaker father-and-son team of John and William Bartram, had lived and conducted business. (Their homestead and forty-five acres survive as the nation's oldest botanic garden.) King George III, President

'DR. HUEY'

George Washington, and other loyal customers ordered native flora such as *Rosa pennsylvanica*, grown from seeds the Bartrams collected in the wild. Across the Schuylkill, America's earliest commercial seed producer, David Landreth, had established his company in 1784. The firm's list of rose hybrids included **'Landreth's Carmine'**, a climbing Noisette with immense clusters of carmine blooms. William Buist, proprietor of a top-drawer nineteenth-century Philadelphia rose nursery, got his start in Landreth's employ. Buist also worked as a gardener at Woodlands, the estate of William Hamilton, upriver from the Bartrams. Hamilton's grounds displayed many of the first China roses introduced to the United States, notably **'Hamilton Monthly'** (now extinct).

Huey decided to record some of his personal history during the First World War, a conflict that would soon obliterate his precious garden. In the 1917 *American Rose Annual*, he flashed back to pre–Civil War Philadelphia. "My earliest rose recollection," he wrote, "is of an attempt to pluck a moss rose in my grandmother's garden and of getting my fingers pricked by the sharp thorns. Rescued by the nurse, the thorns were removed, and I was turned loose in the belief that a lesson had been taught. Nevertheless, I wanted that rose, and returned to the attack with a like result. Mother then appeared on the scene, took in the situation, cut the rose, removed the thorns, and made me happy with the flower. I have loved roses ever since." Unfortunately, failure dogged Huey's initial adult attempts at growing his own blooms: "the flowers that resulted compared most unfavorably with the illustrations in the catalogues, while the plants would die by the dozen." But the good doctor soldiered on, working his way through the inventories of local nurseries until he had achieved a measure of success and confidence. "Knowing that many others were thirsting for knowledge," he recalled, "I began writing and talking of my experiences and how my difficulties were overcome, thus doing a sort of rose missionary work."

Huey's reputation as a serious amateur eventually persuaded several Pennsylvania rose nurseries to send him samples of their latest hybrids for testing.

In 1898 Scott's Roses in nearby Sharon Hill brought Huey three **'Killarney'** hybrid teas, newly imported from Ireland. Grafted onto R. *canina,* the root-stock of choice in Europe, these were the first "budded" rosebushes Huey had ever grown—and, to his amazement, they outperformed every other rose in his garden. Besides fostering a friendship with the creator of 'Killarney'—Alex Dickson, who released a pink hybrid tea, **'Robert Huey'**, in 1911—this suc-cess led Huey to study the suitability of various rootstocks for North Amer-ica. Diligent research persuaded him that R. *multiflora* yielded the best results within a broad range of soils and climatic conditions, and his published find-ings convinced important growers to bud their cultivars onto that wild species. Early-twentieth-century gardeners had Huey to thank for the larger, healthier bushes they could now grow at home. By the same token, Huey upbraided the American Rose Society for catering to professional florists rather than supply-ing amateur horticulturists with practical information and advice. He even quit the ARS for two years in protest, rejoining only after he felt the society had mended its ways.

He practiced his preaching through generous acts, such as a gift of fifty rosebushes to fellow Philadelphian gardener George Thomas Jr., who had ex-pressed a lack of interest in the whole genus *Rosa.* Huey contendedly watched as Thomas "got the rose fever too." Indeed, Thomas became one of America's most prolific amateur rose breeders—and returned the favor. On June 4, 1919, Thomas invited his mentor and a contingent of ARS dignitaries for the official introduction of his latest red climber, 'Dr. Huey'. The man of the hour may well have needed cheering up: The government had recently confiscated his garden for the wartime expansion of nearby shipyards. Huey found genuine

solace in his rose for years to come. Thomas, he wrote, "has surely done splendid work . . . making me very proud of my pupil."

Grafted to *R. multiflora* rootstock, his protégé's tribute brightened dooryards from coast to coast. Huey died in 1928 at age eighty-five, unaware that
repeat-blooming climbers would replace his only-in-June namesake in the
public's heart or that it would ultimately go underground. During the 1950s,
tests conducted by mass-market nurseries determined that the best rootstock
for California's rose fields was 'Dr. Huey'. Acres of it, planted for this purpose, grew around the city of Shafter, hub of the West Coast rose industry.
Wholesalers got to calling the bush — still America's most commonly used rootstock — **'Shafter'**. Maybe public-spirited
Robert Huey would have perceived an ironic appropriateness in this payoff for his advocacy of grafted roses
as a godsend to Everyman. But maybe he'd also be
pleased to know that experts in his native Philadelphia, and throughout most of the colder climates
of North America, still recommend grafting onto
R. multiflora — just what the doctor ordered.

DR. ROBERT HUEY, THE DENTIST AND
AMATEUR ROSARIAN FROM PHILADELPHIA

THE WIZARDS

During André Du Pont's service as Empress Joséphine's court rosarian in the first decade of the 1800s, a contemporary called him "an enchanter who submits the rose to his magic wand and forces it to undergo the most surprising and agreeable transformation." This wizardry—an innovative hand-pollination technique—transformed rose breeding from a game of chance into something of a science. Du Pont was also the first hybridizer of many to style himself the "godparent" of seedlings he bred. The painter Redouté labeled one of these, a gallica, **'Rosier du Pont'** in his portrait of the flower. Subsequent chip-off-the-old-block names have carried on this tradition.

'Dr. J. H. Nicolas': A French schoolboy whose industrialist father tended roses as a hobby, ten-year-old Jean Henri Nicolas (1875–1937) fell in love with the scent of a hybrid tea, **'La France'**. He was twenty-seven when a business trip for the family firm took him to the United States where he married an American, settled in Indianapolis, and finally planted his own garden. This return to the soil convinced him to train as a rosarian and—as he wryly remarked in the 1922 *American Rose Annual*— embark on "missionary work to make rose-lovers out of golf-players and other wasters of time." The transplanted Frenchman's new *métier* blossomed quickly: five years after Conard-Pyle hired him as a rose researcher, in 1925 Jackson & Perkins appointed him director of research. A bon vivant with an irreverent wit, Nicolas loved skewering disagreeable or pompous rose names. **'Odorata'** he deemed one of the most "unfortunate" labels ever tied to a stem; mouthfuls like **'Baronesse A. van Hovell tot Westerflier'** provoked guffaws. Simplicity distinguishes the names he gave most of his own thirty-one cultivars, from **'Empire State'** and **'Kismet'** to **'Lucy T. Nicolas'** (after his wife) and **'Smiles'**. Citing Nicolas's achievements as hybridizer, writer, and rose ambassador-at-large, the Sorbonne awarded its alumnus an honorary doctorate in 1934. He died in his sleep three years later, en route from Europe to America. One of his last creations, a pink climber, was introduced posthumously as **'Dr. J. H. Nicolas'**.

'Gene Boerner': "You're our head hybridizer now, Gene . . . you know what we need. Now get out your camel's hair pollen brush and produce it." Thus spake Charlie Perkins, president of Jackson & Perkins, to Eugene S. Boerner (1893–1966) when he joined the business in 1937. During his three decades as J&P's director of research, Boerner would create 181 rose hybrids, 111 of which were floribundas—winning him international fame as "Papa Floribunda." He often greeted visitors to the J&P rose fields by raising his fedora and pulling out a cut rose. The humid warmth under his hat, he explained, would draw out the flower's fragrance. At Gene's Landing, his 160-acre country place in upstate New York, Boerner enjoyed the life of a gentleman farmer, looking after a vineyard, an orchard, and a herd of Hereford cattle, as well as fishing, cooking, collecting antiquarian cookbooks (especially those with recipes calling for rose petals), and breeding dachshunds. A pink floribunda that Papa created shortly before his death, in 1966, was later named **'Gene Boerner'**. His memory also endures in the Eugene S. Boerner Fund, a scholarship he endowed at Cornell University to support the study of rose development, culture, and pathology.

'Harry Wheatcroft': The ebullient nurseryman, author, and lecturer Harry Wheatcroft (1898–1977) attained garden pop-star celebrity as British television's "Mr. Rose." Well before the Peacock Revolution of the sixties, he cut a conspicuous figure on screen and off, wearing muttonchop whiskers and idiosyncratic outfits, such as a houndstooth-tweed suit trimmed in tangerine velvet over an open-collared floral-print shirt. Fellow exhibitors at the staid Chelsea Flower Show gawked at the spectacle of Wheatcroft tearing off his shirt in a frenzy of last-minute rose arranging. This flamboyance belied a good head for business and a keen eye for horticultural distinction, tested by decades of experience (Wheatcroft opened his first rose nursery in 1919, following imprisonment as a conscientious objector during the First World War) and travels around the world in search of promising rose varieties. He was the first UK grower to import and market the phenomenal bestsellers **'Peace'** and **'Queen Elizabeth'**. In 1973 the company he ran with his sons introduced a hybrid tea **'Harry Wheatcroft'**. Everyone who knew the man agreed that, as a portrait in petals, the flaming yellow-and-red-striped flower suited him to a tee.

Noisette: South Carolina rice planter John Champneys can hardly have known when he happened to cross *Rosa moschata* with the China rose **'Old Blush'**, around 1802, that the result would beget an important new class of roses, the Noisettes. Nonetheless, he took pride in his lovely seedling and called it **'Champneys' Pink Cluster'**. This novelty caught the eye of Philippe Noisette, a French nurseryman based in Charleston, who soon bred variations on Champneys's rose and sent them to his brother-cum-business partner in Paris, who cannily introduced them as "Noisette" roses. Early nineteenth-century Americans protested that these roses should properly be called, after

J. H. NICOLAS POLLINATING ROSES

their countryman, "Champneyana." New York nurseryman William Prince entered the fray in 1846, writing, "The origin of the first varieties of this remarkable group has been announced erroneously to the world by various writers, arising first, from the want of candor on the part of the late Philippe Noisette . . . " Wrongly or not, Noisettes they remain.

Pernetiana: When Joseph Pernet (1851–1928) of Lyon, France, married Marie Ducher in 1882, the union joined two rose families. Pernet's father, Jean, a highly respected nurseryman, had hybrids such as **'Triomphe de Pernet Père'** and **'Jean Pernet'** to his credit.

Marie was the daughter of Claude Ducher (**'Gloire de Ducher'**) and his wife, Marie, who had bred hybrids she named for their children: **'Marie Ducher'**, **'Jean Ducher'**, and **'Antoine Ducher'**. (Jean and Antoine started their own nursery, under the name Ducher, which is currently run by Antoine's great-great-great-great-grandson, Fabian). A spat with his father caused Joseph to amend his name, and that of his business, to Pernet-Ducher. Perhaps in the interest of pronounceability, "Ducher" stayed off the labels of his gorgeous yellow hybrids, which came to be known as Pernetiana Roses. Regrettably, they tend to attract fungus.

'Wilhelm Kordes': Building upon his father's success as a commercial rose grower in Germany, Wilhelm Kordes II (1891–1976) opened his own nursery in England in 1912 in partnership with a compatriot, Max Krause. At the start of the First World War, British authorities shut down the business and interned both partners; in 1919 they were deported as "undesirable aliens." "Willi" cheerfully reestablished his rose business in Sparrieshoop, near Hamburg, while maintaining close ties in England and cultivating new friends in the United States. Rosarians everywhere continue to benefit from his introduction in 1922 of a less fungus-prone Pernetiana—sunset-colored **'Wilhelm Kordes'**, a nod to his father and namesake—which made possible numerous disease-resistant strains. A decade later, the robust health and beauty of Kordes's almost black hybrid tea **'Crimson Glory'** further raised his international standing as a virtuoso of rose hardiness. A different sort of ingenuity emerged during the next war, when he saved more than two thousand of his rosebushes (a verboten crop during the conflict) by hiding them in a legal field of rye. Peacetime found Kordes as resilient as ever, developing a series of shrub roses, the Kordesii, that fear neither black spot nor mildew. Among the best known of these hybrids is red-flowered **'Dortmund'**. Introduced in 1955, this climber takes its name from the hometown of the German Rose Society, an organization Kordes resurrected after the war. His nursery, now directed by Wilhelm Kordes III and as vibrant as it was in Willi's day, still specializes in disease-resistant roses.

EGLANTINE

MADAME EGLENTYNE, THE HIGHFALUTIN English prioress in Geoffrey Chaucer's *Canterbury Tales*, took pride in her schoolgirl French and genteel manners. This superior Mother Superior would have adored being named after a blossom with a fancy-sounding French label—as long as no fellow pilgrim (that coarse wife of Bath, *par exemple*) made cracks about a wickedly thorny rose running wild in hedgerows throughout Christendom.

With all due respect, that actually is a fair description of this plant. Mellifluous *eglantine* comes from the Latin for "needle" and "sting," by way of the Medieval French *aiglent* and the Middle English *eglentyn*. The Old English *brer* ("briar" or "bramble") behind eglantine's other common name, sweet briar, also denotes its prickliness. What struck Anglo-Saxons as the sweet side of the shrub seems not to have been its light pink, five-petaled spring flowers, pretty though they are, or its ruddy autumn hips (the source of its botanical name, *Rosa rubiginosa*, from the Latin for "rusty"), but the crisp apple scent of its dark green leaves. "The eglentine is much like the common brer but the leues [leaves] are swete and pleasant to smel to," wrote the botanist William Turner in his exhaustively titled *A New Herball: Wherein are Conteyned the Names of Herbes in Greke, Latin, Englysh, Duch, Frenche, and in the Potecaries*

Rosa rubiginosa ε
Double Red Sweet Brie

and Herbaries Latin, with the Properties Degrees and Naturall Places of the Same, published in 1551.

A less pedantic take on fragrance inspired Shakespeare to entwine this rose with other aromatic vegetation in *A Midsummer Night's Dream*: "I know a bank where the wild thyme blows, / Where oxlips and the nodding violet grows, / Quite overcanopied with luscious woodbine, / With sweet musk-roses, and with eglantine: / There sleeps Titania sometime of the night, / Lulled in these flowers with dances and delight." Lest anyone doubt that the Bard indeed knew this briar well, consider the following lines from *Cymbeline*: "Thou shalt not lack / The flower that's like thy face, pale primrose, nor / The azured harebell, like thy veins; no, nor / The leaf of eglantine, whom not to slander, / Outsweetened not thy breath"; or these from *All's Well that Ends Well*: "the time will bring on summer, / When briers shall have leaves as well as thorns, / And be as sweet as sharp."

English poets from Spenser to Keats, Wordsworth, and Tennyson also perfumed pages with eglantine, punctuating sentiment with thorns. One of Spenser's sonnets touches on a recurrent theme: "Sweet is the Rose, but growes vpon a brere; / . . . Sweet is the Eglantine, but pricketh nere." In North America, eglantine transplanted by homesick colonists rapidly escaped into the wild — and found its way into literature, prickles and all. Nathaniel Hawthorne described Hester Prynne, the adulterous heroine of *The Scarlet Letter*, gathering sweet-briar leaves from a stream bank for her illegitimate child. (Elsewhere in the novel, a wild rosebush symbolizes perseverence in the

ENGLISH BOTANICAL ARTIST MARY LAWRANCE PAINTED THIS DOUBLE EGLANTINE IN 1799.

face of social condemnation.) A scandalous shade of scarlet, the rose **'Hester Prynne'** is a floribunda, not an eglantine hybrid. Henry David Thoreau wrote of picking eglantine in bud as he hiked along Walden's railroad causeway, on one of his meditative pilgrimages. A journal entry observes: "Nature imitates all things in flowers. They are at once the most beautiful and the ugliest objects, the most fragrant and the most offensive to the nostrils."

Had Madame Eglentyne foreseen the unsavory company her namesake would keep — scribblers, fallen women, idlers — she doubtless would have asked to be excused from the library. A more suitable alter ego finally appeared in 1969, when the English rose breeder David Austin introduced a hybrid shrub with lightly scented flowers in a tasteful shade of pale pink that he christened **'The Prioress'** (its genealogy doesn't show a drop of common eglantine blood and even includes a Bourbon). Austin subsequently allowed that this plant required way too much cosseting, and therefore should be grown only by "collectors." Madame Eglentyne would certainly have liked that. On the other hand, she might have been miffed by Austin's decision in 1994 to name another pink shrub rose **'Eglantyne'**, after Eglantyne Jebb, the founder of the British Save the Children Fund. Not only is the newer flower more beautiful and fragrant than 'The Prioress', but its truly benevolent namesake never provoked a poet's satire.

BOOKISH BLOOMS

W ell-read rosarians will be pleased to note that their favorite flower crops up in many literary circles. Regrettably, some of the varieties cited below have gone "out of print," being extinct or no longer listed in nursery catalogs.

Sappho: Three nineteenth-century roses named **'Sappho'** honor the ancient Greek poet, who lived on the island of Lesbos. William Paul, the English hybridizer of the latest in the trio, an 1889 pink tea, quoted the Athenian biographer Philostratus: "Sappho was enamoured of the Rose, and bestows upon it always some distinguished praise: she likens it to the most beautiful of maidens."

Anacreon: This Greek bon vivant's verse sings of wine and roses, usually in that order. All four of the nineteenth-century gallicas called **'Anacréon'**, two of which are extinct, had wine-colored flowers.

Pierre de Ronsard: Roses symbolize fleeting amours in Ronsard's sonnet *Roses* and other works. Mary, Queen of Scots (and, for a time, queen of the French, too) presented the poet a silver rose as a token of admiration. In the United States, the pink and white French climber **'Pierre de Ronsard'** goes by the prosaic **'Eden 88'**.

Miguel de Cervantes: Don Quixote worships Dulcinea, "for her hairs are gold . . . her eyebrows rainbows, her eyes suns, her cheeks roses," and promises his right-hand man, Sancho Panza, a pastoral retreat where "the roses will lend their perfume." An international rose competition takes place every May at the Parc de Cervantes i Roserar, a public park in Barcelona. Seeking to buy the hard-to-find European roses **'Cervantes'**, **'Don Quichotte'**, and **'Dulcinea'** in the United States can prove a quixotic mission.

William Shakespeare: The crimson gallica **'Shakespeare'**, bred in France before 1843, is also known as **'Kean'**, after Edmund Kean (1789–1833), a British actor famed for playing Shakespearean roles. Displeased by his 1987 shrub **'William**

Shakespeare', a horticultural flop, English breeder David Austin introduced a sequel, and now his crimson-to-purple **'William Shakespeare 2000'** grows at the playwright's birthplace in Stratford-upon-Avon. Thereby hangs a long tale of Shakespearean names: **'A Midsummer Night's Dream'**, **'Proud Titania'**, **'Oberon'**, and **'Puck'**; **'Mistress Quickly'** and **'Falstaff'**; **'Desdemona'** (apparently extinct) and **'Othello'**; **'Prins Hamlet'**; **'Romeo'** and **'Juliet'**; **'Admired Miranda'** and **'Prospero'**; **'The Dark Lady'** (dark red, of course) of the sonnets; and more.

Christopher Marlowe: In "The Passionate Shepherd to His Love," a man woos his sweetheart, saying, "Come live with me and be my love . . . / There I will make thee beds of roses." The orange-red bloom of the shrub **'Christopher Marlowe'** befits the writer's notorious temper.

Wolfgang von Goethe: The philosopher, poet, and dramatist grew up in Frankfurt and trained **'Frankfort Rose'** (*Rosa* x *francofurtana*) over his treasured garden house in Weimar. As a visitor noted, "he actually lived in the middle of a rosebush." German nurseries produced the moss rose **'Goethe'** in 1911 and the hybrid perpetual **'Wolfgang von Goethe'** in 1933. Neither has *R.* x *francofurtana* in its lineage. Two **'Faust'** roses and one **'Dr. Faust'** (an infernal mix of yellow, orange, and pink) recall the famous Goethean character.

Robert Burns: "A Rose-Bud in My Early Walk," "Yon Rosy Brier," and "A Red, Red Rose" belong to a garland of works by Scotland's national bard. One floral namesake, the red hybrid tea **'Rabbie Burns'**, is Scottish; the other, the white shrub **'Robbie Burns'**, is English.

Lord Byron: His "Love's Last Adieu" gives perspective on garden maintenance: "The roses of Love glad the garden of life, / Though nurtur'd 'mid weeds dropping pestilent dew, / Till Time crops the leaves with unmerciful knife, / Or prunes them for ever, in Love's last adieu!" The early gallica **'Lord Byron'** has bid the world adieu, but an apricot-colored climber by the same name, bred in 1991, has taken its place.

Sir Walter Scott: Since the mid-nineteenth century, rosarians have linked flowers to the novelist's legion of historical characters. The Victorian grower Lord Penzance gave Scott names to no fewer than thirteen of his hybrid eglantines, including **'Flora McIvor'**, **'Jeanie Deans'**, **'Meg Merrilies'**, all of which are available today.

George Sand: Upon the birth of this French writer (née Amandine-Aurore-Lucile Dupin), during a country-house dance, an aunt said, "She will be fortunate, she was born among the roses to the sound of music." The heroines of Sand's first novel were Rose, an actress, and Blanche, a nun. Two roses, a rugosa and a hybrid tea, bear the nom de plume **'George Sand'**.

Charles Dickens: A rose garden was one of the author's favorite spots at his last home, Gad's Hill. He named Oliver Twist's angelic aunt Rose, and in *Martin Chuzzlewit* he wrote of a widow: "[In] full bloom she was now; with roses on her ample skirts, and roses on her bodice . . . aye, and roses, worth the gathering too, on her lips, for that matter." After Dickens's

death, in 1870, a grateful nation blanketed his coffin with roses. **'Charles Dickens'** tells a tale of two roses: an 1886 hybrid perpetual and a centenary floribunda. Other Dickensian plants include **'Great Expectations'**, **'Miss Havisham'**, **'Oliver Twist'**, and **'Artful Dodger'**.

Rainer Maria Rilke: An infected wound from a rose thorn in his garden may have precipitated the illness that killed Rilke in 1926 at the age of fifty-one. The German poet composed his own epitaph: "Rose, oh sheer contradiction. Desire to be no one's sleep under so many eyelids." The floribunda **'Rainer Maria Rilke'** is a wide-awake orange.

Colette: Three twentieth-century **'Colette'** cultivars honor the author who knew roses intimately. In *The House of Claudine* she wrote: "The beak of secateurs snaps along the rose alleys. Another replies in the orchard. Later on in the rose garden there will be a swath of tender openings, red with daybreak on the summit, green and juicy at the base." One 'Colette', a French hybrid tea, was exported to the United Kingdom under the name **'John Keats'**.

Isak Dinesen: The pseudonymous author of *Out of Africa*—Karen Blixen in private life—loved to arrange the flowers she grew on her Kenyan farm and at her family home in Rungstedlund, Denmark (now a museum). A Danish breeder developed the hardy white hybrid tea **'Karen Blixen'**, which thrives at Rungstedlund today. Some say that orange, yellow, and pink **'Out of Africa'**, also a hybrid tea, resembles an African sunset.

Agatha Christie: Preferring a poison pen to a trowel, the British mystery writer let others look after her garden in Devon. Her sleuth Miss Marple, on the other hand, tends roses for enjoyment as well as detective work. "Gardening," she explains, "is as good as a smoke screen." A pinkish red floribunda and a clear pink climber, both called **'Agatha Christie'**, commemorate the author.

Antoine de Saint-Exupéry: His Little Prince from an asteroid tells earthly rosebushes about the plant he loves more than anything else, "She alone was the most important of you all, because I watered her . . . Because I killed the caterpillars for her (except two or three for butterflies). Because I listened to her when she complained, or even sometimes to her silence. Because she is my rose." One of the two **'Saint-Exupéry'** hybrid teas bred in France provided pollen for the breeding of **'Vol de Nuit'** ('Night Flight'), named after the author's poem with that title. An aviator, Saint-Exupéry died in a wartime plane crash, but the red polyantha **'Petit Prince'** keeps his memory bright.

Raymond Carver: The American short-story writer and poet grew roses at home and brought them into his work. In the poem "Cherish" a man watches his wife in the garden pruning: "She's alone / with roses and with something else I can only think, not / say. I know the names of those bushes." After the author's death, his publisher encouraged English hybridizer Peter Beales to name the apricot yellow shrub **'Raymond Carver'**.

EMPRESS JOSÉPHINE

"I AWAKE FILLED WITH THOUGHTS of you," Napoléon wrote to Rose de Beauharnais, in 1795, four months before their wedding; "the intoxicating pleasures of last night, allow my senses no rest. Sweet and incomparable Joséphine, how strangely you work upon my heart!!" This is the first record of the young general addressing his beloved as Joséphine. Did he give her a new name to erase her dubious past? All we know is this: As Joséphine she would make her name as one of the greatest champions a rose ever had.

The future French empress was born on the West Indian island of Martinique in 1763 as Marie Josèphe Rose de Tascher de la Pagerie — "Rose," from the cradle on, to friends and family. An arranged marriage to Alexandre, vicomte de Beauharnais, took the pretty Creole to Paris as a sixteen-year-old.

'EMPRESS JOSÉPHINE', AS PORTRAYED
BY PIERRE JOSEPH REDOUTÉ IN 1817

This unhappy union, marked by infidelities on both sides, produced two children. The couple was imprisoned during the Reign of Terror, but Rose—unlike her spouse—escaped the guillotine, thanks, perhaps, to an influential cousin of the Marquis de Sade who became her lover. After the Revolution, the resilient widow clung to the upper rungs of the social ladder as a *merveilleuse* ("marvelous one") in the smart set of that era. Through friends she met the up-and-coming Citizen Bonaparte. For him, it was love at first sight. For her, it was a hunch that the ladder could reach even higher than she had imagined.

The Bonaparte formerly known as Rose didn't set her sights on gardening until 1799, when she purchased the Château de Malmaison, a relatively

THE CHÂTEAU DE MALMAISON ROSE GARDEN IN AN EARLY-TWENTIETH-CENTURY VIEW

modest country place about ten miles from Paris. Bored with the ceremonial duties of a political wife, Joséphine had yearned for a private refuge. Secluded Malmaison came with a mature *jardin anglais*, an English parklike setting with curved pathways, islands of trees and shrubs, and meandering streams and flower beds reminiscent of her childhood plantation. Preferring this informality to rigid French landscapes, Joséphine hired Alexander Howatson, a Scottish gardener, to embellish the existing design with choice ornamental plants. She began spending time with Howatson and his staff, learning botany and horticulture and shopping at nurseries. She commissioned the botanical artist Pierre-Joseph Redouté to paint flowers from her gardens and decorate rooms inside the château with floral motifs. And she befriended the distinguished Parisian gardener André Du Pont, whose consuming passion for roses ensnared her.

By 1804, the year Napoléon crowned Joséphine empress, she had granted Du Pont carte blanche to collect and hybridize rose varieties for Malmaison. Her collection rapidly expanded to comprise more than two hundred varieties, a compendium of every rose then known in the Western world, and the largest *roseraie* in all of France. These treasures resided in the Emperor's Garden, a rectangular plot of symmetrical beds, straight paths, and clipped hedges designed by the architect Pierre Fontaine, a classicist who disdained the rest of Joséphine's rambling arcadia. Geometrical formality didn't cramp her style, though, when it came to plant names. At Malmaison, staid old *Rosa alba incarnata* metamorphosed into **'Cuisse de Nymphe Emue'** ("thigh of an aroused nymph") and flowered shamelessly beside **'Parure des Vierges'** ("virgins' jewelry"). **'La Roxelane'** honored a river in Martinique. **'Grand**

Turban' ("large turban") and **'Manteau Rouge'** ("red cloak") got their labels from current Paris fashions. **'La Belle Sultane'** probably alluded to Aimée Dubucq de Rivery, a cousin of Joséphine's, who, at age thirteen, had been captured at sea by pirates and sold into the harem of Ottoman sultan Abdul Hamid I. **'L'Empereur'** and **'Le Grand Napoléon'** required no annotation.

Like her conquering husband, Joséphine collected showpieces from around the world. Malmaison's menagerie included Australian black swans, Swiss cows (and cowherds), African gazelles, and an orangutan that entertained dinner guests. A conservatory sheltered tropical plants grown from Martinican seeds and cuttings. Garden beds displayed North American species roses such as *R. carolina*, *R. virginiana*, and *R. setigera*, probably shipped as plants or seeds by the botanist André Michaux, whose expeditions the empress underwrote. She imported the latest hybrids from Belgium and England, regardless of political or military obstacles. Eight months before the Treaty of Amiens, while France and Britain were still at war, Napoléon wrote to Joséphine: "Some plants have come for you from London, which I have sent to your gardener."

The emperor's personal secretary later recalled: "Nowhere, except on the field of battle, did I ever see Bonaparte more happy than in the gardens of Malmaison." This happiness ended in 1809, when Napoléon reluctantly divorced Joséphine, who had borne him no children. Although he went on to marry the nubile Princess Marie Louise of Austria, he permitted his ex-wife to retain her imperial title and stay on at her château.

Joséphine's successor as empress had no interest in gardening, but fashion and protocol virtually demanded that a rose bear her name. To remain in Napoléon's good graces, Joséphine made the arrangements. Her gardeners recycled a variety that had grown at Malmaison for some time as **'Agathe Rose'** and stuck on a new label: **'Marie Louise'**.

Joséphine died in 1814, a year before Napoléon went into exile on St. Helena. Debts that Joséphine had accrued forced her children to sell Malmaison. During the many years the house stood vacant, vandals ransacked the gardens and all documentary records of the roses disappeared, save for Redouté's botanical portraits. A skirmish during the Franco-Prussian War nearly destroyed the château, which later became a French army barracks.

At the turn of the twentieth century, French philanthropist Daniel Osiris, American expatriate Edward Tuck, and Paris department store tycoon and rose enthusiast Jules Gravereaux joined forces to establish Malmaison as a museum of the Napoleonic epoch. To improve the grounds, Gravereaux donated 197 rose varieties believed to have been in cultivation during Joséphine's reign. After this gallant attempt at a renaissance, however, the rose collection suffered from wartime neglect and economic hardship. Today, instead of Empire-period gallicas, teas, and other antique roses, modern hybrids such as **'Queen Elizabeth'**, **'Dorothy Perkins'**, and **'American Pillar'** greet visitors at the entrance to the Musée du Château de Malmaison, in now-suburban Rueil-Malmaison. Hidden behind an allée of trees, the ghostly outlines of Fontaine's geometric beds frame remnants of abortive efforts to restore the original *roseraie*.

Several nineteenth-century roses that honor Joséphine's legacy still thrive in many gardens. The most popular, **'Souvenir de la Malmaison'**, a light pink very fragrant Bourbon, dates to 1844, thirty years after her death. Lesser-known **'Eugène de Beauharnais'**, a purple China named after her son, was introduced in 1838 ('**Hortense de Beauharnais**', an 1834 pink gallica honoring her daughter, who married Napoléon's brother Louis, is now extinct). The most beautiful of all these tributes, **'L'Impératrice Joséphine'** (**'Empress Joséphine'**), a deep pink ruffled bloom with a heavenly fragrance, acquired that name sometime between 1814 and 1816. This gallica is actually a much older hybrid, recorded in the sixteenth century, but its rendezvous with destiny was worth the wait.

NAPOLÉON COMPLEX

Joséphine might have hesitated to plant **'Grand Napoléon'**, a mauve Belgian Gallica, because it came out during the year of her divorce. She didn't live long enough to contemplate the damask **'Folie de Bonaparte'**, bred in 1821, the year Napoléon died on St. Helena (and now extinct). No one who mourned his passing would have hesitated to plant either of the later varieties named **'Napoléon'**: an 1835 repeat-blooming pink China and an 1846 once-blooming mauve gallica. Another tribute, the Bourbon **'Cendres de Napoléon'** ("Napoléon's ashes"), dates to 1841, when the emperor's mummified remains traveled from St. Helena to Paris, for reburial in a monumental tomb at Les Invalides.

The French nurseryman Jean-Pierre Vibert—a veteran of Napoléon's army and a disciple of Joséphine's rosarian, Du Pont—kept a special place in his heart for the imperial family. In 1826, three years after introducing the pale pink alba **'Joséphine de Beauharnais'**, he gave *Rosa* x *centifolia* **'Cristata'** the name **'Chapeau de Napoléon'** ("Napoléon's hat"), because the fringed silhouette of its green sepal-covered flower bud resembles Bonaparte's signature bicorne. The bud unfurls richly perfumed deep pink petals.

THE FAIRY

I F YOU BELIEVE IN fairies, clap your hands, but if you want to grow **'The Fairy'**, put on your thickest gloves. That way, the prickles on this rose's wandlike stems won't break the enchantment of its flowers. As if by magic, little pink pompoms keep appearing on 'The Fairy' all summer long, and the plant's exceptional disease resistance can turn any thumb green. Bred in England in 1932, a child of the Edwardian rambler **'Lady Gay'**, the shrub has a low spreading habit ideally suited to the landscape of fairies and sprites.

British grown-ups found escape from the Great Depression in Andrew Lang's *The Blue Fairy Book*, J. M. Barrie's *Peter Pan,* and Rose Fyleman's *Fairies and Friends.* A poem Fyleman published in 1917 begins: "There are fairies at the bottom of our garden! / It's not so very, very far away; / You pass the gardner's shed and you just keep straight ahead— / I do so hope they've really come to stay."

A century earlier, the visionary

'THE FAIRY'

poet and artist William Blake made drawings of kindred spirits and wrote about fairies, which he claimed to see with his own eyes. To the astonishment of a woman seated beside him at a party, Blake once matter-of-factly described a fairy funeral held in his garden earlier that day. This ceremony, he told her, had entailed "a procession of creatures of the size and colour of green and grey grasshoppers, bearing a body laid out on a rose-leaf, which they buried with songs."

The plant that British gardeners first knew as "fairy rose" (formally *Rosa chinensis minima* or **'Miss Lawrance's Rose'**, in honor of the botanical artist Mary Lawrance) is a diminutive species that came to England from the Far East in 1810. A favorite of city dwellers, who shoehorned it into pots and window boxes, this undemanding, ever-blooming little bush proved remarkably easy to propagate. New York nurseryman William Prince listed sixteen fairy rose varieties, with blossoms "no larger than a five or ten cent piece," in his 1846 catalog. Small was beautiful then. But as silver-dollar-sized flowers became the gold standard of late-nineteenth-century horticulture, the term *fairy rose*—and the plant itself—gradually dropped out of circulation.

In 1932 hybridizer Ann Bentall labeled a polyantha 'The Fairy', banking on the name's nostalgic appeal. Robust sales confirmed her hunch. When a different breeder made a match between 'The Fairy' and the floribunda **'Goldilocks'**, in 1960, he sensibly called it **'Fairy Tale'**. And when 'The Fairy' became a parent yet again, almost forty years on, that baby appeared under the slightly pixilated **'Happy Ever After'**.

A WREATH OF ROSES, ENGRAVED AFTER A 1799 DRAWING BY MARY LAWRANCE

Frontispiece

MAGIC KINGDOM

Another fairy tale came true when Dutch rose hybridizer Gerrit de Ruiter brought forth his Seven Dwarfs series, starting with **'Doc'** in 1954 and ending with **'Grumpy'** two years later. The members of this septet legitimately qualify as "dwarf" shrubs, and each displays proportionately minuscule flowers. Other breeders had already produced four white roses, ranging from miniature to full-sized hybrid tea, all named **'Snow White'**. The first, produced by Spaniard Pedro Dot, appeared in 1938, shortly after the release of Walt Disney's *Snow White and the Seven Dwarfs*.

The brothers Grimm—commemorated in the 1932 German climber **'Grimm'**—wrote their story "Dörnroschen" ("Little Briar-Rose"), the classic German version of "Sleeping Beauty," in 1812. Nevertheless, a German-bred **'Dörnroschen'** rose (marketed in the United States as **'Sleeping Beauty'**) didn't make its entrance until 1960, right on the heels of Disney's cinematic *Sleeping Beauty*. Commercial growers have always kept close tabs on box-office results. Two roses dubbed **'Prince Charming'**—a 1953 Dutch miniature and a 1958 Canadian shrub—succeeded an extinct hybrid tea with the same title, introduced around the turn of the twentieth century or earlier.

'Hans Christian Andersen', a red floribunda hybridized in Denmark in 1986, salutes the great nineteenth-century Danish storyteller who is virtually unrecognizable in the title character of the 1952 Hollywood musical *Hans Christian Andersen*, played by Danny Kaye. Although the real-life author was no song-and-dance man, he did slip fresh rose petals into letters. California hybridizer Ralph Moore, whose wryly named Sequoia Nursery specializes in miniature roses, has honored two of Andersen's most famous characters. **'Thumbelina'**, a 1954 red mini, recalls the girl so tiny she slept in a walnut shell under a rose-petal blanket. **'Little Mermaid'**, a yellow mini climber, celebrates the wistful naiad with skin "as clear and delicate as a rose leaf." Of course, most of the people who have planted Moore's rose since it came on the market, in 1995, probably envision the perky bikini-clad Little Mermaid of yet another Disney blockbuster.

FANTIN-LATOUR

"THERE IS NOTHING MORE difficult for a truly creative painter than to paint a rose," said Henri Matisse, "because before he can do so he has first to forget all the roses that were ever painted." If that's true, French artist Henri Fantin-Latour must have longed to contract amnesia. For nearly half a century, from the 1860s until his death in 1904, he enjoyed success as Europe's foremost floral still life painter, producing roughly six hundred canvases in that genre (far outnumbering his other claim to fame, group portraits of musicians, writers, and fellow artists). Roses became his signature. "The rose—so complicated in its design, contours, and colour, in its rolls and curls, now fluted like the decoration of a fashionable hat, round and smooth, now like a button or a woman's breast—no one understood them better than Fantin," wrote the French art critic Jacques-Emile Blanche.

Unlike the Impressionists, many of whom were his friends, Fantin-Latour rarely painted outdoors; and yet he had a deep love of the countryside. After marrying another prolific flower painter, Victoria Dubourg, in 1876, Fantin-Latour regularly summered at her family's estate in Normandy. Local residents reported that he breathed his last, as many a gardener would hope to, during a walk among his rosebushes.

Mystery enfolds **"Fantin-Latour,"** a richly fragrant hybrid Bourbon with

pale blush petals ringing a deeper pink cupped center. Officially of unknown origin, this tall arching shrub was first recorded around 1900, but seems to have remained anonymous until the English rosarian and flower painter Graham Stuart Thomas rediscovered it decades later in a garden where an unknown hand had labeled it "Best Garden Rose." Agreeing that the shrub merited this kudos, Thomas apparently named it after one of his favorite artists. His own writings, however, don't specify whether he came up with the name or got it from someone else. "So far," he noted in 1955, without further explanation, "I have been unable to trace the name in any nineteenth-century book." In any case, romantics like to think that "Fantin-Latour" grew in the French artist's garden during his lifetime or even came into being under his care. Only one thing is sure: "Fantin-Latour" strongly resembles many of the roses in his paintings.

THERE'S NO QUESTION WHY a handful of rose varieties invoke the name of an earlier French flower painter, Pierre-Joseph Redouté (1759–1840), who has been called the "Raphael of roses." Colored engravings of his 167 watercolors for the book *Les roses*, published between 1817 and 1824, probably hang on more walls than do images from John James Audubon's equally iconic *Birds of America*, issued about twenty years later. (With characteristic generosity, Redouté personally introduced Audubon to the future King Louis Philippe and other influential Parisians in 1828.)

Who knows how many decorators have used "Redouté" as shorthand

THE ROSY WEALTH OF JUNE BY HENRI FANTIN-LATOUR, 1881

for "botanical print, suitable for framing"? An amiable fellow and a patient teacher — to the likes of Marie Antoinette, both of Napoléon's wives, and Louis Philippe's queen — Redouté would probably have loved to hear that generations of nonhorticultural admirers have made his beautiful rose portraits an interior-design cliché (*cliché*, after all, started out as the French term for a printer's metal plate). And yet, he might also have enjoyed being called a peeping botanist. Although not academically trained in botany, like Claude-Antoine Thory, who wrote the authoritative texts that accompany the images in *Les roses*, Redouté was a knowledgeable experimental gardener and a stickler for scientific accuracy. If Thory's reference to a "pectinate stipule" or "spatulate pinnule" puzzles you, just look at the clear, detailed picture on the facing page for elucidation.

Rose historians regularly consult *Les roses* as an indispensable resource for plant classification and nomenclature, including many names that Redouté and Thory devised. At one international rose conference, a French delegate with a limited command of English and an American equally deficient in French clashed over the identity of an old hybrid. With a finger pointed at his adversary's face, the American told her where to go for the correct answer: "You'll find it in Ray Doot!" The Frenchwoman's blank stare showed that she hadn't a clue what he meant.

It's likely that Thory urged his collaborator to introduce two recently discovered plants in their book as **'Rosier Redouté à feuilles glauques'** ("Redouté's rose with glaucous leaves") and **'Rosier Redouté à tiges et à épines rouges'** ("Redouté's rose with red stems and prickles"). They named others after friends and colleagues: The caption for a pink-to-yellow damask,

'Rosier Aurore Poniatowska', honors Aurore Poniatowska, a pupil of Redouté; *Rosa L'Heritieranea* acknowledges the tutelage and financial support that the botanist Charles Louis L'Héritier de Brutelle gave Redouté when he was starting out; light pink *R. damascena Celsiana* (now known simply as **'Celsiana'**) recalls horticulturist Jacques-Martin Cels, who introduced French gardeners to this old Dutch variety, a favorite subject of the floral still-life painter Jan van Huysum (1682–1749). In his youth, Redouté was bowled over by Van Huysum's work, which inspired him to abandon human portraiture for botanical art.

Two hybrids—one a centifolia, the other a moss—both came to be known in France as **'Rose des Peintres'** ("painters' rose"), because they recall flowers painted again and again by the Dutch. Their deliberately allegorical bouquets seduce the eye and engage the mind with moral and religious emblems. Every dewdrop poised on a petal, every leaf nibbled by an insect was meant to heighten the illusion of ephemeral reality—and symbolize the vanity of earthly things. The trompe l'oeil of these "vanitas" paintings can't quite trick a gardener or botanist, though. In picture after picture, flowers that bloom at different times improbably synchronize peak displays for their moment in a painted vase. Individual roses combine the charms of several cultivars, as if they indeed belong to an otherworldly class of "Roses des Peintres."

Although Van Huysum also played fast and loose with the horticultural calendar by composing multiseasonal arrangements, he refused to deal in humbug roses. His then uncommon insistence on having the real thing "sit" for its portrait caused him to inform one patron that she would just have to wait for a picture she had commissioned until a certain yellow rose came into flower the following year. So accurate are van Huysum's likenesses that rosarians have no trouble identifying his favorite models. One rose — 'Celsiana' — goes by **'Van Huysum'** in some gardens (not to be confused with **'Van Huyssum'**, a violet-red gallica that gained an extra *s* upon its introduction in 1845).

YOU COULD FILL A museum with roses that have been named after painters since the turn of the nineteenth century — in France, the hybrid perpetuals **'Raphael'**, **'Rubens'**, and **'Ingres'** (all introduced prior to 1855), the Delbard nursery's current "Les Roses de Peintres" series of shrubs and hybrid teas that includes **'Paul Cézanne'**, **'Edgar Degas'**, and **'Camille Pissaro'**; in the Netherlands, **'Jan Steen'** and **'Vincent van Gogh'**; in Germany, **'Albrecht Dürer'** and **'Emil Nolde'**; and in England, **'Gainsborough'**. Others celebrate movements (**'The Impressionist'** and **'Modern Art'**) or individual paintings (**'Mona Lisa'** and **'September Morn'**).

Some names virtually frame the living plant as a work of art. Its colors, shapes, and textures provide a medium for the hybridizer's creativity; the nursery serves as art dealer; the gardener collects and displays. One of the oldest examples, **'Painted Damask'**, which dates at least to the 1830s, has white petals with edges that look as if the anonymous artist dipped them in red pigment. Similar modern titles, by contrast, usually belong to signed originals with documented provenance (e.g., red-, white-, and pink-striped **'Painter's Palette'**, soft pink **'Watercolor'**, and mottled orange **'Work of Art'**, all miniatures from grower Ralph Moore's studio). Sam McGredy describes the series of vibrant, splashy, spotted, blotched, and streaked roses he started producing in 1971 as "hand-painted." To stress their bold contemporaneity, he chose to call the first in this oeuvre—a mottled pink floribunda with silvery highlights—**'Picasso'**. When McGredy politely requested a signed letter of permission from Pablo himself, the artist refused, explaining that he wasn't about to give away an autograph then worth $10,000 on the international market. The patent office had to settle for a note from Picasso's manager, and McGredy learned a timely lesson in painting by numbers.

THE COLLECTOR

The small but valuable class of Portland roses, among the first repeat-blooming European hybrids ever bred from Chinese imports, commemorates an Englishwoman of extraordinary taste and accomplishments: Margaret Cavendish, Duchess of Portland (1715–1785). Her circle of friends included Samuel Johnson, Jean-Jacques Rousseau, and Horace Walpole. The latter wrote that, "In an age of great collectors she rivalled the greatest." She also possessed the wealth to transform her country house into a full-fledged museum of art and natural history, replete with Roman sculpture and Old Master drawings, porcelain and silver of her own design; collections of shells, fossils, spiders, fungi, and exotic flora. Besides funding expeditions by Captain Cook and Joseph Banks, the duchess established a private zoo, aviary, and botanical garden, which disappeared long ago. There's no record of how the fragrant red **'Duchess of Portland'** came to grow on the Cavendish estate or even when it acquired that title; the famously unpretentious duchess probably had nothing to do with naming it. At some point, though, the plant reached France where Empress Joséphine eagerly added it to her own collection and Redouté portrayed it in *Les roses* with the label **'Rosier de Portland'**.

FASHION

THINK PINK, PUT ON lots of manure, don't stint on fragrance, and knock 'em dead. Words to that effect passed through the mind of hybridizer Gene Boerner, as he primped his most promising creation for the Jackson & Perkins nursery's 1949 line. Certain that its unique coral salmon hue and heady perfume—a first among the otherwise faint-scented floribundas—would make this rose a trendsetter, Boerner's boss, Charles Perkins, propagated a huge crop of 350,000 bushes. Boerner and Perkins were still trying on names, however, until a stylist from Neiman Marcus, the upscale Dallas department store, chanced to drop by their upstate New York nursery. As soon as the visitor glimpsed the rose, inspiration struck: Here, in these anonymous petals, he saw a color so fresh, so chic, so directional, he could conceive an entire Neiman's fashion show around it! But was a mere seedling ready for the runway?

Faster than you can say "retail," Boerner labeled the floribunda **'Fashion'** (a powder pink sibling came out as **'Vogue'** in 1951), and Perkins boxed up a shipment of twenty-five hundred plants, so that Neiman Marcus decorators could transform selling floors into gilt-edged rose beds. Live mannequins modeled coral salmon outfits, while matching accessories, bed linens, and other merchandise color-coordinated the rest of the store. After this well-publicized

premiere, Jackson & Perkins could hardly keep enough 'Fashion' on the racks
to satisfy nationwide demand. Sales during the early 1950s—five hundred
thousand plants per year—topped those of **'Peace'**, a best seller since 1945.

Boerner bred his modish floribunda in 1947, the year Christian Dior presented the New Look, a voluptuous silhouette that revolutionized couture and
gave the war-ravaged garment industry a much-needed shot in the shoulder
pad. Although Dior said he designed his wasp-waisted ensembles with long,
full-blown skirts for modern "flower women," the New Look also recalled the
billowing crinolines and hothouse
existence of society belles a century earlier. Roses had been essential components of Victorian
wardrobes, for both day and evening, and smart women knew exactly which floral varieties were
au courant or passé. The debu-
tante of the 1880s who flaunted
tea roses and hybrid perpetuals
wouldn't have been caught dead
in the Provence roses that Grand-
mama had worn to her first ball.
Textile manufacturers keyed dyes
to the tints of stylish cultivars and

The New 1950 ★ Floribunda Rose—FASHION—a glorious new color in Roses. $2 each; 3 for $5

STAR ROSES *Fall 1949*

'FASHION', THE NEW LOOK ROSE

named fabrics accordingly, so that a pink gown of the 1890s might be cut from **'La France'** duchesse lace or **'American Beauty'** silk. A properly attired gentleman started the day with a fresh rosebud in his lapel, and not just any old kind. Wearing buff yellow **'Safrano'** showed impeccable taste. Shell pink **'Duchesse de Brabant'**, Theodore Roosevelt's favorite, became so popular it was nicknamed the "buttonhole rose."

Victorian gallants often compared women to roses, but J. J. Grandville literally illustrated that metaphor in his whimsical *Les fleurs animées*, or *The Flowers Personified*, first published in Paris and New York in 1847. Among the blooms that morph into humans within the book's satiric bower, *Rosa centifolia* cuts an especially stylish figure. Beneath her petal mantilla, crowned by a rose-hip coronet, more petals mold a bodice and sleeves. Rosebuds frame the décolletage and rose leaves trim a bouffant skirt.

Real-world dressmakers and milliners concocted similar finery well past the turn of the next century. Perhaps the apogee of rose attire occurred in 1910, during an acclaimed exhibition of roses at the International Floral Show in Paris. The American garden writer Georgia Torrey Drennan gushed, "Rose parties were the order of the day. Ladies' evening gowns were deftly and lightly covered with cut-roses, exquisitely fresh and fragrant. Even men appeared in court dress of pale evening shades with wreaths of cut-roses to match around the neck as a kind of decoration."

Roses moved in exclusive circles, but snobbery delayed the appearance of garment-related rose names. Growers and their clientele, who strove to preserve an aristocratic air about the queen of flowers, sniffed at the slightest whiff of "trade." Even after Charles Frederick Worth, the English-born designer to the court of Second Empire France, played a key role in shaping the institution later called haute couture, it was not until 1889 that the Lyonnaise hybridizer "La Veuve" ("the Widow") Schwartz bred the rosy carmine hybrid rugosa **'Madame Charles Frédéric Worth'**. By recognizing madame rather than monsieur, who ran the House of Worth, the rose suggests a polite compliment untainted by commerce.

The first entrepreneur to purchase a rose name solely for advertising was probably the French dressmaker Caroline Testout. A silk-buying trip may have taken her to textile mills in Lyon as well as to the nearby nursery of Joseph Pernet-Ducher, *the* breeder of ultrachic hybrid teas. Testout's business had done so well that she planned to open a London branch and wanted a signature rose to promote it. Pernet-Ducher drove a hard bargain—he later admitted to a fellow rosarian that he had written off the seedling as "mediocre"—but the couturière got her **'Madame Caroline Testout'**. Back then, way before the invention of designer-logo scarves and bags, this was a bold coup de PR.

A PLATE FROM J. J. GRANDVILLE'S
THE FLOWERS PERSONIFIED, 1847

Applause greeted Testout's rose when its fragrant shell-shaped pink petals first appeared at horticultural and fashion shows in 1890, and the accolades resounded halfway around the world. In 1893, the *New York Times* reported on that spring's Madison Square Garden flower show: "In glass vases near the cut-flower booth were great, splendid bunches of Mermet, La France, American Beauty . . . and most splendid of all, the enormous pink silky balls of the princess among the roses, the Mme. Caroline Testout." By the 1920s bushes of this celebrated variety fringed the sidewalks of Portland, Oregon, "the Rose City." Today, the few documentary scraps of Caroline Testout's existence pale beside the perennial beauty of her signature flower. It will forever head the still-growing rose parade of designers, from **'Coco'** (as in Chanel), **'Christian Dior'**, **'Givenchy'**, and **'Lanvin'** to **'Lagerfeld'**, **'Montana'** (think Claude), **'Paris d'Yves Saint Laurent'**, and **'Sonia Rykiel'**.

The post–World War II rediscovery of sensuous fabrics, piqued by Dior's New Look, seduced rosarians, too. Petal textures inspired **'Taffeta'** (1947); **'Crêpe de Chine'** (1970); **'Cashmere'** and **'French Lace'** (both 1980); and **'Velveteen'** (1994). In

'MADAME CAROLINE TESTOUT',
NAMED FOR A DRESSMAKER FROM LYON

search of flattering analogies to flower shapes and colors, hybridizers raided closets and bureau drawers. The results include large-flowered **'Crinoline'** (1964); orange-red **'Hot Pants'** (1979); miniature **'Charm Bracelet'** (1992); as well as the upright shrub **'Four Inch Heels'** and the spreading mini **'Flip Flop'** (both 2003). Each season brings its must-haves. But whatever the current vogue, if anyone asks that perennial question, "How do I look?," a white floribunda bred in 1998 has the answer—**'Fabulous!'**

HAIR AND MAKEUP

In 1932 Mathias Leenders, a prominent Dutch hybridizer, bred a medium red rose with attractive curly petals, which he dubbed **'Mevrouw van Straaten van Nes'**. Devotees of stiff, upright hybrid teas—then the rose world's reigning class—were shocked when this bushy plant with densely clustered flowers garnered the Prix de Bagatelle. Jackson & Perkins was eager to capitalize on rising interest in floribundas by introducing the plant in the United States but worried that its clunky name would impede sales. When nursery representative Jean Henri Nicolas relayed this concern to Leenders, the breeder's daughter gamely replied, "Why not name it **'Permanent Wave'**?" This alternative clicked, thanks largely to the marcelled hairdos that were all the rage in Hollywood. Another Dutch grower, Verschuren, uncapped deep cerise **'Lipstick'** in 1940 and creamy white **'Beauty Cream'** in 1956 (both floribundas). Kordes, a German nursery formulated bronze orange **'Coppertone'**, a hybrid tea, in 1969, and America's Griffith J. Buck brought out red-spotted **'Freckle Face'**, a shrub rose, seven years later. A scarlet-rimmed white "eye" accounts for **'Eyepaint'**, the 1975 floribunda Sam McGredy created in New Zealand; **'Mascara'**, a 1992 florist's rose by Meilland, of France, is pink with a darker edge.

FORTUNE'S
FIVE-COLORED ROSE

WHY ON EARTH WOULD a fellow setting out to hunt for plants and seeds require a double-barreled shotgun, a pair of pistols, and a blackjack? Botanist Robert Fortune's demand for weapons baffled his employers at the Horticultural Society of London, as they prepared to send the thirty-year-old Scot on a solo plant-collecting expedition in China in 1842. With the first Opium War having concluded in a treaty favorable to British trade, society members argued that a stout spade, some trowels, and a Chinese dictionary were all an explorer would need to gather rare Asian breeds of orange and peach trees, azaleas, lilies, bamboos, and a fabled blue peony. But Fortune stuck to his guns, literally—a wise move, as his perilous three-year Eastern sojourn would confirm.

Attacked by bandits, pirates, and hostile villagers, he repeatedly had to shoot or bluff his way out of danger. Granted, as Fortune revealed later in his published memoirs, he brought trouble upon himself by disobeying imperial dictates that strictly confined all foreigners except French Jesuit missionaries to Shanghai, Ningbo, Fuzhou, Xiamen, and Guangzhou. To scope out flora in forbidden territory, such as the city of Suzhou (where he bagged a smashing gardenia), he traveled incognito in Chinese garb with a long queue on his otherwise shaved head. Amazingly, he eluded detection; when locals questioned his strange pronunciation or grammar, he'd explain that he spoke the dialect of a far-off province.

Less romantically, Fortune made some of his finest discoveries at commercial nurseries and private gardens inside the authorized "treaty ports." Shopping trips to the excellent rose department at Guangzhou's Fa Tee nursery yielded many of the goodies he eventually shipped home to England in twenty-six wardian cases, terrarium-like containers designed for botanical travelers. Fortune came upon two ancient hybrids that now bear his name inside a Ningbo mandarin's compound. "On entering one of the gardens on

a fine morning in May," he wrote, "I was struck with a mass of yellow flowers which completely covered a distant part of the wall. The colour was not a common yellow, but had something of buff in it, which gave the flowers a striking uncommon appearance. I immediately ran up to the place and, to my surprise and delight, found that it was a most beautiful new

'FORTUNE'S FIVE-COLORED ROSE' IN ITS MULTIPINK FORM, AS ILLUSTRATED IN FERENTZEL KOMLOSY'S *ROSEN-ALBUM*, 1868–1875

double yellow climbing rose. I have no doubt, from what I afterwards learned, that this rose is from the more northern districts of the empire and will prove perfectly hardy in Europe. Another rose, which the Chinese call **'Five Coloured'**, was also found in one of these gardens at the time. It belongs to the section commonly called the China roses in this country [Great Britain], but grows in a very strange and beautiful manner. Sometimes it produces self-coloured blooms, being either red or French white and frequently having flowers of both on one plant at the same time—while at other times the flowers are striped with two of the colours."

In the West, those vivid finds became **'Fortune's Double Yellow'** and **'Fortune's Five-colored Rose'**. The latter, a tea, eventually vanished from cultivation in Europe and America, only to resurface in 1953 as a mystery rose in Bermuda, where islanders called it **"Smith's Parish,"** after the district in which it survived.

Mystery of a different sort attends *Rosa* x *fortuneana*, another of Fortune's Chinese hybrids. The large white flowers, though sweet smelling, are nothing to write home about, and the plant fares badly in cold climates; but in warm regions—from California to Bermuda—it supplies one of the best rootstocks for grafting rose varieties that otherwise might languish. In Florida, where **'Dr. Huey'** and other rootstocks commonly used throughout most of the United States succumb to nematodes in the soil, only roses propagated on nematode-resistant *R.* x *fortuneana* last more than a couple of years. Because this horticultural mainstay does its work underground, however, supporting the stems, foliage, and flowers of the different cultivar identified on the nursery label, many gardeners are unaware that *R.* x *fortuneana* lurks on the premises.

Western botanists welcomed the more than 120 "new" plants — from *Daphne fortunei* and the kumquat, *Fortunella*, to *Rhododendron fortunei* and the palm *Trachycarpus fortunei* — that Fortune brought from the Far East on five voyages he made before retiring in 1862. By then, two French hybridizers had introduced **'Robert Fortune'** roses, a moss and a hybrid perpetual, neither of which has lasted long enough to perpetuate his memory. Fortune's best-known feat, outside horticultural circles, involved tea — not a tea rose but the tea tree, *Camellia sinensis,* whose leaves are steeped to brew Britain's favorite beverage. On behalf of the East India Company, which paid him at a rate five times higher than the Horticultural Society's, Fortune arranged for some twenty thousand Chinese tea plants (and several tea experts) to be spirited into India, enabling the British Raj to break China's monopoly on tea production.

MODERN COMMENTATORS HAVE NOTED that Fortune's five books about his Asian exploits fail to mention his wife and children, who stayed in Britain throughout his nineteen years abroad. Perhaps Mrs. Fortune never asked for a well-earned equivalent to the **'Lady Banks Rose'**, or *R. banksiae* var. *banksiae.* That fragrant white-flowered shrub, found in China on a British plant-gathering mission and brought to England in 1807, had been named after the wife of Sir Joseph Banks, an eminent naturalist and a founder of the Horticultural Society. Banks's own scientific travels included a round-the-world voyage with Captain James Cook. Considering the huge contribution to global horticulture made by plant hunters and their long-suffering spouses, it's appropriate that the largest rosebush on earth is a 'Lady Banks Rose' in Tombstone, Arizona, grown from a root brought from Scotland in the 1880s. The trunk measures thirteen feet in circumference, and the flowering stems cover eighty-five-hundred square feet.

Although not Guinness record-setters, other roses also commemorate illustrious wanderers and, in a few instances, the helpmates they left behind. In 1855 a French rosarian named his velvety purple and pink moss **'William Lobb'**, as an homage to the contemporary English botanist whose spectacular finds in Chile and the Pacific Northwest included the monkey puzzle tree and the redwood. *R. wichurana*, or **'Memorial Rose'**, recalls the German jurist and botanist Max Ernst Wichura, who found this species on a Japanese riverbank in 1861 and sent samples back to Europe. Wichura's accidental death five years later cut short a distinguished career (Charles Darwin cites his studies of hybridizing in *The Origin of Species*), and the wild Japanese rose he had collected was almost forgotten. It remained anonymous until 1886, when the Belgian botanist François Crépin rediscovered it in the Brussels Botanical Garden and conferred the name, originally *R. wichuraiana*, that gives Max Wichura proper credit.

The multitalented adventurer James Edward Tierney Aitcheson, a naturalist and surgeon-major in the British Army, made his name in late Victorian botanical circles by publishing scholarly studies of the indigenous flora he encountered while on Her Majesty's service in India and Afghanistan. No rose recalls J. E. T. Aitcheson himself, but he devised a discreetly cryptic tribute to his better half, whose initials were E. C. A., by tagging a shrubby, yellow-flowered Afghan species with the acronymic *R. ecae*.

Another enigmatic title, **'The Engineer's Rose'**, commemorates an amateur garden traveler, the British engineer Robert (or Albert) Smith who fell for this red-flowered climber while traveling in Japan, where it was called *Sukara Ibara,* meaning "scholar's briar." Appreciative friends in Scotland, with whom Smith shared his find, switched the vocational name to suit his profession. An enterprising nurseryman, Charles Turner, acquired the plant in 1893 and renamed it **'Turner's Crimson Rambler'**. It rapidly became a best seller on both sides of the Atlantic.

A gargantuan white-flowering climber with the largest leaves of any rose, *R. sinowilsonii,* preserves the nickname of English plant hunter Ernest Henry "Chinese" Wilson (*Sino* is Greco-Latin for "Chinese"). In 1902, after a three-year sojourn in mountainous northwestern China for James Veitch & Sons' Royal Exotic Nursery, Wilson brought home more than four hundred previously unknown species, including the kiwi fruit and the paperbark maple. He pressed on despite acts of God and man—such as the plague that deprived him of an interpreter and the house builder who felled a legendary handkerchief tree, *Davidia involucrata,* right before Wilson's arrival. Later, working for the Arnold Arboretum, in Boston, Massachusetts, where he became the director in 1927, Wilson not only combed China for more living treasure but also ventured into Korea, Japan, Australia, India, and the African continent.

Among the seventy-odd roses Wilson collected for the Arnold Arboretum is a Himalayan musk he named *R. helenae* in appreciation of his

ERNEST HENRY "CHINESE" WILSON AT HARVARD'S
ARNOLD ARBORETUM WITH SOME OF HIS ASIAN PRIZES

wife, Helen, whose married life had much in common with Mrs. Fortune's. The rosarian Jean Henri Nicolas recalled, "Mrs Wilson had been at our house and had told my wife about her husband once leaving her with a three-months-old baby, years ago, to go for a long absence in the wilds of China. My wife could not refrain from mentioning that to Miss Willmott [the British gardener and writer Ellen Willmott]. Miss Willmott prided herself on having fostered Wilson's career and having been instrumental in sending him on his first expedition to China for James Veitch. To my wife she remarked: 'A man must leave his wife and family for science.' After she left my wife remarked, 'That is an old maid's point of view.'"

MISSIONARY ZEAL

Time and again, E. H. Wilson would reach some remote part of China, only to find that a French or British missionary had already been there in search of plants. Clergymen who headed east often had training in botany and other scientific subjects, which Chinese officials encouraged them to teach as a public service. Moreover, prolonged residence enabled missionaries to earn the respect and trust of local nurserymen, gardeners, and naturalists. The following men of the cloth may not have converted throngs of Chinese to Christianity, but they did help guide many an Asian rose into the West.

Jean Pierre Armand David: A Franciscan friar, Père David was renowned as a naturalist in France before he departed for missionary work in China in 1862. Church authorities allowed David to collect herbarium specimens for the Natural History Museum in Paris. Plant hunting led him into Mongolia and other far-flung regions where his kindly manner gained him a warm hospitality few foreigners received. In 1869, on a trek through rugged western Sichuan, he came upon the pink single-flowered shrub that a French botanist named *Rosa davidii* (aka **'Father David's Rose'**) in his honor.

Ernst Faber: Historians of Eastern philosophy and religion recognize this German sinologist as a specialist on Confucianism; botanists know Dr. Faber for the plants he discovered during his four decades as a missionary in China. In 1887 he found the rose that he dubbed *R. omeiensis*—a species with delicate foliage, translucent scarlet thorns, and unusual four-petaled white flowers reminiscent of Maltese crosses—while exploring Mount Omei (Emei in modern Pinyin), a peak that is sacred to Buddhism.

Paul Guillaume Farges: In China from 1867 until his death in 1912, the French missionary and naturalist identified hundreds of plant species. The weirdly beautiful blue bean tree, *Decaisnea fargesii*, is one of his most memorable exotics. Strong pink *R. moyesii* **'Fargesii'**, native to Sichuan and Yunnan, is the only rose bearing his name.

J. Moyes: The Reverend Moyes joined the China Inland Mission, a Protestant organization whose members wore Chinese dress and pigtails and conducted services in Chinese homes. Some rosarians credit Moyes with discovering *R. moyesii*, a shrub with crimson flowers and bottle-shaped orange hips. Rose historian Peter Harkness, however, asserts that E. H. Wilson found the plant, and named it in gratitude to the missionary, who had hosted him in China.

Hugh (Hugo) Scallan: This Welsh Catholic missionary's place in European and American gardens is assured by the brilliant lemon yellow flowers and dainty foliage of **'Father Hugo's Rose'** (*R. hugonis*). When Scallan encountered the rose in north-central China and collected its seed, circa 1899, he was probably assisted by Padre Giuseppe Giraldi, a Franciscan priest and botanist. Scallon sent seeds to London, and plants first came on the market at the Veitch nursery. In 1917 Conard-Pyle introduced *R. hugonis* to America with an exotically secular label: **'Golden Rose of China'**.

FRAU KARL DRUSCHKI

J UST AS SAUERKRAUT BECAME liberty cabbage during World War I and
French fries turned into freedom fries amid the Iraqi conflict, rose
names have often changed with the political climate. Foreign-sounding
plants are an obvious target for secateur-wielding patriots. On August 7,
1915—exactly three months after a German U-boat sank the ocean liner RMS
Lusitania, with 159 U.S. civilians on board—the *New York Times* quoted a
headline from the French newspaper *Le Matin*: "Unboche our roses" (*Boche*
was the French equivalent of "Hun"). Even though the United States had not
yet entered the Great War against the Central Powers, the majority of Americans' sympathies lay with France and her allies. The *Times* reported that *Le
Matin* was urging French horticulturists to replace German flower names, and
it wasn't long before Yanks heeded the call.

Leading the list of enemy Teutons was the rose **'Frau Karl Druschki'**. Although bred by a German, Peter Lambert, this hybrid perpetual had—*quelle
horreur!*—French parents: **'Madame Caroline Testout'** and **'Merveille de
Lyon'**. When the as yet nameless seedling premiered at the Stuttgart Exhibition of 1899, visitors voted to call it **'Schneekönigin'** (**'Snow Queen'**), because of the large snowy blooms that some rosarians still consider the finest
white flowers ever. But Lambert refused to introduce his rose under that label,

certain that it would triumph at the more prestigious 1900 German Rose Society Exhibition where the winner was to be named for the elderly statesman Prince Otto von Bismarck, virtually ensuring commercial success.

Lambert's scheme backfired. Ruling that no rose colored a meek white could adequately symbolize the power of the Iron Chancellor, the exhibition committee tapped a strong silvery pink bloom instead. Privately, however, committee member Karl Druschki, the president of the German Rose Society and director of a major European nursery, negotiated with Lambert to name the magnificent seedling after his wife. A hefty fee changed hands, and 'Frau Karl Druschki' was formally presented at the society's 1901 exhibition in Berlin. French nurserymen began selling the plant a year later, as **'Madame Charles Druschki'**.

In turn-of-the-century America, the rose remained *auf Deutsch* until World War I stirred distrust of all things German. Families named Schmidt switched to Smith and dachsunds trotted out as "liberty pups." Overseas, 'Frau Karl Druschki' became **'La Reine des Neiges'** ("the queen of the

'FRAU KARL DRUSCHKI', WHICH
TURNED INTO 'WHITE AMERICAN BEAUTY'
DURING THE FIRST WORLD WAR

snows") in France and **'Snow Queen'**, a translation of the French, in Great Britain. U.S. growers opted for **'White American Beauty'**. Other roses were similarly naturalized. **'Grüss an Teplitz'**, which had been popular in America since 1897, reemerged as **'Virginia R. Coxe'**, honoring a contemporary writer. German imports recovered their original tags in peacetime — and then, from the outbreak of World War II well into the postwar era, roses once again assumed aliases. **'Direktor Benschop'**, created in Ütersen, Germany, in 1939, turned into **'City of York'** (as in York, Pennsylvania) after it reached the United States. The 1944 floribunda **'August Seebauer'** landed in Britain as **'Queen Mother'**.

Other name changes reflect longer-lasting cultural hostilities. During the 1930s, the American Rose Society's president, Horace J. McFarland, launched a campaign to shorten the names of imported roses, on the grounds that linguistically challenged American gardeners stumbled over the spelling and pronunciation of foreign words. An editorial by E. S. Trott in the 1931 *American Rose Annual* added that roses whose names start with an

'MADAME GRÉGOIRE STAECHELIN',
AKA 'SPANISH BEAUTY'

alien "zizzing" sound, such as **'Zéphirine Drouhin'** and **'Ghisilaine de Féligonde'**, are "apt to have something queer about them." Trott never cited the zizz in xenophobia.

Between the wars, American nurseries issued contracts to foreign rose growers that reserved the right of approving extant names and, if necessary, abbreviating them or assigning new ones better suited to the U.S. market. Even cosmopolitan rosarians, such the Franco-American Jean Henri Nicolas, condemned long names as a liability. Before his Pennsylvania-based employer, Conard-Pyle, introduced a rose from Spain, **'Madame Grégoire Staechelin'**, in 1929, Nicolas cut its name to 'Staechelin' and distributed a phonetic guide: "[T]hink of a good beefsteak, and use the last syllable." But this tip failed to boost sales. Only when Conard-Pyle altered 'Staechelin' to **'Spanish Beauty'** did the pink climber become a best seller.

An Italian rosarian, Countess Senni, voiced the chagrin of fellow Europeans in a letter to the 1933 *American Rose Annual*. She remarked that ARS members' ignorance of foreign languages was their misfortune and should not be inflicted on the rest of the world by imposing American names as the global standard, a proposal then under discussion. Italians, she noted, had uncomplainingly accepted American roses with such hard-to-pronounce monickers as **'Chicago'** (a hybrid tea). For decades to come, American provincialism continued to rankle rosarians abroad—and sometimes tickle them. Case in point: Only after **'Misty'**, an award-winner at home, flopped in Germany during the 1960s did the hybrid tea's California breeder, Armstrong Nursery, discover that *Mist* in German means "bullshit."

THE IMPOSTERS

Numerous flowering plants that do not belong to the genus *Rosa* nevertheless have "rose" in their common names. Here are some impostors with their proper botanical labels.

Alpine rose: *Rhododendron ferrugineum*

Christmas rose: *Helleborus niger*

Cotton rose: *Hibiscus mutabilis*

Desert rose: *Adenium*

Egyptian rose: *Scabiosa atropurpurea*

Fen rose: *Kosteletzkya*

Guelder rose: *Viburnum opulus*

Japanese rose: *Kerria*

Lenten rose: *Helleborus orientalis*

Montpellier rock rose: *Cistus monspeliensis*

Moss rose: *Portulaca grandiflora*

Rock rose: *Cistus* and *Helianthemum*

Rose mallow: *Hibiscus moscheutos*

Rose of China: *Hibiscus rosa-sinensis*

Rose of Heaven: *Silene coeli-rosa*

Rose of Jericho: *Anastatica hierochuntica* and *Selaginella lepidophylla*

Rose of Sharon: *Hibiscus syriacus* and *Hypericum calycinum*

Rose of Venezuela: *Brownea ariza*

Sand rose: *Anacampseros telephiastrum*

Sun rose: *Cistus* and *Helianthemum*

Sydney rock rose: *Boronia serrulata*

Velvet rose: *Aeonium canariense*

Wind rose: *Roemeria hybrida*

Wood rose: *Merremia tuberosa*

GLOIRE DE DIJON

'GLOIRE DE DIJON'

Not to be confused with the golden brown grandiflora **'Honey Dijon'**, which takes its name from supermarket mustard, **'Gloire de Dijon'** ("glory of Dijon") is the caviar of roses. The World Federation of Rose Societies has ensconced this incomparable climber in the Old Rose Hall of Fame, an honor as coveted as Michelin's four stars.

Dijon, the French city, has a lot more than mustard on the menu. As the capital of Burgundy, it boasts a history of superb cuisine, noble wines from nearby domaines, and *premier cru* roses from the region's distinguished nurseries. When visitors flocked to Dijon's annual floral exhibition in June 1852, they expected to view nothing less than the crème de la crème of modern hybrids. And they found it in a new tea-Noisette from Dijonais nurseryman Edmé-Henry Jacotot whose large fragrant flowers displayed a translucent blend of rose, salmon, and yellow. With great fanfare, the jury of the Société d'Horticulture de la Côte-d'Or announced that Jacotot's seedling had captured the exhibition's top prize and would be given the name 'Gloire de Dijon'.

The English rosarian S. Reynolds Hole wrote in 1869, "[If] ever, for some heinous crime, I were miserably sentenced, for the rest of my life, to possess but a single Rose-tree, I should desire to be supplied, on leaving the dock, with a strong plant of Gloire de Dijon." Generations of rose lovers have agreed. One of the more sensational tributes occurred in New Orleans at a trial held in 1894. Gertrude "Queen Gertie" Livingston, reigning madam of Storyville, the Crescent City's tenderloin, testified on behalf of one of her girls, who had bitten off a rival's finger. A hush fell over the courtroom as Livingston made a grand entrance. "Her majesty, Queen Gertie, was dressed in a most becoming, tailor-made gown, trimmed with green," a newspaper reported. "On her maidenly breast she wore Gloire de Dijon."

While delayed in Dijon on his way to the front in December 1917, U.S. Army ordnance sergeant John Caspar Wister—a Philadelphia landscape architect later acclaimed as the doyen of American horticulturists—searched for the exact birthplace of his favorite rose. He found one scraggly specimen among the odds and ends inside a ramshackle greenhouse run by Jacotot's grandson. This survivor was all the more precious because the small nursery had never introduced another rose before or after 'Gloire de Dijon'. On a return visit in 1922, Wister discovered that even that lone remnant had perished.

'Gloire de Dijon' is one of many French roses celebrating glorious places, such as **'Gloire de France'**, a gallica, of course, bred before 1819, and **'Gloire de Lyon'**, an 1857 hybrid perpetual. Other "Gloires" spotlight a state of mind, like the 1825 Bourbon **'Gloire des Rosomanes'**. *Rosomanes* translates as "rose maniacs" or "rose nuts," which is probably how this Gloire's breeders, Plantier and Vibert, regarded some of their more exacting customers.

JUST AS FRANCOPHONES USE *gloire* to pay a compliment, German speakers turn to *Grüss*. Rose names beginning *Grüss an* mean "Greetings to," and the recipients of these salutations range from Bavaria and Berlin to Weimar and Zweibrücken. A 1927 American rose catalog caught the spirit in its description of **'Grüss an Teplitz'** (*Teplitz* is the German name for Teplice, a Czech spa town) as "a great big lusty fellow, always nodding 'howdy-do' with bunches of red posies."

Rosarians harbor especially warm feelings toward **'Grüss an Aachen'**. Besides offering lavish clusters of silken rosette-shaped blooms in a pearly pink suffused with pale yellow, this German-bred hybrid has given botanists the pleasure of arguing over how to classify it. The plant's ancestry is so complex that rosarians can't agree whether it's a floribunda, a hybrid tea, a polyantha, or a Bourbon. Its cultivar name salutes Aachen (Aix-la-Chapelle to the French, who call this rose **'Salut d'Aix la Chapelle'**), the imperial capital and burial place of Charlemagne, a part-time gardener, who was himself honored by three nineteenth-century pink roses named **'Charlemagne'**: a gallica and two hybrid perpetuals. In the early 800s he issued the Latin edict *Capitulare de Villis Imperiabilis*, which specifies seventy-three plants to be cultivated throughout the Holy Roman Empire and includes the earliest references to rose propagation in Germany.

Like faithful pen pals, rose breeders around the world have sent forth plants with names that read like souvenir postcards: **'Privet iz Alma-Aty'** (**'Greetings from Alma-Aty'**), a Russian hybrid tea; **'Donau!'** ("Danube!"), a Czech climber; **'Spirit of Ocean City'**, an American florist's rose dedicated to the New Jersey resort. Current rose catalogs also deliver the garden counterparts of all-purpose blank-message cards, from the formal **'Greetings'** (a reddish purple and white shrub rose) to the casual **'Hi'** (a light pink micro-miniature) and the folksy **'Hi Neighbor'** (a red shrub). Large vases of **'Aloha'**, a pink apple-scented American climber, are often set out to welcome participants at international rose events. Sad to say, bright yellow **'Esperanto'**, a 1932 Czech hybrid tea, can be hard to come by these days.

GLORY OF NEW ORLEANS

I n Plaquemines Parish, Louisiana, across the Mississippi from New Orleans, gardener Peggy Martin nurtured cuttings from an anomyous old rose that an acquaintance in the Big Easy had given her. After Hurricane Katrina hit in 2005, twenty feet of brackish water covered Martin's yard for more than two weeks. She returned to find that the only relic of her garden was this rose, as vigorous as ever and in bloom. At the urging of her friend William C. Welch, a horticulture professor at Texas A&M University, six nurseries in Texas and Alabama propagated cuttings of the thornless pink-flowered rambler and sold them in the fall of 2006 as a fund-raiser for horticultural restoration throughout the storm-ravaged region. The rose appears in catalogs as **"Peggy Martin,"** with the double quotation marks of a found variety. But Martin is determined to discover her rambler's original name and replace the temporary label.

GOURMET POPCORN

L IKE CHEFS AND WAITERS, professional rose growers never tire of hearing customers say "delicious," "luscious," and "Oh, all right—I really shouldn't, but I'll take a smidgen more." Some gardeners need only a whiff of spicy rose aroma or a glance at tender, succulent petals before they start to salivate; others confess that a weakness for intoxicating colors lures them off the path of moderation again and again. The inevitable result is a smorgasbord of rose names taken from foods and beverages. **'Gourmet Popcorn'**, an ever-popular miniature shrub (about three feet high and wide), has puffy clusters of white blooms with butter yellow centers. There's climbing **'Fried Egg Rose'**—as Bermudians call *Rosa bracteata* (aka **'Macartney Rose'**), because of its broad white single petals and prominent yolk gold center. The floribunda **'Orange Juice'** and miniature **'Orange Marmalade'** both come in the color on the label. The robust café-au-lait hue of **'Café Olé'**, a miniature, and the rich russet of **'Hot Cocoa'**, a floribunda, provide a wakeup call for gardeners weary of conventional pastels. Sizzling colors inspired **'Hot Tamale'**, a shocking pink and yellow miniature, as well as **'Barbecue'**, a red, strong-scented floribunda bred in Northern Ireland and currently available only in Europe (go figure). Add orange-red **'Paprika'**, **'Cayenne'**, or **'Cajun Spice'** to taste.

Miniature **'Gourmet Pheasant'** has flowers in the deep pink to medium red of a game bird roasted rare. Epicures might choose to pair this with the wine red, cup-shaped blooms of the shrub **'Chianti'** rather than rose *ordinaire* **"House Red,"** which a Canadian rosarian found growing outside her house. A vintage hybrid tea with a mild bouquet, like medium yellow **'Chardonnay'** or off-white **'Chablis'**, would be better suited to **'Golden Salmon Supérieur'**, a deep orange polyantha cooked up by a Dutch breeder. At the Villa Reale, in Monza, Italy, they grow the deep yellow floribunda **'Polenta'**, which has not been exported to the United States.

Only-in-America specialties include **'Peanut Butter & Jelly'**, a russet miniature; **'Cherry Cola'**, a dark red hybrid tea; **'Iced Tea'**, a brisk russet and peach, but not a tea; **'Pink Lemonade'**, a yellow-to-pink hybrid tea; and **'Bubble Gum'**, a juicy pink floribunda.

(**'Hamburger Phoenix'**, however, may not match your expectations: This medium red floribunda, bred in 1954, celebrates the rise of the German port after wartime bombing.) If you still crave something sweet, try pink-and-white-swirled **'Berries 'n' Cream'**, a large flowered climber; light yellow **'Crème Brûlée'**, a shrub; white-to-golden **'Cheesecake'**, a miniature; icing

'GOURMET POPCORN', A 1986 MINIATURE

pink **'Cupcake'**, a mini that looks piped through a pastry tube; or chocolaty **'Brownie'**, a floribunda in a peculiar mix of tan, gold, and pink with hints of brown that's definitely an acquired taste.

Rosarians keep the outdoor bar fully stocked, so gardeners can toast their health with **'Champagne Cocktail'**, an apricot-flushed floribunda; **'Piña Colada'**, a light yellow miniature; **'Mint Julep'**, a greenish pink hybrid tea; or **'Whisky Mac'**, a hybrid tea in the same rich amber as the cocktail made with whisky and green-ginger wine. Although 'Whisky Mac' comes from Germany, two of its genetic by-products—**'Climbing Whisky Mac'** and **'Drambuie'**—are as Scottish as their names. Brand-name Scotches (hold the rocks) include **'Johnnie Walker'**, a golden buff hybrid tea blended in England; **'Glenfiddich'**, a deep yellow floribunda straight from Scotland; and **'Arthur Bell'**, a clear yellow Northern Irish floribunda ("My reward for this," wrote nurseryman Sam McGredy, "was innumerable cases of whiskey").

None of the above names predates 1900; most, in fact, are mid-twentieth century or later. Prior to that, rose growers rarely played with palatable metaphors, because roses were a standard ingredient for cooks around the world. A chronicle of annual customs and festivals in Beijing describes seasonal dishes such as rose cakes, eaten during the fourth lunar month, and a summertime sour-prune drink incorporating rose petals, which is "cooled with ice water until it chills the teeth." In India the favorite hot-weather refreshment, or *sharbart*, is a rose water–based syrup that often contains essences of other flowers and herbs such as portulaca, water lily, mint, and coriander.

In some cultures long ago, if a particular variety had exceptionally flavorful or aromatic petals or hips it acquired a label such as **'Conditorum'** (Latin for "of the confectioners") or **'Tidbit Rose'**. These are interchangeable names for a gallica native to Central Europe that, for more than five hundred years, has been used to make preserves, sweetmeats, and other goodies, like Hungarian rose-hip butter, Swiss rose-hip jam, and Turkish rose-hip tea.

Early Americans coated young shoots of sweet briar and freshly picked rosebuds with sugar—an expensive luxury—to serve as after-dinner comfits. At Mount Airy, their Virginia plantation, the Tayloe family drank wine made from the petals of damask roses in their boxwood parterre. The following recipe for conserve of red roses, a domestic staple, comes from *Adam's Luxury, and Eve's Cookery; or the Kitchen-Garden display'd*, published in London in 1744: "Take one pound of rose buds and bruise them with a wooden pestle in a marble mortar, adding by degrees of white loaf-sugar powdered and sifted, three pounds, continue beating them till no particles of the rose can be seen and till the mass is all alike." A century later, Catharine E. Beecher, the Martha Stewart of her time, supplied American readers with this "receipt" for rose butter: "Take a glass jar, put on the bottom a layer of butter, and each day put in rose leaves, adding layers of butter, and when full, cover tight, and use the butter for articles to be flavored with rose water."

Most early culinary names pertain to familiar kitchen scents. Among the oldest is the cinnamon rose, *R. majalis* (formerly *R. cinnamomea*), a species of which John Parkinson, royal botanist to Charles I of England, wrote in 1629: "The small sent of Cinamon that is found in the flowers hath caused it to beare the name." Some herbalists have taken issue with this etymology,

THE DOUBLE-FLOWERED CINNAMON ROSE, BY GERMAN BOTANIST GEORG DIONYSIUS EHRET, 1768

The double Cinnamon Rose

citing instead the visual resemblance between the rose's woody stems and those of the spice tree's bark. But no one disputes that Parkinson and his contemporaries gobbled up toothsome rose shoots, aromatic rose petals, and ripe rose hips.

Such was not the case with nineteenth-century **'Cinnamon-scented Rose'**, an unrelated China so called for the aroma of its dark red flowers; **'Sweet Anise Rose'**, a licorice-scented yellow tea; or **'A Odeur de Pâte d'Amandes'** ("scent of almond paste"). By design, these fancy confections ended up in a vase, not on a plate, tempting only the nostrils and eyes. They let wasp-waisted belles satisfy a yen for flowers without ingesting fattening rose confections. Our pragmatic era rewards similar restraint with the spicily fragrant yellow and pink hybrid tea **'Weight Watchers Success'**.

POTTED ROSES

Samuel Parsons relays an enticing rose recipe that the third-century Hellenistic writer Athenaeus picked up from the king of Sicily's chef. "This is what I call potted roses," the cook told him, "and it is thus prepared: I first pound some of the most fragrant roses in a mortar; then I take the brains of birds and pigs, well boiled and stripped of every particle of meat; I then add the yolks of some eggs, some oil, a little cordial, some pepper, and some wine: after having beaten and mixed it well together, I throw it in a new pot, and place it over a slow but steady fire." Athenaeus reported, "As he said these things, the cook uncovered the pot, and there issued forth a most delicious fragrance, perfuming the whole dining-hall, and overcoming the guests with delight."

GREEN ROSE

ONLY PROFESSIONAL ONE-UPMANSHIP CAN explain why the green-est thumbs in early-nineteenth-century French horticulture com-peted to create the world's first green-flowered rose. One method, recommended by Jean Louis Marie Guillemeau in his *Histoire naturelle de la rose* of 1800, involved planting a rosebush with pale pink or white blooms close to holly and or-ange trees, and waiting for the flowers to go green. Guillemeau also advocated hyp-notizing trees to keep them from dropping their leaves in the fall. History fails to re-cord whether either technique worked, but when a green-flowered rosebush, *Rosa chinensis* **'Viridiflora'**, finally did materialize in American nurseries dur-ing the 1830s, horticultural hocus-pocus had played no part. 'Viridiflora' developed as a bona

A PERENNIAL CURIOSITY: THE 'GREEN ROSE',
ROSA CHINENSIS 'VIRIDIFLORA'

fide natural phenomenon. The deep green petals tinged with bronze and pink, as opaque and firm as sepals, are one-of-a-kind among roses. Some rosarians consider them a freak of nature.

After touring Robert Buist's nursery in Philadelphia in 1849, the landscape designer and architect Andrew Jackson Downing wrote, "The most singular, though least beautiful [rose is] the **'Green Rose'**, a curious example of vegetable morphology, the petals of the flower being all green, like the leaves of the plant." Documentary evidence suggests that, even though it is classed as a China rose, *R. chinensis* 'Viridiflora' may have originated in South Carolina or Georgia. Buist's first specimens came from stock acquired in Charleston in 1833. A decade later, a Savannah cotton merchant planted 'Viridiflora' at his country place (now Barnsley Gardens Resort, where cuttings from the original bush still grow). The rose set sail from Baltimore for its long-awaited French première, at the Paris Exposition Universelle in 1856, only to be jeered by horticultural pundits: "This is a little monstrosity or an error of nature. Nothing more!" The London *Gardeners' Chronicle and Agricultural Gazette* agreed that "a green eyed monster like this is not inviting."

The 'Green Rose' continues to receive mixed reviews. It makes a good cut flower because the sturdy foliage-like petals last longer in a vase than those of most roses, and it's a surefire garden conversation piece. This bizarre flower plays a pivotal role in *The Green Rose of Furley Hall*, a historical novel about Quakers guiding slaves to freedom along the Underground Railroad during the Civil War. Author Helen Corse Barney drew upon stories of her Quaker ancestors, such as William Corse, a Baltimore nurseryman with abolitionist sympathies who planted 'Viridiflora' at his estate, Furley Hall. Plants survived there until the property was bulldozed for row-house construction in 1953, the year Barney published her book. Local legend—arising, perhaps, from the novel—says that Underground Railroad conductors signaled to one another by wearing a 'Green Rose'.

Few modern breeders have attempted to copy nature's emerald rose, and the results of their efforts—generally white or yellow flowers with just a tincture of chartreuse, like the miniature **'Green Diamonds'** or the florist's roses **'Green Success'** and **'Lovely Green'**—pale by comparison.

FAR MORE ELUSIVE, AND so alluring that rose hybridizers have called it their Holy Grail, is the creation of a blue rose. Reports of "Arabian" roses in tones of lapis lazuli and sky blue tantalized generations of Western gardeners. In *The Old Rose Informant*, historian Brent C. Dickerson mentions that in 1810 an English nobleman, Lord Milford, got his hands on an apparent breakthrough: a China rose, not yet in bloom, labeled **'Blue Rose'**. To his lordship's dismay, when the flowers unfurled, they were purple. Nurseries made sure that the offspring of that deceiver entered catalogs under more accurate names: **'Indica Purpurea'**, **'Pourpre'**, and **'Purple'**.

Although the splendid German rambler **'Veilchenblau'** (**'Violet Blue'**), bred in 1909, leans more toward blue than any predecessor, the *Veilchen* definitely dominates the *Blau*. English hybridizer Harry Wheatcroft compared the splash of its newly opened blooms to "a spilt pot of violet ink." Perhaps he remembered shortcuts used by Victorians too impatient for the slow progress of cross-breeding. In 1842 William Paul had recommended watering white- or pale-pink-flowered rosebushes with dilute indigo dye. The October 1884 issue of *Journal des Roses* supplied how-to for dipping pale flowers in a solution of carbonate of potash and then soaking them in blue aniline powder dissolved in water.

True blue, like the cerulean pigment found in salvias, delphiniums, hyacinths, and forget-me-nots, simply does not exist in roses. The ancient Greeks and Romans, of course, explained this absence with a myth. To console Chloris, or Flora, the goddess of flowers and spring, after her favorite nymph had died, fellow deities transformed the corpse into a blossom more beautiful than any other: the rose. Chloris endowed this new creation with every color except blue, which reminded her of death. Try as they might, hybridizers have not filled that gap in the spectrum. Neither **'Blue Girl'**, **'Blue Mist'**, **'Blue Bayou'**, **'Moody Blues'**, **'Rhapsody in Blue'** nor any other would-be blue lives up to its name. All embody shades of lavender or mauve, often turning a melancholy gray as they mature.

A 1910 ADVERTISEMENT EXAGGERATES THE AZURE OF 'VIOLET BLUE' ('VEILCHENBLAU'), THEN A NOVELTY RAMBLER.

SHORTLY AFTER THE SECOND World War, New York rose hybridizer Gene Boerner brought a hybrid tea from the McGredy nursery in Northern Ireland, hoping that its unusual hue of lavender gray with brownish under-tones might be a useful addition to his breeding palette. At first, neither he nor the McGredys, who had puckishly named it **'The Mouse'**, figured on marketing the plant. Sam McGredy—whose uncle handed off the rose, "providing it's understood that it's none of my doing"—later wrote that this flower was, "to most people, a revolting colour." But others, including Boerner's em-ployer, Charles Perkins, begged to differ. When Perkins showed 'The Mouse' to Helen Jepson, a star soprano at the Metropolitan Opera, she warbled that it perfectly matched her new pearl necklace, and said, "Why don't you name it 'Gray Pearl'?" Boerner gave his okay after a quick trip to Tiffany's, where a salesman showed him the real thing—and its impressive price tag.

Although **'Grey Pearl'** (Americans adopted the British spelling, presum-ably for snob appeal) got no bravos for its lackluster performance in gardens, varieties bred from it displayed promising hints of lavender blue. In 1948 came **'Lavender Pinocchio'**, a floribunda that begat **'Lavender Garnette'**, **'Lavender Princess'**, and **'Lavender Girl'**. Another child of 'Grey Pearl', **'Sterling Silver'**, became a celebrity and florist's pet in the late 1950s, after gossip columnists revealed that Richard Burton gave bouquets of the mauve rose to Elizabeth Taylor because it matched her eyes. A seedling of 'Sterling Silver' bred in 1964, **'Blue Moon'** is still the bluest hybrid tea around, not-withstanding its pronounced lavender tone.

Research into the chemical structure of plant pigmentation began in Ger-many around the time that 'Veilchenblau' first bloomed, although these two

developments had no connection. Within the past two decades, a consortium
of Australian and Japanese molecular geneticists have concentrated on grafting a "blue gene" from pansies and other flowers to bioengineer a blue rose.
In Tennessee, Vanderbilt University biochemists investigating treatments for
cancer and Alzheimer's disease have isolated a liver enzyme that turns human
tissue blue—and can produce the same color in plants. So far, splicing the
liver gene into roses has yielded erratic results: bluish stems and bluish prickles but no thoroughly blue flower. We're afraid to ask whether the ultimate
outcome will be 'Blue Cross' or 'Blue Shield'.

THE WHITE ALBUM

Alba means "white" in Latin, although many roses classed as albas are softly
tinged with pink. Modern rosarians have searched in vain for a surviving specimen of the original parent strain, but they generally assume that the earliest
examples originated in central or southern Europe as a cross between a damask or a gallica
and some form of *Rosa canina*. Roman soldiers or colonists brought albas to Britain, and the
roses became so plentiful that Pliny cited them as a possible reason why England came to be
called Albion. A descendant of those imports, *R.* x *alba* **'Semiplena'**, later won renown as
'The White Rose of York'.

Early in the eighteenth century, white *R.* x *alba* **'Maxima'** became a secret sign of soli-
darity among the Jacobites, supporters of the exiled James III and his son Prince Charles.
After government forces vanquished Charles's troops, he fled to the Outer Hebrides where
Flora Macdonald—foster child of the local British commander—helped him slip away to
France by disguising him as her maid, decorating his cap with the Jacobite rose. This legend
gives *R.* x *alba* 'Maxima' its alternative name, **'Bonnie Prince Charlie's Rose'**.

HEBE'S CUP

'HEBE'S LIP'

POOR HEBE. SHE SEEMED to have it made on Mount Olympus as cupbearer to her fellow Greek gods. A double nectar for Athena, a refill for Ares, a nice dessert wine to go with Poseidon's ambrosia. Everything was fine until—damn it to Hades!—Hebe suddenly slipped on the golden floor and fell. Word came down, like a bolt out of the blue, that her services were no longer required. Worse yet, her replacement was a mere mortal: Ganymede (as in **'Ganymed'**, a red floribunda), boy toy of Hebe's own father, Zeus. Maybe **'Hebe's Lip'** (a white eglantine) refers to what the fired waitgoddess gave Dad when she heard this news. Luckily, Hebe hadn't quit her day job as goddess of youth and forgiveness. The rest, as they say, is mythology.

By the time the deep-pink French hybrid Bourbon **'Coupe d'Hébé'**, or **'Hebe's Cup'**, appeared in 1840 ('Hebe's Lip' was bred in England six years later), nearly a century of neoclassical revivals—in art, literature, architecture, and every other area of design—had left a deep impression on rose culture in Europe and North America. As a result, our gardens resound with echoes of Greek and Roman myths. The choice of a particular deity's Hellenic name over its Latin counterpart seems to reflect common usage in the breeder's own language, and an individual sense of euphony, rather than botanical convention or historical bias. Latin names dominate the list, perhaps because the revels of rose-crowned Greeks (rose garlands were standard festive wear) couldn't hold an oil lamp to the toga parties where orgiastic Romans smothered their guests, sometimes literally, with flowers. Two **'Bacchus'** roses—an 1855 hybrid perpetual and a 1951 hybrid tea—toasted the Roman god of wine long before the 2002 floribunda **'Dionisia'** became the only salute to Dionysus, his Grecian double.

'HEBE'S CUP'

Like many gods and humans, rose breeders have given in to the intoxicating effects of beauty and love, so floral paeans to Venus and Cupid (or their Greek alter egos, Aphrodite and Eros) abound. In *The Birth of Venus*, the Renaissance artist Sandro Botticelli painted the goddess emerging from the sea, shell-borne amid a heavenly downpour of roses. Hence **'Conque de Vénus'** (*conque* is "shell" in French), a pre-1844 white

Noisette, and **'Naissance de Vénus'**, (*naissance* is "birth"), an 1826 medium pink alba, whose Gallic name belies the plant's German origin. Only **'Vénus Mère'**, or "Mother Venus," a medium pink Dutch gallica bred before 1811, refers to the deity's role as Cupid's mother, maybe because her parenting left much to be desired.

Venus didn't intervene, for instance, when Cupid started sneaking wine from Bacchus. Until the little scamp spilled a drink on some rose petals, staining them red, all roses had been pristine white. Mother certainly rued the day she let sonny play with arrows. First he angrily shot a quiverful into some rosebushes after a bee stung his lip as he tried to kiss a flower; that's how roses got thorns. Then one of Cupid's arrows accidentally wounded Venus, causing her to moon over the handsome Adonis. This affair came to a gory conclusion on the tusks of a wild boar, explaining why the earliest of the four roses called **'Adonis'**, a gallica bred before 1814, has blood red flowers. Amazingly, after Cupid pricked himself with an arrowhead and fell for a comely mortal, Psyche, the pair breezed through one challenge after another to wed and live happily ever after. As befits the marriage of god and mortal, the first **'Psyche'**, bred in France before 1836, is a hybrid perpetual.

Zeus, or Jupiter, takes the prize for divinely versatile lovemaking. **'Danaë'**, a 1913 hybrid musk, recalls the maiden he ravished by disguising himself as a shower of gold. Her rose, of course, is pale yellow; **'Zeus'**, bred in 1959, is a golden climber. The god turned into a swan to seduce the human princess Leda, fathering the egg that hatched Helen of Troy. Beginning with an 1827 damask, several roses have invoked Leda's name and alluded to her rendezvous with Zeus through a blur of pink and white blossoms. If a latter-day Zeus had wanted to appease his famously jealous wife, Hera, he could have sent some of the roses that bear her Roman name, Juno (the earliest is a red gallica bred before 1811). Or maybe not. Writing in 1869 about **'Juno'**, an 1847 white hybrid China, the English rosarian S. Reynolds Hole called it "a Rose, which, like the goddess, may justly complain of neglect, appearing in few gardens, and well deserving a place in all."

SUB ROSA

A synonym for "in secret" since the 1650s, the English phrase *sub rosa* comes from the Latin for "under the rose." Greek mythology told that Cupid slipped a rose to Harpocrates, the god of silence, as a payoff for holding his tongue about Venus's dalliances. The ancients consequently hung roses above dining tables to remind guests that they must not repeat anything said in confidence—under penalty of divine retribution. This tradition spread throughout Europe, and ceilings with carved or painted roses became a common feature of banquet halls, meeting chambers, and church confessionals. It was even said that Queen Elizabeth I of England wore a rose behind her ear to indicate royal discretion (a custom that Elizabeth II must have prayed, more than once, her own family would adopt). The symbolism persists in the names of modern roses such as **'Dark Secret'**, a crimson American hybrid tea; **'Discretion'**, a salmon pink French hybrid tea; **'Golden Silence'**, a yellow Canadian miniature; and **'Harmonia Sub Rosa'**, a pink and white French hybrid tea.

HELEN KELLER

AFTER SCARLET FEVER LEFT her blind and deaf at the age of nineteen months, Helen Keller could neither see a flower nor hear its name, but she always held roses dear. In *The Story of My Life*, published in 1903, shortly before her graduation from Radcliffe College, the Alabama native wrote: "Never have I found in the greenhouses of the North such

heart-satisfying roses as the climbing roses of my southern home. They used to hang in long festoons from our porch, filling the whole air with their fragrance, untainted by any earthly smell; and in the early morning, washed in the dew, they felt so soft, so pure, I could not help wondering if they did not resemble the asphodels of God's garden."

Flowers also stimulated the child's intellectual curiosity, which she learned to apply under the guidance of her teacher Anne

HELEN KELLER WITH SOME OF THE MANY ROSES
SHE KNEW BY SMELL AND TOUCH

Sullivan, a tutelage dramatized on stage and screen in *The Miracle Worker*. When Keller visited Pennsylvania nurseryman Robert Pyle at the Star Rose Gardens in 1942, she asked him to demonstrate, by touch, the propagation technique known as budding. She already had a rose of her own: **'Helen Keller'**, a suitably fragrant deep pink hybrid perpetual introduced by an Irish grower in 1895, the year she turned fifteen. By then, reports of her prodigious determination and accomplishments — newspapers ran photographs of the young Keller reading Shakespeare in braille — had made Keller a popular heroine. President Grover Cleveland met with her at the White House. Alexander Graham Bell, a longtime friend whose deaf wife also adored roses,

enjoyed chatting with this brilliant girl and her teacher (via manual alphabet and lip reading) while they sat in his garden.

"As the soil brings forth thistles and as roses have thorns," Keller wrote, "human life will have its trials." Any gardener who has braved prickly canes to prune a rosebush — or watched one bloom despite the ravages of aphids, black

Thé Sombreuil.

Journal des Roses et des Vergers, pl XVIII

spot, cane borers, galls, Japanese beetles, midges, rust, sawflies, thrips, and other natural foes — is inclined to view its beauty as a profile in courage. Hard-won respect has likewise moved rose growers to name a host of plants after valiant women. When Helen Keller took a rare turn at acting in the 1919 silent film *Deliverance*, she played Joan of Arc, one of history's many heroines for whom roses are named. In addition to the pink gallica **'La Pucelle'** (*La pucelle d'Orléans*, "the Maid of Orleans," was Joan's nom de guerre), four white **'Jeanne d'Arc'** roses commemorate the medieval warrior-saint known for her virginal white armor, horse, and banner.

A heroic maiden from French Revolutionary days lives on in **'Mademoiselle de Sombreuil'**, a creamy white tea rose, and **'Sombreuil'**, a white climber. During the September Massacres of 1792, a Paris mob dragged the young woman's aged father, a former government official, from his prison cell for summary execution. When Marie-Maurille rushed forward to plead for mercy, swearing that the marquis opposed the Royalist cause in spite of his noble title, the throng demanded that she affirm solidarity with the common man by drinking the blood of slain aristocrats. She swallowed a full glass of this grisly draft without flinching, and her father was spared. Her death, in 1823, moved Victor Hugo to pen an ode to her filial sacrifice.

Down the social ladder and across the North Sea, an English lighthouse keeper's daughter inspired the hybrid tea **'Grace Darling'**. During a storm in 1838, Grace and her father repeatedly rowed a small boat through gale-force winds and turbulent water to rescue the survivors of a shipwreck off their island home. Sensational reports in the British press and a slew of semifictional books endowed this unassuming twenty-three-year-old with superhuman strength and angelic kindness. Queen Victoria sent a personal letter of praise; William Wordsworth wrote a laudatory poem; admirers begged for snippets of her clothing; and images of "the girl with windswept hair" adorned tea caddies, candy boxes, and china. The embarrassed object of this attention, who declined the many monetary awards she was offered, complained that she had better things to do than answer fan mail: "I have seven apartments in the house to keep in a state fit to be inspected everyday by Gentlemen." Her domestic rounds came to a halt in 1842, when Grace Darling—worn out, it is said, by contending with celebrity—expired of consumption in her father's arms. Fate had supplied the perfect ending to a legend that biographers continued to embellish. Bathed in this sentimental aura, creamy pink 'Grace Darling' met with great success in the 1880s.

The garden's tributes to bravery and humanitarian relief also include **'Clara Barton'**, a hybrid tea named for the shy New Englander who became a pioneering Civil War nurse, suffragist, and founder of the American Red Cross. Off duty, she enjoyed tending rosebushes. Barton felt personally tied to red roses through forebears who hailed from Lancashire, England. Her cousin William Eleazar Barton wrote in 1922: "In the Wars of the Roses the Bartons were with the house of Lancaster, and the Red Rose is the traditional flower of the Barton family. Clara Barton, when she wore flowers, habitually wore red roses; and whatever her attire there was almost invariably about it somewhere a touch of red, 'her color,' she called it, as it had been the color of her ancestors for many generations." Genealogy aside, when the Conard & Jones nursery requested permission to name a rose for her in 1898, the Red Cross president could have been miffed—not because the plant lacked horticultural merit, but because its flowers were, as the breeder's catalog boasted, "a rare and exquisite shade of delicate amber pink." Barton appreciated the rose's publicity value for the Red Cross, however, and gave it her blessing.

Although the English nurse Edith Cavell was a gifted artist, who loved to paint flowers near her father's Norfolk vicarage, she had no reason to expect that a rose would ever bear her name—let alone *two* roses: **'Miss Edith Cavell'**, a scarlet Dutch polyantha bred in 1917, and **'Edith Cavell'**, a pale yellow English hybrid tea of 1918. Sadly, those dates explain why this gallant woman never laid eyes on either plant. Cavell's distinguished career and fluency in French led to her appointment in 1905 as matron of the Berkendael Medical Institute, a progressive nursing school in Brussels. Soon after the First World War began, German occupying forces in Belgium arrested her for helping Allied prisoners escape to the Netherlands, and sentenced her to death as a spy. An appeal from the Belgian minister of the United States, then officially a neutral power, failed to stop the German firing squad that executed Cavell at dawn on October 12, 1915. Only hours before, she told a chaplain, "I realize that patriotism is not enough, I must have no hatred or bitterness towards anyone." Various monuments honor her, from a statue in London to plaques in South African churches, a hospital in Brussels, a mountain in Canada, and a solitary 'Edith Cavell' rosebush at the Nurses' Memorial Chapel in Christchurch, New Zealand.

A ROSE OF ONE'S OWN

You don't have to swim through storm-tossed waters or stand before a firing squad to have a rose named for you. All you need is a checkbook. Every major rose company maintains a portfolio of unnamed seedlings that are available for a price, but several smaller operations—such as the Antique Rose Emporium in Brenham, Texas—also offer this service. J. B. Williams and Associates, in Silver Spring, Maryland, has specialized in naming roses for private individuals since 1972. The Brooklyn Botanic Garden honored its director emeritus Elizabeth Scholtz with a Williams orange-pink grandiflora, **'Elizabeth Scholtz'**, which was sold as a fund-raiser for the garden in 1981. Banker and philanthropist David Rockefeller purchased a Williams rose and gave it to his wife, Peggy, in 1992. Not by chance, the red hybrid tea **'Peggy Rockefeller'** occupies a prominent location in the Peggy Rockefeller Rose Garden at the New York Botanical Garden.

To find out whether your favorite rose nursery will name a plant to order, contact its public relations department. Fees vary, averaging about $15,000 or more. This includes rights to all sales in the United States. (Unless you make special arrangements, the breeder is entitled to pocket any foreign proceeds.) If you wish to patent the rose—usually a two-year process that's necessary only if you plan on selling the rose to the general public—most breeders will assist you for an additional fee. Public release also requires a search to ensure that the name you've chosen isn't already in use, after which you and the nursery should submit the name to the International Registration Authority for Roses. To list a custom-labeled variety in a retail catalog, most growers require a minimum initial order, typically 250 plants.

Patience is key. Even if you decide to commission a rose only for private enjoyment, it could take at least a year before you receive bushes that are ready to plant. And then there's another essential delay: Wait a season or two to see how your namesake performs in the garden before you give seedlings to friends and colleagues. Do you really want the world to know that you're prone to black spot?

HOLY ROSE OF ABYSSINIA

HALOED IN MYSTERY, THIS pink single-flowered species may have the most venerable lineage of any Western garden rose. Historians suspect that a fourth-century Christian saint, the freed slave Frumentius, imported it from his native Phoenicia (now Syria) to Abyssinia (Ethiopia) where he gathered a vast flock of converts and became the first bishop of Axum. One of the churches he founded there, St. Mary of Zion, claims to house the Ark of the Covenant (the same lost ark pursued on-screen by Indiana Jones). The shrub rose associated with Abba Salama, "Father of Peace," as Frumentius is known in his adopted land, still grew in Ethiopian churchyards in the late 1840s, when the French botanist Achille Richard labeled it *Rosa sancta*, meaning "holy rose." After a British archaeologist found garlands strung with dried blossoms of that rose, or a similar variety, inside ancient Egyptian tombs, the plant acquired the alias **'Tomb Rose'**. To avoid confusion with an unrelated plant already called *R. sancta*, botanists renamed Richard's holy rose *R. richardii*. But St. Frumentius must be pleased to know that nonscientists persist in calling it **'Holy Rose of Abyssinia'**.

The geographical ID helps to distinguish this rose from a throng of other sanctified blooms. By the Middle Ages, Christian lore had endowed the whole rose family with complex religious symbolism. The Roman Catholic Church exalted the rose as a generic emblem of paradise, of divinity made flesh, and of the Virgin Mary ("God's rose garden" in Latin hymns). Church iconographers assigned specific meanings to flower colors: red roses signified the blood of martyrs and the Passion of Christ; white, the Virgin's immaculate purity; and yellow, her golden wisdom (for more than a thousand years, popes have bestowed the gift of a solid-gold rose on people or institutions they esteem). Rose stems supplied a legendary source for the crown of thorns as well as an epithet for the sinless Virgin, "the rose without thorns."

The twentieth-century rose hybrids **'Rosary'**, or **'Roserie'** (a pink rambler), and **'Ave Maria'** (a white hybrid tea, now extinct, and a red one, as well as a white polyantha) invoke a tangible bond among the mother of Jesus, her flower, and divine mysteries. For Catholics, "rosary" refers both to a form of prayer involving the recitation of 150 Hail Marys, or Ave Marias, and to the string of beads used to keep count during that meditative sequence. The word stems from the Latin *rosarium*, "rose garden"—still the secular definition of "rosary"—and *rosarius*, "rose garland or bouquet."

THE VENERABLE *ROSA SANCTA*, OR "HOLY ROSE"

In the Middle Ages, even unlettered Christians linked rosary beads to roses, thanks to a legend repeated from northern Europe to Abyssinia. The story tells of a devout youth who places a homemade wreath of 150 roses on the Virgin's altar every day. After joining a monastery, where his schedule can't accommodate flower weaving, he substitutes a Hail Mary for each of the roses he used to offer. All goes well until the young man travels through a forest, where bandits creep up on him as he kneels to pray. Suddenly, the thieves stop in their tracks, terrified by a radiant apparition of the Blessed Mother. She plucks 150 roses from the monk's open mouth and entwines them into a garland, which she drapes around his neck. The brigands flee, and their intended victim possesses the world's first rosary. In one narrative, the flowers miraculously solidify, reinforcing some historians' belief that early rosaries were strung with rose hips.

ALTHOUGH IT IS A miniature rose, **'Rose Window'**, a medley of red, yellow, and orange, pays homage to the monumental stained-glass rose windows of gothic cathedrals. In *Mont-Saint-Michel and Chartres*, Henry Adams wrote, "[T]he Gothic architect . . . felt the value of the rose in art, and perhaps still more in religion, for the rose was Mary's emblem. One is fairly sure that the great Chartres rose of the west front was put there to please her, since it was to be always before her eyes, the most conspicuous object she would see from the high altar, and therefore the most carefully considered ornament in the whole church."

Individual rose names commemorate sightings of Mary in farflung places. **'Our Lady of Guadalupe'**, an American floribunda, honors the visions of Juan Diego Cuauhtlatoatzin, a Mexican Indian who converted to Christianity. He was alone on chilly Tepeyac hill in December 1531, headed for mass in Mexico City, when the Virgin Mary came to him. She told Cuauhtlatoatzin that she wished to have a shrine built on the hillside, and instructed him to convey her desire to his bishop. Skeptical, the clergyman demanded proof of divine intervention. Mary obliged by causing Castilian roses to bloom amid the frozen rocks. Cuauhtlatoatzin picked a bunch of flowers, wrapped them in his cactus-cloth cloak, and rushed back to the bishop. When he unfolded his mantle to present the flowers—mirabile dictu—its coarse fabric displayed a life-sized image of a dark-skinned Virgin.

Pilgrims still climb Tepeyac to pray before that icon inside the Basilica of Our Lady of Guadalupe. How Guadalupe came to be part of this Virgin's name puzzles linguists and historians, but the Vatican unequivocally recognizes her as the patron saint of North and South America. Rome has also declared Juan Diego Cuauhtlatoatzin the first American Indian saint. Rose grower Jackson & Perkins created 'Our Lady of Guadalupe' in 2000, after receiving requests from farmworkers employed in the nursery's fields and from a Catholic priest active in the hispanic community of Los Angeles. Proceeds from rose sales help to fund a scholarship for Latino students.

The French floribunda **'Centenaire de Lourdes'** was introduced in 1958, one hundred years after a poor shepherdess, fourteen-year-old Bernadette Soubirous, announced that Mary had appeared to her in a cave near Lourdes, in southwestern France. The girl said: "I saw a Lady dressed in white, wearing a white dress, a blue girdle and a yellow rose on each foot, the same color as the chain of her rosary." During the ninth of eighteen visitations, this figure guided Bernadette to dig for an underground spring, later revered for its healing waters. Upon her canonization in 1933, Bernadette joined an illustrious company of saints tied to roses.

The Agathes, a group of nearly thornless gallicas, recall the third-century Sicilian virgin martyr St. Agatha. A lecherous Roman senator had her breasts cut off after she spurned him. Three roses have been named **'Saint Fiacre'**, for the Irish-born patron saint of gardeners and cab drivers (the first taxi was probably a carriage in seventeenth-century Paris known as a fiacre, because it could be hired at the Hôtel de Saint Fiacre). An Italian folktale relates that St. Francis—memorialized in the bright pink gallica **'Saint François'**—resisted temptation by jumping naked into a thicket of brambles. The bloody thorns put forth roses, which he laid on a chapel altar. St. Rita of Cascia—as in **'Santa Rita'**, an orange-pink hybrid tea—claimed that the Savior pressed a thorn into her forehead, causing a wound that never healed and blessing her with empathy for his agony on the cross. Divine providence also enabled Rita, the patron of impossible causes, to make a rose bloom in midwinter.

IN THE BEGINNING

Roses grew in Palestine during biblical times, but where the word *rose* appears in English translations of the Old Testament, it probably does not refer to the plant we know by that name. The rose in Isaiah 35:1, for example, may in fact be a narcissus or an autumn crocus. The rose of Sharon in the Songs of Solomon is also thought to be a tuber, not the shrub *Hibiscus syriacus*, which carries that name today. Nevertheless, latter-day hybridizers have created true roses that bring Bible stories to life.

'Genesis': A mauve miniature. One of its parents is **'Angel Face'**.

'Eden 88': This temptingly fragrant pink climber is exceptionally disease resistant.

'Adam': The salmon pink climbing tea commemorates the French breeder Michel Adam, who produced it in 1838.

'Eve': Coral hybrid tea with yellow shading. A legend says that when Eve learned she could take only one flower out of Eden, she chose a white rose, which blushed with pleasure.

'Samson': The strongman's namesake is a red miniature.

'Delilah': This mauve hybrid tea needs careful pruning.

'Couronne de Salomon' ('Solomon's Crown'): Each flower of the deep pink gallica is ringed by a "crown" of eight to ten buds. It is no longer available commercially.

'Ruth': The Reverend Joseph Pemberton bred this orange hybrid tea.

'Queen Esther': One ancestor of this pink-edged white hybrid tea is regal **'Golden Scepter'**. The crimson gallica honoring the king Esther married, **'Ahasuerus'**, has disappeared.

IRISH GOLD

WHEN A LEPRECHAUN PLAYS center for the Boston Celtics and a Highlander swaps his kilt for trousers, you might see a rose supplant the shamrock of Ireland or the thistle of Scotland. The wise gardener would sooner prune poison ivy with bare hands than mess with national symbols—especially on patches of the old, or auld, sod where England's rose can be a touchy subject. But the Irish and Scots have fine, distinctive roses of their own, whose names resound with Hibernian and Caledonian pride. Among the oldest are the **'Wild Irish Rose'**, *Rosa* x *hibernica*, beloved of tenors, and the **'Scots Rose'**,

SCOTLAND'S 'AYRSHIRE ROSE' WAS
FIRST RECORDED IN 1768.

R. spinosissima (aka *R. pimpinellifolia*), which only Englishmen and other out-landers call "Scotch." Modern varieties include a list to warm the cockles of a tourist board director's heart: **'Rose of Tralee'**, **'Celtic Honey'**, and **'River-dance'**; **'Bonnie Scotland'**, **'Rabbie Burns'**, and **'Highland Fling'**. Some hybrids have a mixed heritage connecting both shores of the Irish Sea—nota-bly, **'Irish Gold'**, which was bred by a family of Scots-Irish stock.

Dual nationality is also an issue for Scotland's **'Ayrshire Rose'**, which first bloomed in 1768 at Loudon Castle in the western county of Ayr. The Earl of Loudon, who had commanded all British troops during the French and In-dian War, grew the rose from seeds collected in North America. Its fragrant white flowers attracted the attention of nurserymen in Scotland and abroad, who bred hybrids like pink **'Ayrshire Queen'** and **'Tea-scented Ayrshire'** (possibly created in Italy). These plants' pliable canes make them excellent choices for training as "weeping" standards—memorials of a sort to the origi-nal 'Ayrshire Rose', which is now extinct.

Botanists scouting in western Scotland first identified the prickly low-growing 'Scots Rose', or **'Scots Briar'**, with small cupped white flowers of nine to sixteen petals, in 1771. A double, more abundantly petaled form cropped up in 1802 at the Perth nursery of Robert Brown (the namesake of *R. brunonii*, an import from more distant highlands, the Himalayas). Hundreds of dou-ble cultivars, such as Brown's **'King of Scotland'** and French-bred **'Petite Ecossaise'** ("little Scotswoman"), both pink, crowded European and Ameri-can plant catalogs by the 1820s. Brown himself eventually immigrated to the United States, as did his countrymen Robert Buist and Peter Henderson, who established major rose nurseries in Philadelphia and Jersey City.

It was Ireland, however, that beckoned to Brown's Scottish business partner, Alexander Dickson. In 1836 he founded a nursery at Newtownards, on the outskirts of Belfast in County Down. Belfast was then an industrial boomtown with a prosperous elite intent on acquiring grand new gardens. By the late 1870s, when Dickson's son, George, focused on breeding roses, gardeners throughout the British Isles had come to resent the French monopoly on fashionable hybrids, which was reflected in the prevalence of Gallic names. George and his sons, Alexander II and George II, charged into the nativist vanguard, determined to match or surpass the horticultural caliber of imported roses and stamp their creations "made in Great Britain." Until then, Ireland's chief claim to rose fame had been *R.* x *hibernica*, a naturally occurring hybrid of two species.

One of Alexander II's early successes was **'Earl of Dufferin'**, a crimson maroon hybrid perpetual honoring the Irish viceroy of India, who also had Scottish forbears and owned property in County Down. Ivory and pink **'Marchioness of Londonderry'**, an 1893 hybrid perpetual, curtseyed to the wife of Britain's former lord lieutenant of Ireland and a vocal opponent of Irish home rule. The Dicksons occasionally ventured beyond the northern counties of Ulster to label plants such as **'Killarney'**, an 1898 hybrid tea, which commemorates the far-off southwestern beauty spot famous for its lakes.

During the turmoil of 1916 to 1921, which culminated in the separation of the Irish Free State from Northern Ireland, the simple act of naming a flower could be inflammatory. But as the English rosarian Jack Harkness observed decades later, in his biographical compendium *The Makers of Heavenly Roses*, "The Dicksons got on with their work, being gentle and decent people who saw nothing but trouble in politics." A glance at the list of names they've bestowed on roses confirms the constant focus on work and family that has sustained their firm through six generations. **'Margaret Dickson'** (1891), **'Hugh Dickson'** (1905), **'George Dickson'** (1912), and **'Grandpa Dickson'** (1966) all thrive in gardens today. The last, honoring Alexander Dickson III, was introduced by his grandson Alexander Patrick "Pat" Dickson (whose son Colin Dickson currently runs the show), and garnered every major award on the international rose circuit. Assuming that Americans wouldn't know a Dickson from a Dougherty, however, marketers rechristened this yellow hybrid tea **'Irish Gold'** for customers in the United States. And, should Grandpa protest, the younger Dicksons could cite *his* father's 1914 **'Irish Fireflame'**—a single-flowered stunner—as precedent.

Meanwhile, Northern Ireland's *other* rose dynasty, the McGredy clan, had been collecting its own trove of horticultural gold medals. Forty years after Alexander

SINGLE-FLOWERED HYBRID TEAS FROM IRELAND, SUCH AS 'IRISH FIREFLAME' (*CENTER LEFT*), WERE FASHIONABLE DURING THE EARLY TWENTIETH CENTURY.

Dickson I set up shop, Samuel McGredy, previously a gardener on a private estate, opened a nursery in Portadown, also near Belfast. A specialist in pansies, he dabbled in roses only as a hobby, but his son Sam II made rose hybridizing the family business—and a personal passion. By the time of his death in 1926, Sam II had produced hundreds of new varieties, earning him the nickname the Irish Wizard. The following year, Sam III released **'Irish Hope'** and **'Irish Courage'**, simultaneously affirming familial continuity and patriotic resolve.

A happy marriage and a strong woman stand behind **'Mrs. Sam McGredy'**, a large-flowered scarlet and orange hybrid tea Sam III bred in 1929. Asked to select "her" wifely rose from a group of candidates that Sam considered the pick of the nursery, Ruth Darragh McGredy said no to the whole bunch. Instead, she chose a plant he had cast aside because of its thin stems and insisted that he distribute it with her name on the label. Neither McGredy could foresee that the rose would come to mark an untimely parting. In 1934 Sam died of a sudden heart attack at age thirty-eight, leaving Ruth with three young children to care for and a business to run. Sam IV, who took over in 1952, later brushed aside **'Sam McGredy'**, a memorial to his father introduced in 1937, as "an absolute dud, which should never have been given that name. It just wouldn't grow, producing normally one big shoot with one or two absolutely perfect hybrid-tea blooms on top." Commercially, though, the occasional flop made little difference: by the late 1930s, a quarter of all hybrid teas sold in America were of Irish origin. 'Mrs. Sam McGredy' became an international best seller and remained one of the firm's biggest moneymakers for decades.

Another chapter of McGredy history ended in 1972, when—frustrated by the high costs of running a winter greenhouse operation in Northern Ireland and "very depressed by the unending troubles all around me"—Sam IV transplanted his family and his business to New Zealand. As a parting gesture before pulling up roots, he created the red rose **'City of Belfast'**, a tribute to the ambitious City of Belfast International Rose Garden then being planned. Today heirlooms bred by every generation of Dicksons and McGredys bloom at the center of that garden, Irish gold from the mother lode.

THE ELUSIVE BANSHEE

The banshee's wail is a presage; her origins are a mystery. Like this spirit in Gaelic folklore, the **"Banshee"** rose—also called **"The Baffling Banshee"** or **"The Great Impersonator"**—keeps its true identity hidden. Few early rose books mention the plant despite its lovely blush-colored spring flowers and bewitching fragrance. In *Old Garden Roses* (1937) E. A. Bunyard describes the aroma as an "Eau de Cologne scent [that] will delight all lovers of scented roses, being 'sui generis' in this."

Curiously, "Banshee" appears to grow only in the United States—primarily the Northeast—and in Canada, although records indicate that members of the MacLeod clan transported a rose of this name from Scotland to the American colonies. After the outbreak of the American Revolution, Tory emigrants took "Banshee" to Canada where it is also called **"Loyalist Rose."** The shrub has mainly been sighted in old cemeteries, lending credence to legends that its fearsome thorns ward off evil spirits. Skeptics pooh-pooh this as an example of the Irish tradition commemorated by a climbing tea bred in California in 1934: **'Blarney'**.

JARDINS DE BAGATELLE

IRDS TRILL AN OBBLIGATO to the chamber music piped onto a Parisian terrace as white-gloved waiters pour café au lait and Champagne beside trays of breakfast pastries. Behind them, potted citrus trees and palms line the stately arcaded orangerie of the Jardins de Bagatelle, a cluster of former royal gardens amid the public woodland of the Bois de Boulogne. Guests in smart summer frocks and suits chat, nibble, and sip in the sunshine until a bell rings, signaling them to take their seats inside the orangerie beneath chandeliers strung with ivy, moss, and freshly cut roses. This is the annual Concours International de Roses Nouvelles (the International New Rose Trials), a competition sponsored by the city of Paris since 1907. Jury duty is about to commence.

The jurors, one hundred rosarians invited from ten countries, know that only a short walk away, one corner of Bagatelle's formal rose garden has housed a collection of new hybrids for the past

'JARDINS DE BAGATELLE'

two years. Throughout that time, a *commission permanente* made up of Bagatelle staff and leading French rosarians has subjected each bush to continuous scrutiny, scoring it monthly for number of flowers, recurrence of bloom, disease resistance, and overall performance. On this day in 2006 (as always, the third Thursday in June), the jury will pass final judgment. The ninety-six rose finalists represent twenty-seven hybridizers from nine countries. Four plants will receive a certificate of merit; one will be singled out for exceptional fragrance (the pink-flushed white French hybrid tea **'Jardins de Bagatelle'** captured this award in 1986); one will win second prize; and one will take the top honor — generally considered Europe's most prestigious — the Gold

JUDGES REVIEW ENTRANTS IN THE 1933 INTERNATIONAL NEW ROSE TRIALS AT THE JARDINS DE BAGATELLE.

Medal. That rose will be planted in the "beds of honor" adjoining the orange-rie terrace where every gold medalist since 1907 remains on display. The rest will be composted.

All of a sudden, loudspeakers blast the allegro *Country Dance* from Vivaldi's *Spring*: The moment has come for the jury to enter the trial garden. Equipped with sharp pencils and clipboards holding the commission's assessment of every finalist, the jurors will spend the next two hours awarding points to each rose for overall quality and for fragrance. Only numbered tags identify the roses, to conceal their origins. Although the pretrial briefing instructs participants to focus only on the bushes, jurors can't help but notice that prominent breeders, such as Wilhelm Kordes III and Alain Meilland, happen to loiter near certain specimens. Short roses stand at a disadvantage in the fragrance competition, since they're out of nose reach for all but limber jurors (miniskirts and low décolletages have been known to cause wardrobe malfunctions in the call of duty). How jurors with cigars or pipes in their mouths—and there's at least one every year—can detect subtle scents presents a perpetual mystery. The studious silence is occasionally broken by viva voce comments: "Oooh, that one's lovely" and "Horrible. It's knickers pink!"

Precisely at noon, the judging ends and luncheon is served: filet mignon and asparagus tips, endive salad, sorbet, cheese, and wine. After coffee, a hush settles over the room as Deputy Mayor Yves Contassot rises to read off the list of winners. When he reveals the extraordinary news that this year's Prix du Parfum (Fragrance Award) and Médaille d'Or (Gold Medal) will go to a single rose—a pinkish violet floribunda bred by Georges Delbard, as yet labeled only with its provisional nursery-code ID, **'DELgramo'**—the jury delivers a rousing ovation. A highly competitive breeder who had been a prominent contender is seen to depart in haste.

'DELgramo' (as of this writing, Delbard has yet to settle on a marketable cultivar name) has taken its place in history in a garden that still looks just as it did a century ago, when the first Gold Medal went to **'Marquise de Sinéty'**, a redolent golden yellow hybrid tea flushed with bronzy red, which the breeder, Joseph Pernet-Ducher, named after a Norman châtelaine. The geometrically arranged beds of Bagatelle's formal *roseraie* still follow the 1907 design by Jean C. N. Forestier, then the director of parks for Paris. (Twelve years later, the Bagatelle gold medalist was the carmine hybrid tea, **'Jean C. N. Forestier'**.) His friend Jules Gravereaux initially donated twelve hundred bushes from his private garden to be planted within the framework of tightly clipped miniature boxwood hedges. The two men hatched the idea of an annual concours in hopes of celebrating the beauty of Bagatelle and to promote the introduction of outstanding new hybrids.

Gravereaux, a top executive at the Paris department store Bon Marché, first became interested in roses through his business. Buying trips often took him to the textile center of Lille, where he met a M. Nicolas, a cotton manufacturer and amateur gardener. It became an annual custom for Gravereaux to visit Nicolas's estate, the Domaine de Cartigny, near Roubaix. During one of these get-togethers, in June 1885, Nicolas's ten-year-old son Jean-Henri (later a rose breeder) overheard the Parisian say to his father, "I wish I had a *roseraie* like this," to which the elder Nicolas replied, 'Gravereaux, if I had your fortune I would retire from business and devote my life to the Rose."

'MADAME JULES GRAVEREAUX', A CLIMBING TEA ROSE FROM 1901

Seven years later, the forty-eight-year-old retailer took this advice. His wife, who had worried that his health suffered from a lack of fresh air and exercise, was thrilled when he began planting roses in the kitchen garden of their modest home in l'Haÿ, a village south of Paris. Before long, Gravereaux began hybridizing, too, and hired the eminent landscape designer Edouard André to lay out a plot capable of accommodating more than sixteen hundred species and cultivars. They dedicated a central bed to the owner's twenty-seven personal creations. Although he reserved some of these varieties as a private source for rose oil, others became available commercially, such as **'Amélie Gravereaux'**, **'Rose à Parfum de l'Haÿ'**, and **'La France Victorieuse'**.

Besides donating roses to Bagatelle, Gravereaux contributed plants to the derelict grounds at the Château de Malmaison in an effort to replicate what the empress Joséphine had once grown there (a section of the garden at l'Haÿ included a duplicate of everything sent to the château). A devotee of drama and literature, he installed the Théâtre de la Rose on his property and frequently played host to Les Rosati, a circle of poets and artists. Jean Cocteau recited his verse and Isadora Duncan danced while the audience watched from turfed benches. Gravereaux's colleagues dedicated several hybrids to the man (**'Rosomane Gravereaux'**, **'Rhodologue Jules Gravereaux'**, **'Rhodophile Gravereaux'**), to his supportive wife (**'Madame Jules Gravereaux'**), and to his entire collection (**'Roseraie de l'Haÿ'**). The garden expanded until it reached peak capacity in 1910, encompassing every known rose type—roughly eight thousand in all. By then, Gravereaux's 3.7 acres had attained international fame. When his plants were in bloom, visitors crammed the streets of sleepy l'Haÿ. In 1914 local boosters renamed their town l'Haÿ les Roses.

Gravereaux's domain now flourishes as the publicly owned and accessible
Roseraie du Val-du-Marne.

GHOSTLY GARDENS

Unlike the impeccably maintained Bagatelle and Roseraie du Val-du-Marne,
some landmark rose gardens endure only in the name of a plant.

'Souvenir de la Malmaison': When hybridizer Jean Béluze introduced this
pale pink Bourbon in 1844, the empress Joséphine's rose garden at the Château de Malmaison was indeed only a memory; poachers had stolen or destroyed the imperial plants
decades before. There's no truth to the myth that 'Souvenir de la Malmaison' originated
in a cutting taken from the grounds by a Russian nobleman who once visited the château as Joséphine's guest. Curiously, folklore on the Eastern Shore of Maryland tells of
local roses that came from Malmaison, which a ghostly gardener appears to tend "at the
change of the moon." Perhaps this legend sprang from rumors surrounding Napoléon's
sister-in-law Betsy Bonaparte, a native Marylander.

'Bloomfield Abundance': The Philadelphia banker George Clifford Thomas Jr. was
still in his early thirties when he abandoned a promising career at Drexel & Company, in
1907, to focus on breeding roses at his ancestral home, Bloomfield Farm. Thomas eventually included "Bloomfield" in the names of twenty-two of his thirty-eight acclaimed
hybrids, which read like the titles of a multivolume family saga. The pink shrub **'Bloomfield Abundance'**, one of the first in this series, dates to 1920. An avid golfer, Thomas
sold the bulk of Bloomfield Farm to the Whitemarsh Valley Country Club and converted his gardens into a golf course. The remainder of Bloomfield became part of the
Morris Arboretum after Thomas moved to California in 1922. Besides planning golf links
for the Bel-Air and Los Angeles country clubs, the former Philadelphian bred roses in

the benign climate of Beverly Hills, but his heart never left the City of Horticultural Love: "The purpose of my experiments was to produce a hardy, everblooming climber for the Philadelphia district in which I lived." One of his California roses, **'Bloomfield Beverly'**, straddles the continent.

'Breeze Hill': Tired of row-house life in downtown Harrisburg, Pennsylvania, where he had to put up with a tiny "handkerchief garden" and "twenty hours of trolley cars that banged past every five minutes," horticultural printer J. Horace McFarland searched for a larger patch of earth blessed with peace and quiet. In 1909 he found it: a wind-swept site, just outside the city, which he called Breeze Hill. The rose garden he estab-lished there soon developed into America's largest private rosarium. McFarland opened it to the public and invited the American Rose Society to set up its headquarters at his office. Even people who never visited came to know Breeze Hill through pictures that McFarland, a pioneer in color-photographic printing, shot to illustrate his books. As ARS president, and editor of the society's influential *Annual*, McFarland advocated "American made" roses, such as 'Breeze Hill', a pale apricot climber that breeder Walter Van Fleet named to honor this garden. Nevertheless, two of his favorites among the thousands of plants at Breeze Hill—the hybrid teas **'Editor McFarland'** and **'Horace McFarland'**—were French. As president of the American Civic Association, he was a leading advocate for conservation and urban planning nationwide. His "Crusade Against Ugliness" (1904) cited Harrisburg to exemplify a cityscape improved by rosebushes. A few years after McFarland's passing, in 1948, Harrisburg's Polyclinic Hospital bulldozed Breeze Hill to install a parking lot.

'Chevy Chase': To the Indians of southern Maryland, *Nanjemoy* means "Haunt of the Raccoon"; to the residents of suburban Chevy Chase, Maryland, Nanjemoy is the name of a handsome Colonial revival house. Back in 1921, when Dr. Charles Whitman Cross, newly retired from the U.S. Geological Survey, and his wife, Virginia, bought what was then a two-acre property, they planted more than five hundred roses, including sixty varieties of climber, their favorite. Founding members of the Potomac Rose Society and early proponents of a National Rosarium (a short-lived institution in Arlington, Virginia), Dr. and Mrs. Cross hybridized two roses in their garden: **'Nanjemoy'** (now extinct) and **'Mrs. Whitman Cross'**. The couple's gardener, Niels J. Hansen, created the vibrant red rambler **'Chevy Chase'** there in 1939. After the Second World War, much of the land was subdivided and developed, though the house survives along with part of the terraced garden that Rose Isabel Greely designed for the Crosses in 1924. A sunset-colored rose climbing one garden wall may be the only known planting of 'Mrs. Whitman Cross', but the Chevy Chase Historical Society sells potted specimens of 'Chevy Chase' at its annual fund-raiser.

'Triomphe du Luxembourg': Present-day visitors to the Jardin du Luxembourg (Luxembourg Gardens) in the heart of Paris's Left Bank see but a shadow of the illustrious rose display that master rosarian Julien-Alexandre Hardy tended there in the early nineteenth century. Hardy started breeding roses as early as 1818. The gallica **'La Parisienne'**, one of his first creations, was followed by numerous varieties dedicated to the palatial landscape where he demonstrated his artistry, such as the Noisette **'Du Luxembourg'** ("of the Luxembourg"), the China **'Gaufrée du Luxembourg'** (*gaufrée* means "crinkled" or "embossed"), the hybrid perpetual **'Ornement du Luxembourg'**, and the moss **'Pourpre du Luxembourg'** (*pourpre* means "purple"). Hardy's contemporaries hailed his salmon-infused pink tea **'Triomphe du Luxembourg'**, created in 1832, as a triumph indeed. Over the years, the Luxembourg has downsized its rose collection. Hardy's greenhouses no longer exist; nor does 'Triomphe du Luxembourg'. Now and then, a pink rose is sold under this name, but it is a phony, lacking the essential salmon tint.

JUST JOEY

WHETHER FISHING FOR COMPLIMENTS or deflecting criticism, gardeners excel at false modesty. Ask about their roses, and they'll allow, "Yes, it has put out a few nice flowers this year in spite of my terrible pruning," or "Well, at least they're colorful, and they do hide that ugly wall." So when garden visitors first encounter a breathtaking ruffly apricot rose, only to be told it's **'Just Joey'**, they naturally put this down as self-deprecation. But that isn't the case at all. When English nurseryman Roger Pawsey set about naming his gorgeous new hybrid tea early in the 1970s, his first choice was **'Joey Pawsey'**, to honor his wife, Joanna, by her nickname. But because those almost-rhyming syllables twisted every tongue at the nursery, Roger's father proposed an edit: "You could call it just 'Joey'." Which, in a way, Roger did.

Although earlier, more formal generations of hybridizers might have judged this term of endearment too casual, they certainly would have tipped their hats to Roger Pawsey's intention. A thick family album of roses going back almost two hundred years honors growers' nearest and dearest—of the *non*flowering kind. Among the multitude of spouses, no namesake supersedes **'Madame Hardy'**. This damask seedling first flowered for its creator, Madame's husband, Julien Alexandre Hardy, in 1831. One hundred sixty years later, the World Federation of Rose Societies voted it one of the top ten varieties of all time. As head gardener at the Jardins du Luxembourg in Paris, Julien Hardy raised thousands of cultivars and took pleasure in sharing them. He never sold his plants, gladly trading them with fellow rose fanciers. "M. Hardy is very courteous to foreigners," the English nurseryman William Paul commented in 1848, prudently adding, "It is necessary to visit him early in the morning during the Rose season." Unfortunately, with 'Madame Hardy', as with many roses named after nineteenth-century wives, we know a great deal about the flower and the man who bred it but precious little about the woman behind the rose that he himself called **'Félicité Hardy'**.

Another famous French breeder's spouse still blooms as **'Catherine Guillot'**, a fragrant deep pink Bourbon bred by Jean-Baptiste Guillot in 1860. This may have been a tenth-anniversary present—and if so, a thoughtful alternative to the now-traditional gift of tin. Their marriage consolidated two important clans of professional gardeners in the rose-growing district of Lyon, La Guillotière. Catherine's

'JUST JOEY'

ancestors had been horticulturists since the 1690s, and Jean-Baptiste's father, who founded his nursery in 1834, had promoted Lyon's ascendancy over Paris as the center of French rose breeding. Three years after his wedding, Jean-Baptiste left the family firm to establish his own. He earned lasting fame for creating one of the first hybrid teas, **'La France'**, in 1867. Catherine did her part by producing a son and heir, Pierre, who in due course took over the

THE GUILLOT FAMILY ROSE NURSERY IN LYON, FRANCE, DURING THE BELLE ÉPOQUE

nursery. Today, Roseraies Pierre Guillot is managed by Catherine and Jean-Andre's great-great-grandson Jean-Pierre. *Toujours la famille!*

If this Gallic saga calls up Balzac's *Scenes from Provincial Life*, the very British **'Lady Penzance'** of 1894 may sound like a character in Gilbert and Sullivan's *The Pirates of Penzance*. The lady of the plant, a flesh-and-blood Englishwoman of impeccable breeding, plays no part in the opera, but her husband—Sir James Plaisted Wilde, Baron Penzance, judge of the Court of Probate and Divorce—seems the very model of an upper-class eccentric. Off duty, Lord Penzance relaxed with his two hobbies: gathering copious evidence to prove that Sir Francis Bacon—not William Shakespeare—had written the works attributed to the Bard, and hybridizing roses, most of which he named after characters in the works of another favorite author, Sir Walter Scott. These offspring of Scott novels include **'Flora McIvor'** (from *Waverley*; pink with a white center), **'Jeanie Deans'** (from *The Heart of Midlothian*; dark crimson), and **'Meg Merrilies'** (from *Guy Mannering*; crimson pink).

Leaving the vulgar pursuit of showy flowers to breeders of hybrid perpetuals and hybrid teas, Lord Penzance concentrated on the rarefied delights of fragrant leaves, achieved by crossing the species *Rosa eglanteria* with other varieties. In a gently ironic eulogy, the English garden designer and writer Gertrude Jekyll, noted that: "this eminent lawyer, who in some of the years of his mature practice had to put the law in effect in decreeing the separation of unhappy human couples, had sought mental refreshment in the leisure of his latest days by devoting it to the happy marriage of roses."

BUNDLES OF JOY

Rose growers tend to fret over names for a new arrival, just like expecting parents. The twentieth-century American hybridizer Gene Boerner, a bachelor, often spoke of a plant he had bred as his "child," and he anxiously followed the progress of each one after it left the nursery. On his deathbed, Boerner told a friend, "You can't realize the satisfaction it gives me now to know that all those little children of mine—all over the world—will be pushing up their heads when I'm gone."

'FÉLICITÉ PERPÉTUE'

Like parenthood, rose breeding has unpredictable ups and downs. When the wife of Antoine Jacques, head gardener of the duc d'Orléans, unexpectedly gave birth to twins in 1828, Jacques decided to mark the occasion by dedicating roses to his new daughters, Félicité and Perpétue (after the Early Christian saints Felicitas and Perpetua). Having only one untitled rambler on hand, however, he christened the plant with both girls' names. The confusing result, often given as **'Félicité et Perpétue'**, has provoked endless dispute. One of the dozen variants that appear in rose literature, **'Félicité Perpétuelle'**, caused many nineteenth-century gardeners to assume that this creamy white rose blooms nonstop, which it does not. The correct name, as Papa Jacques wrote it, is **'Félicité Perpétue'**.

MAIDEN'S BLUSH

S EX FIRST EXPOSED ITSELF in the garden when the German physician and botanical voyeur Rudolf Jakob Camerarius published *De sexu plantarum epistola* (*A Letter on the Sexuality of Plants*) in 1694. He analyzed reproductive organs in explicit detail, comparing, for instance, a flower's anthers to "the genital parts of the male sex, as their capsules are vessels and containers, in which the semen itself, that powder, the most subtle part of the plant, is produced, collected and from here afterwards given out." Inspired by these revelations, the eighteenth-century Swedish botanist Carl Linneaus devised his groundbreaking system of plant classification and nomenclature, which underlies the Latin names we still use to indicate genus and species (e.g., *Rosa alba*). Linnaeus illustrated the sexual basis of his taxonomy with diagrams of stamens, pistils, and ovaries. Stripped of its fig leaf, botany was no longer deemed a wholesome subject for the young. And because roses symbolized passionate love, censors checked every *Rosa* label for racy allusions to the birds and the bees.

Britons modestly retitled a popular old plant, *R. alba incarnata* ("flesh-colored white rose"), as **'Maiden's Blush'** in 1770. That same year, the English clergyman and nursery owner William Hanbury praised the pink-tinged pallor of its petals: "As to this colour, can we justly form an idea of the finished beauty of a young lady, who is every way perfect in shape and complexion, and whose modesty will give occasion (without any real cause) for the cheeks greatly to glow? Form yourselves an idea of such a colour at that time, and that is the colour of the rose we are treating of, properly termed 'Maiden's Blush'." The German rosarian Carl Gottlob Roessig concurred, noting in *Die Rosen*, a portfolio of rose images published between 1802 and 1820, that the shade of these petals is "analogous to the tint of virgins." Although some French rosarians demonstrated similar delicacy, calling this rose **'La Virginale'**, others formed an idea of *incarnata* at odds with the Rev. Hanbury's. Gallic sensualists embraced the renaming of 'Maiden's Blush' in 1802 as **'Cuisse de Nymphe Emue'** ("thigh of an aroused nymph"). Two alternative synonyms — **'Cuisse de Nymphe à Ovaire Lisse'** ("thigh of a nymphe with a smooth ovary") and prosaic **'La Belle Fille'** (either "the beautiful girl" or "the daughter-in-law") — never caught on. Unable to suppress the popularity of the risqué French name after it reached Britain, guardians of garden morals made do with an ambiguous translation: "thigh of an emoted nymph."

With rose labels like that to browse through, plant shoppers could get rather emoted, too. In *The Coming of the Flowers*, published in 1950, botanist A. W. Anderson described mid-nineteenth-century Londoners visiting the nursery of Thomas Rivers, whose rose catalog offered close to five hundred varieties: "As they inspected the nursery the gentlemen were no doubt delighted with **'Moraga la Favorite'** and **'Infidelities [sic] de Lisette'**, while their wives and daughters tried to assess the charms of **'Assemblage des Beautés'**, **'Oracle du Siècle'**, and **'Desespoir des Amateurs'**, but we cannot help wondering what those Victorian dames thought of the **'Spineless Virgin'**." Anderson adds that a request to name a rose after Queen Mab, the fairy sovereign, prompted the upright rosarian William Paul to exclaim, "Was she a good woman?"

The nymph and company seem downright coy beside modern roses like **'Hot Lips'**, **'Erotika'**, **'X-Rated'**, **'Exhibitionist!'**, **'Kiss of Desire'**, and **'Hanky Panky'** (a child of **'Party Girl'**). When Sam McGredy's floribunda **'Sexy Rexy'** (named for one of the grower's drinking buddies, not the actor Rex Harrison) won the gold medal at Glasgow's 1989 rose trials, grandes dames of the Royal National Rose Society sputtered, "Disgraceful! Vulgar! Coarse!" Nevertheless, after the awards ceremony, some of Rexy's harshest critics shamelessly thrust their noses into the plant's huge clusters of warm pink double flowers.

'MAIDEN'S BLUSH' BY REDOUTÉ, 1817

TEMPTATION

L ike the protective father of a popular teenager, Lyon rose breeder Jean Béluze recommended in 1844 that his new **'Reine des Vierges'** ('Queen of the Virgins'), a pale-pink Bourbon, be kept indoors. That's one way to shelter a pure hybrid from compromising garden companions. No need to worry about modern **'Séduction'**, a salmon pink hybrid tea that's much in demand around Valentine's Day: It is a florist's rose that must be grown under controlled greenhouse conditions. But watch out for **'Passionate Kisses'**, a rosy floribunda from the same French grower that blooms repeatedly, all season long, in many American gardens. France, of course, holds no monopoly on passion. Indeed, the smoldering red hybrid tea **'Passion'** was bred in Japan by Hiroshi Hirabayashi, and the deep pink miniature **'Passion's Flame'** comes from Bruce F. Rennie of Ontario, Canada.

Rosebushes don't share rosarians' obsession with careful breeding. The plants can be downright promiscuous, making it hard to trace the lineage of spontaneous "volunteers" and naturally occuring hybrids. Curators at the San Jose Heritage Rose Garden found an unknown rose in one of their beds, where it had sprouted from seed borne in bird droppings. As the young plant matured, it began to display typical characteristics of several old roses from France, as well as a "freely suckering" habit (i.e., it spreads prolifically by means of suckers, shoots that spring from the plant's base). The San Jose gardeners named their wayward foundling **'The French Strumpet'**.

MARY WASHINGTON

DESPITE ALL THOSE RUMORS that, as a boy, he chopped down his father's cherry tree, George Washington grew up to become a peach of a gardener. Washington was quite particular about the roses that he and his wife, Martha, raised at Mount Vernon, their Virginia estate. Amid a handsome profusion of vegetables, herbs, fruits, and flowers, roses yielded a staple crop for Martha's thrifty household (harvesting the petals used to flavor food and distill rose water was a twelve-day task), but the genus *Rosa* also

'MARY WASHINGTON'

interested George, the experimental horticulturist who maintained a private "Botanick garden" and conservatory.

George purchased the North American swamp rose, *Rosa palustris*, for his extensive collection of native flora, which probably also included **'Prairie Rose'**, *R. setigera*. Some historians speculate that his botanical enthusiasm extended to hybridizing roses; if true, this would make the first president of the United States the country's first rose breeder, too. Virginia tradition credits him with crossing several varieties around 1790 to create a pinkish white seedling, which he purportedly named **'Mary Washington'**, after his mother, Mary Ball Washington. The earliest documentation of this rose growing at Mount Vernon dates to 1891. Two decades later, Georgia Torrey Drennan, a fount of Southern garden lore, wrote that she had often encountered 'Mary Washington'—and a confusingly similar Noisette, **'Lady Washington'**—in family burial plots on old plantations.

Born in 1708, Mary Washington was herself a keen gardener. When General Lafayette came to call on her in Fredericksburg, he is said to have discovered

GARDENS AT MOUNT VERNON SHORTLY AFTER THE CIVIL WAR

the elderly Mrs. Washington puttering among the boxwoods and flowers. A common love of horticulture seems not to have warmed Mary's relationship with the eldest of her six children. George Washington's biographer Joseph J. Ellis, remarks that Mary "lived long enough to see him elected president but never extolled or even acknowledged his public triumphs."

A **'Martha Washington'** has thrived at Mount Vernon since at least 1898, though no evidence links George to the pink climbing rose that recalls his adored wife. The uncertain parentage of Martha's namesake contrasts with her own upper-class Tidewater ancestry; her less well-born husband was the social climber.

Legend has it that George planted the white hybrid musk that has come to be called **'Nelly Custis'**, after Martha's granddaughter from her first marriage, Eleanor Parke Custis. The 1934 Conard-Pyle nursery catalog promoted this variety with the following blurb: "Our stock is from Mt. Vernon, Va. Tradition says that if a young lady will prick her finger on a thorn of the 'Nelly Custis' Rose, and make a wish, her dream the following night will surely come true." Nelly's stepfather might have had a thing or two to say about that. George wrote to "My dear Nelly" in 1796, advising prudence in matters of the heart: "Love is said to be an involuntary passion and it is therefore contended that it cannot be resisted. This is true, in part only; for like all things else when nourished and supplied plentifully with [aliment,] it is rapid in its progress; but let these be withdrawn and it may be stifled in its birth or much stunted in its growth." George Washington lived to see Nelly wed his nephew Lawrence Lewis three years later. Regrettably, their marriage proved to be as miserable as George and Martha's had been happy.

A DEBT OF HONOR

Every June on Hazel Street in Manheim, Pennsylvania, red roses bloom around a fountain outside the Zion Lutheran Church. The fountain marks the site of the congregation's original church, built in 1772 on land leased from Manheim's founder and richest citizen, the ironmaster and glassmaker Henry William Stiegel. His price for the property: "five shillings lawful money of Pennsylvania—yielding and paying therefore unto the said Henry William Stiegel, his heirs or assigns at the said town of Manheim in the month of June yearly forever hereafter the rent of one Red rose." A lordly manner may have entitled this self-made man to style himself "Baron" Stiegel, but financial misfortune ruined him. After receiving only three roses from Zion Lutheran, he was sentenced to debtor's prison and never recovered his wealth.

The rose rent had long been forgotten by 1857, when Manheim's burgeoning Lutheran flock built a larger church to replace its first house of worship. But in 1892, during the construction of a third, even grander structure, the original lease came to light. Grateful congregants established an annual festival to honor the Stiegel family, and that June they presented a red rose to Henry William's great-great-grandson John C. Stiegel of Harrisonburg, Virginia. Ever since, the tradition has continued without a break.

The custom of paying a rose as nominal rent dates back at least to fourteenth-century England. Then, as in Baron Stiegel's day, the flower would have been the esteemed **'Apothecary's Rose'**. Nowadays, however, it's a red hybrid tea—either **'Veterans' Honor'**, which fills the four beds surrounding Zion Lutheran's fountain**, or 'Chrysler Imperial'** or **'Don Juan'**, which grow beside the church. In 2007, despite the best efforts of volunteer gardener Rod Frey Jr., a cool and wet spring meant that Elizabeth Stiegel Rohr of North Bergen, New Jersey, an eighth-generation descendant of the baron, had to settle for a crimson rose from the local florist.

MEMORIAL ROSE

I N THE HARDY MEMORIAL Rose has at last been found the ideal plant for cemeteries," announced a mail-order nursery advertisement in the March 1896 issue of *Ladies' Home Journal*. Although few magazine readers would have recognized the rose's botanical alias, *Rosa wichuraiana*—now *R. wichurana*—many would already have known the plant itself from personal experience. A native of Japan with shiny, disease-resistant foliage that creeps like a ground cover, this rose had been introduced into the United States in 1888 as a self-spreading grave blanket. And spread it did, into graveyards nationwide, propelled by the Victorian obsession with all things funerary.

Early in the nineteenth century, Americans had enthusiastically adopted the old European and Scandinavian custom of planting roses on loved ones' graves. The flowers were also carved on tombstones and memorial statues; forged into iron cemetery fences and gates; and stitched, drawn, or painted onto elegies suitable for framing.

AD IN *LADIES' HOME JOURNAL*, 1896

But many live roses proved so hardy that vestiges of period memorial plant-ings survive to this day. When new, they composed an essential part of grand suburban cemeteries so picturesque that they doubled as public parks. The influential landscape designer and author Andrew Jackson Downing wrote in 1849 that "one of the most remarkable illustrations of the popular taste in this country [is] the rise and progress of our public cemeteries," noting with approval that "a wilderness of roses" fringed the monuments of Philadelphia's Laurel Hill Cemetery.

The fashionable urns, obelisks, and mausoleums in such Elysian garden spots reminded classically educated mourners of burial traditions dating back to antiquity. The Greeks, they knew, had believed that the fragrance of roses purified the ashes of the deceased, while opening buds symbolized renewal. Wealthy Romans had left legacies for the maintenance of rosebushes at their resting places, and instructed heirs to regularly strew the sepulcher with blos-soms. Before falling on his sword, Marc Antony asked Cleopatra to perform the proper floral ceremony at his tomb. Romans of modest means inscribed their grave markers with requests for strangers to leave any roses they could spare. Early Christians also laid roses on the graves of the righteous as a cel-ebration of life.

Time's passage hasn't dimmed the consoling power of this simple gesture. Any Roman citizen would have understood why Joe DiMaggio had fresh-cut roses delivered weekly to the Los Angeles necropolis where Marilyn Monroe was laid to rest. (Di Maggio didn't live to see the apricot hybrid tea **'Marilyn**

'SOUVENIR D'UN AMI'

Monroe', introduced in 2002.) Queen Victoria would have approved the fact that stems of **'Princess Grace'**—Grace's favorite because its red and cream flowers display the state colors of Monaco—are ever present in the cathedral crypt at Monte Carlo where she lies beside Prince Rainier.

Even at the height of the Romantic movement, which reveled in morbidity, most rosarians left the naming of their own memorials to subsequent generations. But funereal homages to others abound. Many incorporate the French *Deuil de*, or "Mourning for," as in the 1845 Bourbon **'Deuil du Duc d'Orléans'**. A considerably less lugubrious phrase, *Souvenir de*, "In Remembrance of"—and its counterparts the German *Andenken an*, the Italian *Ricordo di*, and the Spanish *Recuerdo de*—figures in hundreds of names. Some are anonymous, such as **'Souvenir d'un Ami'** ("in remembrance of a friend"), a fragrant pale pink 1846 tea that served as an all-purpose sympathy card in Victorian England.

As a rule, though, *Souvenirs* honor particular individuals. Some eulogize statesmen, like **'Souvenir du Président Lincoln'**, an 1865 Bourbon of a crimson so dark it can appear almost black, which was dedicated shortly after the American leader's assassination. Others recall eminent writers, artists, and actors, as well as heroes whose fame came after death (one of the most recent examples, **'Souvenir d'Anne Frank'**, a Belgian floribunda, dates to 1960). None is more poignant than a pair of French hybrid teas, **'Souvenir de Claudius Pernet'** and **'Souvenir de Georges Pernet'**, bred in 1920 and 1921, respectively, by Joseph Pernet-Ducher. Claudius and Georges were Joseph's only sons, killed in combat within a few days of each other during the First World War. Looking back in the 1930s, months before his own death, the French rosarian Jean Henri Nicolas wrote: "Father Pernet dedicated his two best roses to his sons. I saw Pernet for the last time ten years later and his eyes still dimmed with tears when he looked at those roses."

COMPELLING PLOTS

Some graveyards, such as the Old City Cemetery in Lynchburg, Virginia, and the Sacramento Historic City Cemetery in Sacramento, California, now maintain gardens for venerable roses grown from cuttings made on their grounds. At Hollywood Cemetery in Richmond, Virginia, visitors can view **"Crenshaw Musk,"** a double white-flowered form of extremely rare *Rosa moschata* planted within the iron-fenced enclosure of the Crenshaw family monument. Now and then, this vigorous bush produces a branch or two with single flowers. Although **"Temple Musk,"** a slightly different double form of *R. moschata* found in the same cemetery's Temple family plot, has mysteriously vanished from Hollywood, another specimen survives and thrives at Elmwood Cemetery in Charlotte, North Carolina.

Unfortunately, many graveyards stand unguarded, and their antique roses fall victim to hungry deer, reckless mowers, and greedy plant poachers. Fear of theft has made rosarians loath to publicize the exact locations of cemetery finds like Texas's **"Old Gay Hill Red China"** and **"China from Andina"** or Louisiana's **"Natchitoches Noisette"** (a local rose expert will divulge only that it turned up "near an old fort"). California offers several cases of studiously hidden provenance. Inquire about the origins of **"Orange Smith"** or **"The Legacy of Joseph Marcilino,"** for example, and you'll be told that they come from "a cemetery in the Sierra foothills"; ask about **"Manchester Guardian Angel"** and you'll learn that it was first spotted draping the carved wings of a memorial seraph somewhere in the vicinity of Manchester, a town in Mendocino County.

NEW DAWN

AS PHOTOGRAPHERS, FLOWER ARRANGERS, and perfumers well know, garden roses reach perfection early in the morning. Colors glow through dew and gentle light; moisture absorbed overnight prolongs the freshness of cut stems; and fragrance gains full strength before the sun starts to warm aromatic oils, dispersing their scent into the air. Combine all that with the spectrum of sunrise pastels in every rose catalog, and it's as clear as day why more than seventy-five roses have "dawn" in their names—from **'Apricot Dawn'** to **'Lady of the Dawn'** and **'Wabash Dawn'**. One outshines the rest, however: reliably cold-hardy, exceptionally disease-resistant, and utterly ravishing **'New Dawn'**.

To begin with, unlike almost all cold-hardy climbers previously available, 'New Dawn' is everblooming, producing clusters of large blush pink flowers from mid-May right up until the first frost. It also holds the distinction of being the first plant ever patented. In 1930, when 'New Dawn' entered the marketplace, the United States Congress passed the Plant Patent Act, which granted anyone who discovered or bred a new plant the sole right to determine who could propagate and sell it during the next seventeen years. (An essential signature on the congressional document matched the name of another rose officially introduced that year, **'President Herbert Hoover'**.) Before the patent act, once a grower introduced a plant to commerce, it became common property, returning little, if any, profit to its originator. "[The] hybridizer of garden Roses has to be content with deposits in the Bank of Glory," wrote J. Horace McFarland, a founder of the American Rose Society, in 1920. Even in those terms, 'New Dawn' yielded a handsome return on investment. The plant was a sport, or mutation, of the once-blooming but otherwise almost identical climber, **'Dr. W. Van Fleet'**, whose creator, Walter Van Fleet, had intended to call it **'Daybreak'**. Despite this modest man's protestations, the nursery that introduced the rose in 1910 insisted on naming it after him.

Van Fleet died before 'New Dawn' emerged, but this respectful allusion to 'Daybreak' would have warmed the doctor's heart.

Soft rosy shades—as in Homer's "rosy-fingered dawn"—have inspired a polyglot chorus of early risers, like **'Aurore'** (for Aurora, the Roman goddess of dawn), a pale pink French alba bred in 1815, and **'Moscow Morn'**, a medium pink Russian hybrid tea from 1952. Although few names evoke the midday hours when roses neither

'NEW DAWN', BY ANNE-MARIE TRECHSLIN

look nor smell their best, vivid yellows triggered America's **'High Noon'**, a hybrid tea released in 1946, six years before the movie Western with that title, and **'Sunny Afternoon'**, a miniature. Mauves tend to call forth dusky labels, such as **'Twilight Secret'**, an Indian floribunda, and **'Twilight Zone'**—attached to both a miniature and a grandiflora—from the United States. Dark reds kindle nocturnal references: Australia's **'Midnight Sun'** and Northern Ireland's blackish crimson **'Night'**.

WHILE PEOPLE AROUND THE world gazed skyward to watch a total eclipse of the sun on August 31, 1932, rosarian Jean Henri Nicolas anxiously bent over a greenhouse workbench in Newark, New York, eyeing a four-inch-tall experimental seedling whose long, slim bud had just begun to re-

veal a glint of gold. He later wrote, "I took a long chance, risking to lose the seedling, and I cut the only two eyes on the little plant, thus destroying it, and budded them on stems of a growing plant. As identification I marked the tags **'Eclipse'**. The eyes grew; the name remained." And that was indeed the name under which Nicolas patented this fine yellow hybrid tea in 1935. His dramatic narrative raised one eyebrow—that of British rosarian Jack Harkness, who decades after Nicolas's death opined: "I am quite certain of two things,

A 1910 PRECURSOR TO THE SHRUB ROSE 'ICEBERG' GROWN TODAY

that most Hybrid Teas in North America are in bloom a little earlier than the end of August, and that nobody seeing the first bloom at that time could possibly introduce the rose three years later, complete with Plant Patent and all. The average time is seven years."

However long they practice their craft, even blasé nurserymen thrill to the spectacle of petals unfolding. Stumped for words to describe that moment, rose breeders often grasp at other awe-inspiring natural phenomena. *Meteor* has figured in the names of roses since the early nineteenth century, when astronomers began to track shooting stars. Fiery red **'Meteor Shower'**, a florist's bloom, belongs to the Cosmic Fiesta Spray Roses series, which also includes hot pink **'Supernova'**. The red floribunda **'Halley's Comet'** went on sale in 1986 to coincide with that celestial body's first appearance since 1910.

The sight of warm sun rays beaming on cool white roses has launched an avalanche of names, like **'Summer Snow'** (a floribunda) and **'Niphetos'** (a tea; *Niphetos* is Greek for "snowy"). Catalan hybridizer Pedro Dot called his most famous shrub rose **'Nevada'** ("snowfall" in Spanish). France's aptly named **'Boule de Neige'** ("snowball") was actually bred in England by a nurseryman who prosaically labeled it **'Globe White Hip'**. The floribunda Americans know as **'Iceberg'** comes from Germany where it goes by the more endearing **'Schneewittchen'**, or "Snow White," as in Seven Dwarfs. **'Polar Ice'**, a French hybrid rugosa introduced to the United States in 2005, has been advertised as remarkably cold hardy. In 1953, **'Sleigh Bells'** provided breeding stock for **'White Christmas'**. Like the two movies in which Bing Crosby crooned Irving Berlin's "White Christmas," both roses were produced in snowy Southern California.

TIME AND AGAIN

The history of the **'Four Seasons Rose'**, *Rosa x damascena bifera*, is a study in hyperbole, because 'Two Seasons Rose' comes closer to the truth. A variety of damask rose, this plant first drew attention in ancient Egypt, because unlike other roses, it not only bloomed in summer but also in the fall (*bifera* means "twice bearing"). During the fifth century BC, Herodotus wrote that Midas himself acquired this phenomenon for his legendary gardens. Romans later imported the off-season exotic from Egypt (another alias, the **'Alexandria Rose'**, honors its Middle Eastern origin) and eventually grew it themselves. The poet Virgil probably had the same fragrant pink-flowered bush in mind when he referred to "the twice-blooming rose of Paestum," naming an Italian city south of Naples.

Until the importation of China roses during the late eighteenth century, *R. x damascena bifera* remained Europe's only repeat-blooming rose, though it picked up various names along the way. The French **'Quatre Saisons'** (**'Four Seasons'**) may have been inspired by the essayist Michel de Montaigne, who in November 1580 saw a rosebush in flower at an Italian monastery. To his amazement, the monks explained that their shrub blossomed year-round. A hundred years later, one of Louis XIV's gardeners made his bid for immortality with a variation on *R. x damascena bifera* called **'Tous-les-Mois'** ("every month"). To be fair, the name didn't say that it *flowered* every month, and now that 'Tous-les-Mois' seems to have vanished, we can't judge for ourselves.

Some optimistic English gardeners called *R. x damascena bifera* the **'Monthly Rose'**, but since the 1700s it has more commonly, and realistically, been known as **'Autumn Damask'**. The eighteenth-century politician and editor Sir Thomas Hanmer gave a sensible explanation: "It beares two or three moneths more in the yeare than the ordinary Damaske, and very plentifully, if it stand warme."

NUR MAHAL

YOU CAN IMAGINE HOW his other wives felt when Jahangir, Mughal emperor of India, publicly changed his eighteenth spouse's name to Nur Mahal, "Light of the Palace," soon after marrying her in 1611. The bride's Persian parents had originally called their daughter Mehr-un-Nisa, "Sun of Women"—scant praise, in Jahangir's estimation, for this paragon of beauty, taste, intelligence, and political acumen. Along the palace corridors in Agra, however, courtiers whispered about an ill-omened background to the latest royal match: infatuation, they said, had driven the emperor to order the murder of Nur Mahal's first husband, the father of her only child. The thirty-something widow—no great catch, given her advanced age—had cold-shouldered Jahangir for years before consenting to wed. And everyone knew that he overindulged in opium and alcohol, dulling his interest in matters of state.

'NUR MAHAL'

Against all odds, Nur Mahal became not only Jahangir's devoted partner but his mainstay—a role he trumpeted by renaming her (again) Nur Jehan, "Light of the World," in 1616. Besides sharing his literary bent, his passion for collecting art, and his flair for architecture and landscape design, she ably shouldered the administrative responsibilities her husband was eager to transfer. "Never has there been a king so subject to the will of his wife," grumbled one Indian general. For almost twenty years, until Jehangir's death in 1627, Nur Jehan and a few close male advisers virtually commanded the realm, even issuing coins in her name.

It is this formidable woman's skill at managing other liquid assets, however, that explains why her names now grace two roses: **'Nur Mahal'**, a crimson hybrid musk bred in England in 1923, and **'Nurjehan'**, a dark pink Indian hybrid tea dated 1980 (other transliterations of *Nur Jehan* include *Noorjehan* and *Nur Jahan*). Both flowers are intensely fragrant, as befits a woman often credited with discovering rose attar, the essential oil that scents the petals.

NUR MAHAL AND HER HUSBAND, MUGHAL EMPEROR JAHANGIR, IN A MODERN DRAWING BY HUGH ROBINSON

The most romantic story has Nur Jehan boating with Jahangir in one of the rose-water-filled canals the couple installed in their palace pleasure gardens, when she realizes that a perfumed slick—pure attar—has formed on the water's surface. Alternatively, Nur Jehan notices an oily film while taking a rose water bath. In both versions, she presents her find to Jahangir, who praises her to the skies.

More prosaically, and plausibly, the emperor himself—in his memoir of court life, *Tuzuk-i-Jahangiri*—attributes this discovery to Nur Jehan's mother, Salima Sultan Begum: "When she was making rose water, a scum formed on the surface of the dishes into which the hot rose water was poured from the jugs. She collected this scum little by little; when much rose water was obtained a sensible quantity of the scum was collected. It is of such strength in perfume that if one drop be rubbed on the palm of the hand it scents a whole assembly, and it appears as if many red rosebuds had bloomed at once. There is no other scent of equal excellence to it. It restores hearts that have gone and brings back withered souls. In reward for that invention, I presented a string of pearls to the inventress. Salima Sultan Begum (may the light of God be upon her tomb) . . . gave this oil the name '*itr-i-Jahangiri* [Jahangir's perfume]."

A pearl necklace was a small price to pay for the secret of making attar—not that it remained an Indian secret for long, if indeed it ever had been. By the mid-seventeenth century, farmers in Bulgaria's Rozova Dolina ("Rose Valley") were cultivating enormous fields of rosebushes and steam-distilling the petals to make top-quality attar, or otto. In business ever since, that industry now produces approximately a third of the world's rose oil, which can retail for more than $300 per ounce. Although perfume distillers in the

Middle East, India, and other countries harvest the same extremely oil-rich rose variety grown in the Bulgarian province of Kazanlik, or Kazanlak—deep pink *Rosa* x *damascena* **'Trigintipetala'**—this rose is known universally as **'Kazanlik'**. French and Moroccan rose-oil producers employ both a different plant—*R.* x *centifolia*, the **'Cabbage Rose'** or **'Rose of Provence'**—and a different method of scent extraction, enfleurage, whereby the petals are steeped in wax. Either way, it can take six hundred pounds of flowers to yield a precious ounce of scent.

JEWELS OF INDIA

There's more than a coincidental kinship between 'Nur Mahal' and **'Taj Mahal'**, a richly fragrant deep pink hybrid tea, bred in California in 1972. The American rose honors the sublime white-marble mausoleum in Agra—its name means "crown of the palace"—that Jahangir's third son and successor, Shah Jehan, erected in memory of *his* favorite wife, Mumtaz Mahal, a niece of Nur Mahal-Nur Jehan. On her deathbed, Mumtaz Mahal supposedly beseeched her husband to build her a tomb "such as the world had never seen before." Her aunt—who outlived Mumtaz Mahal by fifteen years—preferred to create her own monuments and see the results in person. Even after Shah Jehan stripped Nur Jehan of power and imprisoned her, she managed to oversee the design and construction of magnificent tombs for her father and herself. Although the roses she chose for their settings perished long ago, the buildings survive as lustrous gems.

PEACE

As Adolf Hitler started drafting troops for the Third Reich in March 1935, the French rosarian Francis Meilland prepped Seedling No. 3-35-40 for a trial bed at his nursery. He put the young hybrid tea through rigorous tests until in the spring of 1939 it was ready to show the world its mammoth flowers of canary yellow tinged with pink. The international rose growers whom Meilland invited to review No. 3-35-40 liked what they saw, and promptly placed orders for fall shipments to Germany, Italy, and the United States. When delivery time arrived, however, war broke out. Meilland just managed to supply his European customers but could send nothing overseas. Then France required all nurseries to grow food crops for the war effort, and Meilland shoveled two hundred thousand rosebushes to make room for cabbages, rutabagas, and pumpkins, reserving only a small patch for prize hybrids. In 1940, with Nazi occupation under way, the hybridizer spirited a packet of bud eyes from No. 3-35-40 to the American consul in Lyon, pleading that he try to forward this dispatch to Robert Pyle of Conard-Pyle in Pennsylvania. The consul and his bundle caught the last plane out of France.

During the war, Meilland named the plant **'Madame Antoine Meilland'** after his mother, unaware that it was simultaneously being sold in Germany as **'Gloria Dei'** (Latin for "glory of God") and in Italy as **'Gioia'** ("joy"). He hadn't a clue whether his bud eyes had ever touched United States soil, let alone acquired a name there, until the liberation of France in 1944. Almost immediately, a letter arrived from Robert Pyle, informing Meilland that "with our hopes for the future, we dedicate this lovely new rose to Peace." Conard-Pyle representatives released two white doves upon the formal introduction of No. 3-35-40 as **'Peace'** at the Pacific Rose Society exhibition in California, on April 29, 1945 — serendipitously coinciding with the Allied siege of Berlin. When the newly formed United Nations met in San Francisco later that year, each of the forty-nine delegates received a stem of 'Peace'. Thus began an aggressive promotional campaign that helped to make this excellent garden plant the best-selling rose of the twentieth century.

Several American nurseries had been interested in No. 3-35-40 before the war, but walked away from the table when Meilland insisted on a royalty of 33 percent, instead of the customary 15 percent. Conard-Pyle agreed to the Frenchman's terms, in exchange for sole proprietorship of the rose. As Meilland and his family started collecting

EVER-POPULAR 'PEACE' DEBUTED AT THE END OF WORLD WAR II.

the fortune in royalties that 'Peace' would generate, they received a handsome thank-you from Robert Pyle: a brand-new 1946 Chevrolet sedan.

BEFORE A SINGLE AD for 'Peace' appeared, press photos and newsreel clips of civilians greeting troops with flowers had revived ancient associations of roses with victory. But plant names linked to war and peace are inevitably double edged. The truce-flag-white Belgian hybrid musk **'Waterloo'**, for example, has never been popular in France, even though the battle it commemorates took place at peak bloom time. Following Napoléon's defeat, the French rose grower Louis Descemet watched in horror as British troops vandalized his nursery in St. Denis. Only fifteen of the hundred-plus gallicas Descemet had bred are known to have survived; one, still grown today, has the apropos name **'Triomphe de Flore'** ("triumph of Flora"). This blow was so traumatic that he sold his remaining stock to Jean-Pierre Vibert, a veteran who had served under Napoléon. The most prolific hybridizer of his day, Vibert took special pride in cultivars such as **'Général Drouot'** (after one of Bonaparte's trusted commanders), and **'Bougainville'** (for Admiral Louis-Antoine de Bougainville, imperial confidant, amateur gardener, and namesake of the tropical vine bougainvillea). On the verge of death in 1866, Vibert confided to his grandson, "I have loved only Napoléon and roses . . . [and] after all the evils from which I have suffered there remain to me only two objects of profound hatred: the English, who overthrew my idol, and the white worms that destroyed my roses."

Horticulturists used military metaphors to describe the skirmishes that erupt when rosebushes invade other plants' lebensraum. Victorian rose expert

S. Reynolds Hole deployed rose names like toy soldiers to poke fun at his own expansionist policy: "[My] Roses multiplied from a dozen to a score, from a score to a hundred, from a hundred to a thousand . . . Nor were they content with the absolute occupation of that portion of my grounds in which they were first planted . . . So there was a congress of the great military chiefs, Brennus (Hybrid China), Scipio (Gallica), Maréchal Bugeaud (Tea), Duke of Cambridge (Damask), Tippoo Saib (Gallica), Generals Allard, Jacqueminot, Kléber, and Washington (all Hybrid Chinas) . . . They unanimously advised an immediate raid upon the vegetable kingdom which adjoined their own . . . They routed the rhubarb, they carried the asparagus with resistless force, they cut down the raspberries to a cane. They annexed that vegetable kingdom, and they retain it still."

Other rosarians felt less inclined to make light of battle maneuvers. "Do you dare grow roses during wartime?" asked Mrs. Edward W. Biddle of Philadelphia in the 1918 *American Rose Annual*. This question echoed the unease of gardeners worldwide. Biddle's own reply voiced a common thought: "Mercifully there *are* roses to be cultivated while we read of torpedoes and machine guns, of submarines and zeppelins!" American involvement in the "war to end all wars" was too brief to have much impact on native rose names, although Frederick R. M. Undritz of Staten Island, New York, did his part with four patriotic climbers bred in 1917 to 1918: **'General John Pershing'**, **'Freedom'**, **'Silver Star'**, and **'Victory'**. The armistice ending hostilities between the Allies and Germany moved the English clergyman-rosarian Joseph Pemberton to name a white hybrid musk **'Pax'** (Latin for "peace"). Guillot, a French nursery, brought out **'La France Victorieuse'**, a salmon pink hybrid tea.

Uneasy hopes prevailed between the wars. In 1938, the year Neville Chamberlain claimed to guarantee "Peace in Our Time," a South Dakota breeder produced a trio of so-called peace roses: **'Pax Amanda'**, **'Pax Apollo'**, and **'Pax Iola'**. The hybridizer, Niels Ebbsen Hansen, explained that the "Pax" on each label referred not to current events but to the absence of prickles on the plants' "unarmed" stems. "[T]horns," Hansen said, "are no more necessary in roses than war is among humans!"

During the world war that soon followed, roses served as morale boosters on the home front. **'V for Victory'**, a yellow hybrid tea created in 1941 to support the Victory Garden Program, came from the Rhode Island nursery of the Brownell family. (Coincidentally, the Brownells overwintered rose plants in the gun emplacements of an old fort built to protect Naragansett Bay from foreign invaders.) The wife of General George Marshall received a bouquet of her new namesake, **'Katherine T. Marshall'**, when she ceremonially opened the 1942 National Victory Garden Harvest Show. For the launch of the hybrid tea **'Pearl Harbor'** Jackson & Perkins' 1943 catalog quoted war correspondent Raymond Clapper's report on a visit to hospitals and camps: "it is gardening that most of all seems to heal the soul."

The U.S. Department of Agriculture declared in the *House and Garden Annual for 1944*, "We owe it to Johnny and Joan as they come marching home that the old home and the old home town welcome them with more flowers and greenery. What zest will be added then . . . if the meals are graced with bowls of roses, nasturtiums, and other flowers. We must grow more of this food, too—food for our spiritual well-being and our everyday happiness."

DECORATED VETERANS

Given that warriors aren't known for stopping to smell the roses, a surprising number of cultivar names commemorate military heroes and battle sites.

'Admiral Ward': An amateur rosarian, Aaron Ward grew more than three thousand rosebushes on his estate in Roslyn, New York. His favorite French nurseryman, Joseph Pernet-Ducher of Lyon, named this red hybrid tea for him in 1915.

'Audie Murphy': The 1957 hybrid tea is a vivid red badge of courage. It salutes the most decorated American combat soldier in World War II. Murphy proudly tended the rose in his California yard.

'Captain Thomas': George C. Thomas Jr. of Philadelphia interrupted his career as a hybridizer to serve as an aviation instructor in France during World War I. After returning to civilian life, he created a canary yellow climber that came to be known by his rank in the service.

'Duke of Wellington': Bonaparte would have relished the irony that this dark red 1864 hybrid perpetual (aka **'Duc de Wellington'**), like the Iron Duke's two other namesakes, a China and a centifolia, originated in France.

'Ernie Pyle': The Pulitzer Prize–winning war correspondent died under enemy fire during the Battle of Okinawa. His namesake, a medium pink hybrid tea, was introduced posthumously, in 1946.

'Garibaldi': Italian patriot and soldier Giuseppe Garibaldi conquered the Two Sicilies in 1860, the year this dark pink Bourbon got its name.

'Géant des Batailles': In French, the baffling title of this 1846 hybrid perpetual means "giant of battles." The petals are blood red, but neither the flower nor the plant is extraordinarily large.

'Général Jacqueminot': Often called **'General Jack'**, this crimson rose has been one of the most popular hybrid perpetuals ever since its introduction in 1853. Napoleonic commander Jean-François Jacqueminot went on to found a Paris brewery.

'Kitchener of Khartoum': British field marshal Horatio Herbert Kitchener was created Baron Kitchener of Khartoum after a successful campaign in Sudan during the 1890s. The introduction of this red hybrid tea (aka **'K. of K.'**) followed his death in 1916 on a cruiser sunk by a German mine.

'Maréchal Niel': One romantic story tells that Adolphe Niel—a French hero of the Crimean War—was convalescing near Rome when this yellow noisette was found on the Campagna. He sent the rose to France, where the empress Eugénie dedicated it to him.

'Tour de Malakoff': Introduced in 1857, two years after the Battle of Malakoff, this mauve centifolia commemorates a fortified Russian tower (*tour* in French) seized by French troops during the Crimean War.

'Veterans' Honor': Medical research conducted by the U.S. Department of Veterans Affairs benefits from sales of the red hybrid tea.

'Waves': The navy's corps of Women Accepted for Volunteer Emergency Service won its rose, a pink hybrid tea, in 1944.

'World War II Memorial Rose': A percentage of proceeds from sales of this mauve florist's rose goes to the construction of the memorial in Washington, D.C.

'GÉANT DES BATAILLES',
CAPTURED BY HENRY CURTIS IN 1850

PRESIDENT HERBERT HOOVER

A GIDDY WHORL OF ORANGE, pink, and yellow, this fragrant hybrid tea reflected the buoyant mood that swept Herbert Clark Hoover and the Republican party to victory in the 1928 election. After the rose won the gold medal at New York's International Flower Show the following spring, commercial success seemed assured: a chicken in every pot, a car in every garage, a **'President Herbert Hoover'** in every yard. As luck would have it, though, the rose didn't officially go on sale until 1930, after the Wall Street crash of October 1929 had blasted the U.S. economy like a killing frost. Hoover's popularity withered, and the bottom fell out of the market for his namesake. Franklin Delano Roosevelt defeated Hoover in the 1932 election, and rose breeder Gene Boerner never forgot the lesson: he regularly warned colleagues against pinning their hopes on politicians' names.

New York rosarian Lily Shohan tells of how when 'President Herbert Hoover' first came out, her grandmother, Elizabeth Bogen, the lone Republican in a Democratic family, planted a large bed of this variety near her front door in Los Angeles. "Though Grandma really liked the rose, she also got a kick out of annoying her relatives," Shohan says. "Nobody walking by could miss the name printed on the plant label." The Depression deepened, Hoover's promised prosperity wasn't just around the corner, and a disgruntled

Elizabeth Bogen registered Democratic; but she had no intention of ripping out those gorgeous roses. "Grandma simply replaced the label. The new one read: 'Franklin D. Roosevelt'."

The bush legally entitled to bear that name is a solid red hybrid tea bred in 1939, during FDR's second term. His supporters did not have to wait that long, however, to show their loyalty. Roosevelt's campaign song, "Happy Days Are Here Again," had inspired the naming of an orange-red hybrid tea, **'Happy Days'** (now extinct), in 1932. The next year ushered in **'President Franklin D. Roosevelt'**, an orange-red hybrid tea, and **'Mrs. Franklin D. Roosevelt'**,

a deep yellow hybrid tea. Incidentally, *Roosevelt* means "rose field" in Dutch, and the family's coat of arms, dating to the seventeenth century, incorporates three cut roses. When the Roosevelts commissioned a new set of White House china, they had these armorial blooms applied to the rim of every piece. In 1945, at Franklin's request, he was buried in the rose garden on the family estate at Hyde Park, New York, where Eleanor and their Scottish terrier Fala would later lie beside him.

HOOVER'S ROSE STIRRED PARTISAN REACTIONS
DURING THE DEPRESSION

Although our first president, George Washington, supposedly named a variety after his mother (see **'Mary Washington'**, page 185), no one named a rose after the man himself until 1855, when a grower in Washington, D.C., created the crimson tea **'General Washington'**. Five years later, it was joined by a French hybrid perpetual **'Général Washington'**, also cherry red. The lack of a rose honoring George as president—or fellow garden enthusiasts Thomas Jefferson, John Quincy Adams, Andrew Jackson, and Martin Van Buren in any capacity—may reflect early American wariness of aping the titled European tyrants who accepted floral tributes as their due. Abraham Lincoln became the first living occupant of the White House to have a rose named after him. **'Président Lincoln'**, a red hybrid perpetual from the same French breeder who had produced 'Général Washington', came out in 1863, shortly after Lincoln issued the Emancipation Proclamation. The president's assassination two years later elicited three eulogies, all from France (then the leading supplier of roses sold in the United States): **'Abraham Lincoln'**, **'Souvenir d'Abraham Lincoln'**, and **'Souvenir du Président Lincoln'**. Not until 1900 would another rose, the hybrid perpetual **'President McKinley'**, hail an American president. Tragically, it became an unintended memorial one year later, after an anarchist shot McKinley dead.

Given this grim record, some might have feared that the dedication of a new hybrid could jinx a president, which possibly explains why no rose honors Theodore Roosevelt, McKinley's successor. Roosevelt himself thought roses altogether bully, especially given his ancestry. As T. R.'s daughter, Alice Roosevelt Longworth, noted, their entire clan "had roses in book plates and crested rings. Roosevelt babies always had cascades of roses tumbling down

their christening robes." Teddy's affection for the flower transcended genealogy, however. "Upon one of the many memorable visits to the White House
while Roosevelt was President, I saw him take from a vase on his desk a cluster of beautiful roses and present them graciously to a lady who was among
the callers of the day," recalled J. Horace McFarland, the president of the
American Rose Society. When McFarland asked T. R.'s widow, Edith Carow
Roosevelt, which varieties her husband preferred, she replied: 'My husband's
favorite rose, the Duchesse de Brabant, was a very old-fashioned one, which I
have found it impossible to get of late. He associated it with his mother's garden and mine. In White House days he usually wore one in the buttonhole of
his grey suit—as [Joseph] DeCamp painted him. In the portrait, a blue bowl
of the same rose is on the table."

Presidential roses finally resurfaced when two hybrids were named for
William Howard Taft soon after his election in 1908. From then on, the list of
roses pegged to living occupants of the Oval Office includes some presidents
and omits others without any obvious partisan agenda. *Yea*: Wilson, Coolidge,
Franklin Roosevelt, Eisenhower, and Reagan (not just **'Ronald Reagan'**,
but also **'Jelly Bean'**, after the candy he kept on his desk). *Nay*: Harding,
Truman, Kennedy, Ford, Carter, Clinton, and both Bushes. *Undecided*: A
short-lived **'Richard Nixon'** reportedly dropped out of catalogs during the
Watergate scandal. Two posthumous salutes drew all eyes in 1965: **'Mister
Lincoln'** and **'John F. Kennedy'**, aka **'JFK'**. This Lincoln memorial, pegged
to the centennial of that president's assassination, ranks as one of the best red
hybrid teas ever. (**'Honest Abe'**, also red, is the sole presidential miniature, a
floral jest our tallest leader would have enjoyed.) The large flowers of 'JFK' are

white, the color Jacqueline Kennedy chose. Lyndon and Lady Bird Johnson planted beds of this hybrid tea soon after they moved into 1600 Pennsylvania Avenue.

Today, visiting dignitaries and members of the White House press corps will not catch sight of 'John F. Kennedy' in the White House Rose Garden's frequently televised beds adjoining the West Wing. The absence of 'JFK' has less to do with politics or history than with its unreliable winter hardiness and erratic flowering. Nevertheless, Kennedy the man left a lasting mark on

that patch of ground. To make room for the first Rose Garden in 1913, Woodrow Wilson's First Lady, Ellen Axson Wilson, had cleared a Colonial Revival garden that Edith Roosevelt and White House gardener Henry Pfister had installed in 1902. Mrs. Wilson, an accomplished landscape and still-life painter, collaborated with the landscape architect George Burnap to substitute a strictly formal layout of long rectangular beds for Roosevelt's filigree of boxwood ovals and arcs. The Wilson

FDR'S CAMPAIGN SONG INSPIRED THE
HYBRID TEA 'HAPPY DAYS'

arrangement survived until 1961, when President Kennedy, an avid reader of Thomas Jefferson's garden notebooks, decided to enlarge the central lawn to "hold a thousand people for a ceremony" and frame it with French-style borders. The garden's designer, Rachel Lambert Mellon, planted these peripheral parterres with crab apples, which cast shade and, consequently, reduced the number of roses that can grow there. The only varieties in the garden that currently commemorate former residents of the adjoining mansion are **'Pat Nixon'** (a dark red floribunda), 'Ronald Reagan' (a hybrid tea in several shades of red), **'Barbara Bush'** (a coral pink hybrid tea), and **'Laura Bush'** (an orange floribunda).

Oddly, no First Lady roses grow in the First Ladies' Garden, another area of the White House grounds, east of the South Portico. The only tenant is **'Iceberg'**, although many candidates qualify for inclusion. Aside from **'Martha Washington'**, a found rose of unknown origin, few of these preceded **'Mrs. Theodore Roosevelt'**, a light pink hybrid tea of 1903 (**'Abigail Adams'** and **'Dolly** [sic] **Madison'** are twentieth-century creations). Mary Todd Lincoln, the first presidential wife referred to as First Lady, and a perpetually controversial figure, didn't blossom— as **'Mrs. Lincoln'**, a red hybrid tea—until 1997. As intensely as the public had scorned the extravagant, unstable Mary Lincoln, it adored Frances Folsom Cleveland, the first bride of a president ever married in the White House, in 1886. Hucksters exploited the newlywed's youthful good looks and prestige to endorse—without her permission—undergarments, perfume, and face cream. Nurseries expediently retagged **'Général Jacqueminot'**, a French hybrid perpetual, as **'Mrs. Cleveland'**. Mrs. Cleveland, an orchid fancier, may not have noticed or cared.

After the turn of the twentieth century, publicity-savvy hybridizers made a point of requesting official permission for the use of a First Lady's name, not just as a matter of protocol but also for publicity. Aside from the aforementioned Mesdames Roosevelt, Nixon, and Bush, the roster includes '**Madame Taft**', '**Mrs. Warren G. Harding**', '**Mrs. Calvin Coolidge**', '**Mrs. Herbert Hoover**'; '**First Lady**' (a discreet nod to Jacqueline Kennedy from 1961, her first year in Camelot); '**Lady Bird Johnson**' and '**Lady Bird**'; '**Rosalyn Carter**'; '**First Lady Nancy**' and '**Nancy Reagan**' (her husband proclaimed the rose—the entire genus *Rosa*—our national flower in 1986, despite heroic lobbying by the Marigold Society of America); and '**Hillary First Lady**'. The founding mother of the White House Rose Garden, Ellen Wilson, is shamefully absent. Roseless too are Woodrow Wilson's second wife, Edith (she was more involved in affairs of state than the state of the White House gardens); Bess Truman (no connection to '**Dainty Bess**'); and Mamie Eisenhower. Maybe rose breeders suspected what Mamie's husband revealed after leaving office: "Mrs. Eisenhower's favorite flowers are the Violet, the Gardenia, the Azalea, and the Gladiola." Ike added: "I am likewise fond of these particular flowers but my own favorite is the Rose and of all varieties the yellow Rose ranks first in my estimation." (Was he annoyed that the hybrid tea '**President Eisenhower**', inaugurated with him in 1953, is red?) Betty Ford's rose stands apart from the rest: it never needs watering, though it should be dusted now and then, and it's immune to disease and impervious to pests. It is the pink porcelain "Peace Rose" that the former First Lady presents annually, on behalf of the Susan G. Komen Foundation, to a leader in the fight against breast cancer.

WHAT SO PROUDLY WE HAIL

The ancestry of most garden roses grown in the United States today includes immigrant stock: primarily hybrids bred in Europe, the Middle East, and Asia. American nurseries have given patriotic names to numerous plants of varied origins—from **'Amber Waves'** (an apricot-colored floribunda with English and German forebears) and **'Columbia'** (a medium pink rambler of predominantly French extraction) to **'Lady Liberty'** (a creamy hybrid tea that's one-quarter Irish) and **'Stars 'n' Stripes'** (a red-and-white-striped miniature whose family tree has Japanese and Chinese branches). But North America is also home to several indigenous rose species whose provenance shows in their Latin labels. They all produce single (five-petaled) flowers.

Rosa arkansana: Although sometimes called **'Arkansas Rose'**, having been discovered near the Arkansas River in Colorado, this low spreading shrub with pale-to-medium-pink flowers is more commonly known as **'Prairie Wild Rose'**. Both names belie its enormous geographical range, from the Appalachian Mountains west to the Rockies, and from Alberta south to Mexico. Confusingly, the North American species *R. setigera* (the second word means "bristle bearing") goes by **'Prairie Rose'** and **'Climbing Prairie Rose'**. The French botanical explorer André Michaux, who published his monumental *Flora of North America* in 1802, first recorded this white or pink single-flowered plant in the Carolinas, but it can be seen throughout the continental United States—which justifies Michaux's original name for it, **'Rosier d'Amérique'** ("rosebush of America").

R. californica: Found from Southern California to British Columbia, and eastward to Nevada, *R. californica* is one of the Golden State's few native roses. Historians suspect that this upright bush with fragrant single pink blooms is the plant that a Franciscan missionary traveling through California, Fra Junipero Serra, misidentified in 1769 as the perfumed *double*-flowered pink **'Rosal de Castilla'** (**'Rose of Castile'**, aka **'Autumn Damask'**) he had known in Spain. Romanticism and religious fervor may have affected his vision. Fra Junipero noted in his diary, "The branch of a rosebush is at this moment caressing the hand that sets down these lines . . . I bless Thee, Lord, for having created the Rose of Castile." Only after the rose was collected by early-nineteenth-century Russian naturalists at San Francisco's Presidio did it receive its present Latin name.

R. carolina: This robust shrub with pink flowers is native to just about everywhere in the eastern half of North America. The English naturalist John Josselyn encountered the then nameless flower in New England. Writing in 1672, he described it as "Wild Damask Rose, single, but very large and sweet." By "large" he evidently meant just the blossom, since the vigorously spreading **'Carolina Rose'** rarely tops three feet in the wild (it can reach six feet in a garden bed). Because it frequently volunteers in meadows, this plant is also called the **'Pasture Rose'**. We don't know why the eighteenth-century Swedish botanist Carl Linnaeus chose to designate it *carolina*; perhaps he became aware of the plant's existence through specimens from the South.

R. virginiana: Probably the first New World rose cultivated in Europe, this species appears on the 1634 list of plants in the London garden of father-and-son botanical explorers John Tradescant the Elder and John the Younger. Their compatriot John Parkinson discussed the "Virginian Briar Rose" in his *Theatrum Botanicum: The Theater of Plantes*, an herbal published in 1640. In fact, the rose's habitat extends from Newfoundland to Georgia and west to Missouri—most of which lies within the vast swath between the Atlantic and Pacific Oceans that England claimed as "Virginia" during the reign of the Virgin Queen, Elizabeth I. Horticulturists have long prized the four-to-six-foot-tall **'Virginia Rose'** less for its pale pink flowers than for its shiny green leaves (Redouté, who observed this ornamental import in French gardens, labeled it *R. lucida*, "glossy rose"). In autumn, the foliage turns brilliant tones of yellow and red.

QUEEN ELIZABETH

I dreamt the Roses one time went
To meet and sit in Parliament;
The place for these, and for the rest
Of flowers, was thy spotless breast.
Over the which a state was drawn
Of tiffany, or cob-web lawn;
Then in that Parly all those powers
Voted the Rose the Queen of flowers;
But so, as that herself should be
The Maid of Honour unto thee.
— Robert Herrick (1591–1674)

THE ROSE HAS REIGNED as the queen of all flowers since as far back as 600 BC, when Sappho, in her "Ode to the Rose," transformed what Greeks had until then considered the king of flowers into the queen. This idea got a boost from myths about Rhodanthe ("rose flower"), queen of Corinth, whom the god Apollo turned into a rosebush, as retribution for a slight to his sister Artemis. Rhodanthe nevertheless retained royal status, simply making a lateral move to the plant kingdom in 1847, when a French horticulturist named a white Bourbon rose **'Rhodanthe'**.

Old nursery catalogs recite more regal names than you can shake a scepter at, including **'Charlemagne'** (a hybrid perpetual bred in 1836), **'Isabella II'** (gallica, pre 1848), **'Frederick II'** (China, 1847), **'Marie Antoinette'** (gallica, 1829), **'Victor Emmanuel'** (Bourbon, 1859), **'Empress Alexandra of Russia'** (tea, 1897), **'Kaiser Wilhelm II'** (hybrid tea, 1909), and **'Sa Majesté Gustave V'** (hybrid perpetual, 1922). The last was the creation of rose breeder Paul Nabonnand, whose nursery on the French Riviera specialized in plants named for the region's seasonal residents (**'Archiduc Joseph'**, **'Duchesse de Vallombrosa'**, **'Reine Emma des Pays Bas'**, and the like). When Sweden's King Gustav V complained that the Scandinavian climate devastated his rosebushes, Nabonnand encouraged him to sponsor a competition for an everblooming winter-hardy rose. Gustav did just that. Nabonnand gratefully named his own prize-winning entry winner after the king.

At least one crowned plant, **'Rose du Roi'** ("the king's rose"), acquired its title by decree. The forefather of many hybrid perpetuals, it had been bred in 1812 by a gardener at the Château de St. Cloud, a royal property overseen by the comte de Lelieur. This nobleman took such a shine to the seedling's crimson flower that he called it **'Rose Lelieur'**. Unfortunately for the count, after Louis XVIII gained the throne several years later, courtiers eager to curry favor with the king demanded that the name change to glorify him. Lelieur obstinately refused until a higher authority forced him to hand over his rose, at which point the count quit his post at St. Cloud in a huff.

During the 1930s, Jean Henri Nicolas told the story of another plant named by royal request. In Great Britain, he wrote, "It is a great honor when the queen singles out a new rose . . . to be sent to the palace. It was on one of those occasions, in 1917, that Queen Alexandra greatly admired the vivid colors of a McGredy seedling and insisted that it be named **'The Queen Alexandra Rose'** . . . I learned from the late Sam McGredy that he regretted its choice by the queen, as the plant turned out to be of bad habit and difficult to grow."

The current British monarch, represented by **'The Queen Elizabeth Rose'** (just **'Queen Elizabeth'** to most of her American friends), joined the floral royals relatively late. Heraldic roses have served as regal emblems in England since the thirteenth century, when Edward I wielded a golden rose "stalked proper." Hybrids began acquiring British rulers' names in the early 1800s. **'Prince Régent'** (a gallica bred in the Netherlands, almost certainly before George IV's coronation in 1820) and **'William the Fourth'** (a pre-1848 French gallica) preceded **'Reine Victoria'** (1838, French hybrid perpetual), the first of at least seven roses that honored William's niece during her long reign. And that's not counting **'Her Majesty'**, an 1885 hybrid perpetual bred by the English rose hybridizer Henry Bennett, famed for his scientifically bred "Pedigree Roses." Early in

'QUEEN ELIZABETH'

their lives, the queen's garden namesakes consorted with **'Prince Albert'**; and, secluded in a few old-fashioned gardens at the close of the Edwardian era, they lived to greet **'Edward VII'**, bred in 1911 as a memorial to Victoria and Albert's son.

In retrospect, it seems portentous that **'The Princess Elizabeth'**—an orange English hybrid tea introduced in 1927, the year following Elizabeth's birth, when it seemed unlikely she would ever rule—should have been a sport of 'The Queen Alexandra Rose'. Given the name of little Elizabeth Alexandra Mary's younger sister, Margaret Rose, it was inevitable that a **'Princess Margaret Rose'** would follow, as did happen in 1933. (The lineage of this pink hybrid tea—a cross between **'Los Angeles'** and a nameless seedling—may have given Windsor genealogists pause.) **'Lilibet'**, a pale pink American floribunda introduced in 1953, Elizabeth's coronation year, sweetly evokes her childhood nickname, in contrast to the pomp and circumstance of 'The Queen Elizabeth Rose', which came on the market in 1954. Majestically tall (up to eight feet) with large orchid pink flowers, the plant also stands out as the first member of the grandiflora dynasty ever bred.

Credit for this achievement belongs to another Yank, the California hybridizer Walter Lammerts, who started developing his grandiflora, a cross between

a floribunda and a hybrid tea, shortly after the Second World War. In 1952, when Elizabeth became queen upon her father's death,

QUEEN ALEXANDRA BUYING FLOWERS ON ALEXANDRA
ROSE DAY, A CHARITY FUND-RAISER ESTABLISHED IN 1912

Lammerts approached the British consul for permission to name the rose after her. The speed of the affirmative reply stunned British horticulturists. As Sam McGredy, then a loyal subject in Northern Ireland, wrote: "It is remarkable how easily [Lammerts] got permission to use this name. If we in this country want to use a royal name, we have to undergo—and quite rightly—a very strict examination, as I had to when I wanted to call a rose of mine **'Elizabeth of Glamis'** [after the Queen Mother and her Scottish childhood home, Glamis Castle] . . . I was eventually given permission, and we have the letter framed in the office, typed with the giant typewriter that always seems to be used for royal correspondence." But did anybody at Buckingham Palace smile over the parentage of the 1959 floribunda **'Prince Philip'**, bred from **'Independence'** and **'Buccaneer'**, or the 1964 grandiflora **'Improved Prince Philip'**, a cross between 'Prince Philip' and 'The Queen Elizabeth Rose'?

Court protocol played little if any part in the cultivar names inspired by Diana, Princess of Wales. An orange and peach hybrid tea, **'Royal Romance'**, came out in 1982, months after her wedding to Prince Charles but in sync with the release of an American made-for-TV movie *The Royal Romance of Charles and Diana*. The pink American florist's rose **'Lady Diana'**, introduced in 1986, flouted etiquette by using a style of address proper only for the unmarried Diana Spencer. **'People's Princess'**, a pink hybrid tea bred in New Zealand a decade later, reflected both the pop-star celebrity and the common touch of a woman who still seemed destined to become queen. After divorce changed that prospect, Diana continued to receive floral acclaim. In 1997 an English hybridizer presented her with white and ivory **'The Princess of Wales'**—white roses were said to be her favorites—as a tribute to her involvement with the British Lung Foundation. That summer she died in a Paris car crash. Her memorials include the pink hybrid tea **'Diana, Princess of Wales'** as well as two shrubs—apricot **'England's Rose'** and red-and-white-flecked **'Candle in the Wind'**, which echo the song Elton John performed at her funeral in Westminster Abbey.

ROYAL WOES

Uneasy rests the rose that wears the crown—at least in beds where the following blue-blooded cultivars tell their stories.

'Duchesse d'Angoulême': Unlike her parents, Marie Antoinette and Louis XVI, Princess Marie Thérèse Charlotte survived the French Revolution. She married her cousin the duc d'Angoulême and championed the restoration of the Bourbon monarchy. An exile in Austria, the duchess died in 1851. Rosarians debate the exact date when the duchess's centifolia was bred but agree that it received her name while she was alive. Owing to the translucency of its delicate pink petals, this is also known as **'The Wax Rose'**.

'Duchesse de Brabant': Vivacious and charming Archduchess Marie Henriette of Austria was seventeen when she reluctantly wed the aloof Belgian crown prince, Léopold, duc de Brabant, in 1853. That disastrous match, the untimely death of the couple's only son, and the conjugal woes of two of their daughters pushed the duchess into a deep, lifelong depression. Rose gardening became one of her chief consolations. Marie Henriette's namesakes include duchesse lace and the fragrant light pink double tea rose 'Duchesse de Brabant', bred in France in 1857.

'Les Fiançailles de la Princesse Stéphanie et de l'Archiduc Rodolphe': This fittingly extinct rose celebrated the 1880 engagement of the ill-starred Stéphanie of Belgium, daughter of the former duchesse de Brabant (above), and the archduke Rudolf, heir to the Austro-Hungarian throne. Their marriage ended nine years later with the mysterious, possibly suicidal deaths of Rudolf and his mistress in the royal hunting lodge at Mayerling. Stéphanie later married a Hungarian nobleman whose name would have filled an equally long plant label: Elemér Edmund Graf Lónyay de Nagy-Lónya et Vásáros-Namény.

'Erherzog Franz Ferdinand': The death of his cousin Rudolf (above) made Archduke Franz Ferdinand an heir to the Austro-Hungarian imperial throne. His rose, a large, very fragrant red Noisette bred in Luxembourg, dates to 1892. Three years later, he met his wife, Sophie Chotek, a Bohemian countess. Their assassination at Sarajevo in 1914 provoked the outbreak of the First World War.

'Duchess of Windsor': A nod to the divorced American commoner, Wallis Simpson, whose marriage to Britain's Edward VIII forced his abdication, this name is one of several aliases for a red floribunda. Its breeder released the plant in 1932 as **'Permanent Wave'**, which is still the label registered with the American Rose Society. The duchess's royal husband got his own rose, **'Duke of Windsor'**, a hybrid tea, in 1969. Rosarians have noted that the origins of the two cultivars — hers Dutch, his German — seem symbolically apt for spouses who shared a life in exile.

'Duchess of York': Both this and another orange floribunda, **'Fergie'**, honor the redheaded duchess, née Sarah Ferguson. English-bred 'Fergie' appeared in 1987, soon after its namesake wed Prince Andrew, Duke of York. Rumors of their subsequent marital troubles, and photographs of the duchess cavorting topless, made news well before a Northern Irish grower's 'Duchess of York' came out in 1994. Scandal and the Yorks' divorce ultimately persuaded many nurseries to sell the rose under the name on its New Zealand patent: **'Sunseeker'**.

ROSA GALLICA

L IFE WAS A BED of roses for Marie Antoinette, at least for a few hours in May 1770. En route from Vienna to Versailles on the day before her wedding to the dauphin Louis Auguste, the fifteen-year-old Austrian spent the night in the French city of Nancy. To calm her nerves, local historians say, the princess slept on fresh petals of *Rosa gallica*, the **'French Rose'**, a lucrative crop on the nearby farms of Provins. Physicians of that era recommended this flower (especially the variety *R. gallica* **'Officinalis'**, or **'Apothecary's Rose'**) as a source of therapeutic oils for the treatment of hysteria.

R. gallica, one of the oldest roses in existence, takes its name from Gallia, or Gaul, the ancient territory that included France and Belgium. A common wildflower in French hedgerows and fields, the species supplied basic breeding

ROSA GALLICA, FROM BASILIUS BESLER'S
1613 HAND-PAINTED *FLORILEGIUM*

stock for the beginnings of rose hybridization—a revolutionary development in floriculture. The revolution in which Marie Antoinette would lose her head was already under way when a certain M. François, erstwhile gardener to the queen, listed some of the earliest hybrids in his 1790 Paris nursery catalog. The list comprised 112 cultivars, "new double roses" with labels like **'Belle du Monde'** ("beauty of the world") and **'Velours Superbe'** ("superb velvet").

The panache of these names was new and distinctly French, as were the artful shapes, colors, and textures of the flowers they graced. Only decades earlier, a red rose might simply have been identified by its class—damask, say, or gallica—and a notation of its color, *rouge*. But the fashionable taste for the romantic encouraged hybridizers to hawk each plant as if it were the latest novel, with titles like **'Rouge Formidable'**, **'Feu Brillant'** ("shining fire"), **'Rosier d'Amour'** ("rosebush of love"), and **'Enchanteresse'**. Nurserymen also appealed to the aspirations of a rising bourgeoisie by alluding to classical learning (**'Bouquet de Vénus'**) and superior breeding (**'Violette Supérieure'**). No "Liberté" or "Fraternité" emerged from a greenhouse. **'Egalité'** finally appeared after the Second World War, but it was bred by a Dutchman.

ANOTHER RESOURCE FOR HYBRIDIZING, and another resonant French name, came to the fore in 1822 with the advent of Bourbon roses. Despite what their name implies, these flowers did not originate in France (nor are they connected to Kentucky whisky, which honors that state's Bourbon County). They trace their ancestry to the West Indian island Ile de Bourbon, now Réunion, a French colony where planters bounded their fields with double hedges of the vigorous repeat-blooming roses **'Autumn Damask'** and **'Old Blush China'**, segregated in parallel rows. A Creole sugar magnate on the island, Edouard Périchon, noticed that a seedling produced by a chance encounter between the two varieties developed branches and leaves quite unlike those of either parent, although it had inherited their "everblooming" habit. Périchon found this fluke remarkable enough to transplant it into his personal garden and send seeds to France. There they were propagated by Antoine Jacques, head gardener of a blueblood Bourbon, the duc d'Orléans, who would soon ascend the throne as King Louis Philippe.

As with their native gallica, French nurserymen used the import to hybridize a large inventory of elegant *nouveautés* with florid labels: **'Souvenir de la Princesse de Lamballe'**, **'Miroir de Perfection'** ("mirror of perfection"), and **'Enfant d'Ajaccio'** ("child of Ajaccio"), referring to Napoléon's birthplace on the island of Corsica. The correct name of that first West Indian foundling, however, remains in dispute. Some historians insist that it has always been **'Rosier de l'Ile de Bourbon'**, whereas others opt for **'Rose Edouard'**, a nod to M. Périchon and the name by which this rose has long been known in its tropical homeland. A third contingent favors **'Bourbon Jacques'**, after Louis Philippe's loyal retainer. This was the name attached to the plant by Philadelphia nurseryman Thomas Hibbert, the first American to sell a Bourbon rose, in 1828.

American gardeners and florists associated all French roses with those other Gallic luxuries: couture, cuisine, and Champagne—and they likewise became a prestigious commodity. Nurseryman William Prince of New York proudly offered his clientele forty-one varieties of "fine new French Roses' as early as 1820, and Hovey & Company of Boston listed almost two hundred

"French Roses" in its 1846 catalog. The name of one frilly gallica said it all: **'Surpasse Tout'** ("surpasses all"). By the 1860s the majority of roses grown in the United States were of French origin.

Great Britain embraced French roses, too, even if John Bull occasionally held new foreign names at arm's length, suspecting an underlying scheme of bait and switch. In a letter to the editor of *The Gardener's Magazine and Rural Register of Rural and Domestic Improvement*, English nurseryman Thomas Rivers complained: "In forming a collection of roses from the French gardeners, great difficulty is often experienced by their incorrectness in the names of their plants; this inattention, to call it by no worse name, has long been the

MILNE RAMSEY'S *LA FRANCE ROSES*, 1889

bane of commercial gardening." This couldn't be dismissed as mere Franco-phobia. Some of Rivers's French counterparts shared his concern and didn't beat around the rosebush in laying charges. A professional journal in Paris accused the prominent hybridizer Jean-Pierre Vibert of switching plant labels to palm off less desirable varieties at inflated prices.

Regardless of the scandals over bogus names, nothing dampened the enthusiasm in the United States and Great Britain for French fashions. Up-to-date nursery customers wouldn't be caught dead with last season's hybrid gallicas after more stylish Bourbons had arrived. And when one of the earliest examples of a sensational new class of rose—the hybrid tea, which would outdo all others in popularity—came on the scene in 1867, tastemakers in every world capital recognized the inevitability of its name: **'La France'**.

PLUS ÇA CHANGE . . .

Location, location, location. French rosarians learned this mantra back in 1827, when an infestation of root-eating grubs (larvae of the cockchafer beetle) threatened to destroy the nation's major rose fields, which were concentrated in and around Paris. Fleeing the "white worm" plague, rosarians moved south to the grub-free soil and salubrious climate of Angers, Lyon, and Orléans. Soon, new roses reflected this exodus: the lilac-pink moss **'Du Maître d'Ecole'**, named for the Angers neighborhood where nurserymen set up shop; the white and pink hybrid *Rosa roxburghii* **'Triomphe de la Guillotière'**, after the Lyon's rose-growing district; and the velvety mauve Bourbon **'Velours d'Orléans'**. Thanks to its rapid decentralization, the French rose business rebounded, and several provincial rose-growing families, such as the Guillots in Lyon and the Meillands in Provence, became horticultural powerhouses.

Today Meilland International is France's largest dynastic rose company, annually selling more than twelve million rosebushes (not to mention cut flowers) worldwide under the sharp eye and sensitive nose of sixth-generation rosarian Alain Meilland. Although the firm's online catalog contains names that evoke Gallic family ties—**'Papa Meilland'**, for Alain's grandfather; **'Manou Meilland'**, for Alain's mother, Marie-Louise, a formidable hybridizer; and *hommages* to his wife, daughter, and two sons—it also lists roses that don't even whisper "France," such as **'Hello'**, **'Liv Tyler'**, and **'Tequila'**.

Meilland and other major French nurseries have confronted globalization with élan. They retain the aura of *maman-et-papa* firms, but their business models are solidly corporate. International marketing campaigns promote "collections" of new cultivars under thematic brand names: Roseraie Guillot has a line called Rosa Générosa—as in *généreux*, or "generous" (including the apricot shrub **'Paul Bocuse'**, after the well-known chef); Meilland, its Romantica Roses (the deep pink hybrid tea **'Peter Mayle'**, for the author of *A Year in Provence*); and G. Delbard S.A., its Souvenirs d'Amour (the pink shrub **'Madame Bovary'**). Because the good earth of the ancestral *terroir* can no longer meet the demand for Gallic roses, these nurseries also maintain grub-free growing fields in Argentina, Australia, Japan, South Africa, and the United States.

ROSA MULTIFLORA

ASK A BOTANIST WHAT *Rosa multiflora* means, and she'll say, "Rose with many flowers." Ask a gardener, and he'll go on and on about "huge, lovely clusters of small white blossoms spilling from trees and filling the air with a sweet, honeylike fragrance." Ask an environmental-ist, and she'll mutter four-letter words that you won't find in a Latin diction-ary. Like the English sparrow, *R. multiflora* ('**No-ibara**', or "field rose," in its native Japan) was imported into America during the nineteenth century as a prize exotic, only to be fruitful and multiply beyond the wildest expectations. It now heads the list of invasive plants in thirty states, beating out kudzu, the scourge of the South.

Many other names characterize roses by numerical measures. The Latin cultivar name '**Trigintipetala**', for example, indicates a blossom with at least thirty petals. Some counts just don't add up, however. Translated lit-erally, *R. centifolia* denotes "rose with a hundred leaves," even though the number refers not to foliage, but to the multiplicity of petals on this full-bodied flower. That's because, technically speaking, a petal is a modified leaf. And, in any case, the true count is closer to sixty or seventy. (Another

instance of enthusiastic hyperbole comes from the German breeder J. C. Schmidt, who in 1906 called a climber with profuse long pink and white flower clusters **'Tausendschön'** (**'Thousand Beauties'**). Even more baffling, "Hundred-petaled" in a cultivar name does not necessarily mean that the variety belongs to the centifolia class. The **'Hundred-leaved Rose of Auteuil'** and **'Centfeuilles d'Angleterre'** are actually gallicas, and **'Bengal Centfeuilles'** is a China, which obviously traveled west via India.

Size-conscious nineteenth-century breeders aimed for enormous, showy plants, and gave them fittingly hyperbolic labels. French growers preferred the Greek *polyantha* ("many-flowered") to *multiflora* but used it similarly to boast about a plant's abundant blooms. **'Gloire des Polyanthas'** ("glory of the polyanthas"), created in 1887, was one of many shrubs with multiflora and China ancestry that were prized for luxuriant clusters of blooms. A larger-flowered variety produced by crossing polyanthas with hybrid teas became known around 1940 as a "floribunda," from the Latin for "profusely flowered." Then, in 1954, breeders agreed that another superlative, "grandiflora"—previously attached to the names of large-flowered species, such as *R. gallica grandiflora*—would denote a whole new class generated by crossing floribundas with hybrid teas. Rest assured that these terms occasionally perplex rosarians, too.

In general, though, when nurseries have a big flower to sell, they flaunt it with an unambiguous name. Nobody had to ponder whether the 1835 tea rose **'Gigantesque'**, sold as **'Gigantic'** in some United States nurseries, would go unnoticed; likewise the twentieth-century **'Colossus'**, **'Paul Bunyan'**, **'Gentle Giant'**, **'Stephens' Big Purple'**, and **'Super Star Supreme'**. The labels on garden-center rose pots can be strangely reminiscent of those on supermarket olive cans, which range from "large" and "extra large" to "jumbo," "colossal," and "super colossal." The wise rose shopper disregards the label and sizes up the flower himself.

SMALL WONDERS

The idea that the best things come in small packages has sparked breeders' ingenuity. Pennsylvania nurseryman Robert Pyle met the challenge when he introduced the smallest known rose, **'Peon'**, a Dutch miniature, to the United States in 1936. The plant is six inches tall with flowers measuring a scant quarter inch in diameter. Banking on the iconic status of P. T. Barnum's star attraction, "The World-Renowned American Man in Miniature," Pyle renamed the plant **'Tom Thumb'**—and quickly sold out his supply. He had to pull the rose from his catalog until enough fresh stock could be propagated. The success of 'Tom Thumb' reignited interest in miniature roses, turning gigantism on its head. A new breed of rosarians competed to create diminutive varieties with ever-cutesier names, like **'Littlest Angel'**, **'Tiny Tears'**, and **'Baby Betsy McCall'**. The current popularity of container gardening has further encouraged downsizing. Some nurseries now advertise "micro-minis" and "miniflora," although these categories are loosely defined. In general, their blossoms range from a quarter inch to one and a half inches in diameter—smaller than the average hybrid tea, but still larger than 'Tom Thumb'.

'TOM THUMB'

ROSA MUNDI

TABLOID REPORTERS AND PAPARAZZI would instantly break this story if it happened today. Gossip spread more slowly, though, in the Middle Ages, when scandal embroiled England's King Henry II; his consort, Queen Eleanor; his mistress, Rosamund Clifford; and, legend has it, a rose. Henry Plantagenet had been married to Eleanor of Aquitaine for more than a decade when he, then in his thirties, began a passionate affair with the teenage Rosamund. The couple probably met around 1166 at the castle of her ambitious father, Lord Walter de Clifford, who may have encouraged the liaison for political and social advancement. Nonetheless, Henry and Rosamund's mutual affection appears to have been both genuine and lasting.

The king made sure that his paramour lived in regal style, and publicly acknowledged her in 1174, one year after he imprisoned Eleanor during a squabble over property rights and her choice of an heir. This Plantagenet family drama escalated into a battle royal with a tragic subplot involving Rosamund that has been recounted in English ballads, poems, novels, plays, and an opera, and painted by Edward Burne-Jones and Dante Gabriel Rossetti.

Nearly every version of Rosamund's part in the drama sets the scene at Woodstock Palace, a royal hunting lodge near Oxford. There, in a secluded bower Henry built for her, she had a private chapel, cloister, and gardens at her disposal. Meanwhile, the jealous queen plotted to ensnare the mistress shortly before an assignation with the king. Eleanor bribed a servant to sneak her into the bower, but Rosamund happened to look up from her embroidery and caught sight of the queen. Terrified, the younger woman ran for cover in a garden maze. She hastily shoved a skein of thread into her pocket, unaware that one end of the silken strand was still looped through her needlework indoors. The unraveled thread led Eleanor to her rival, whom she confronted with a goblet of poison and a dagger, demanding that Rosamund choose one. Rosamund drank the poison. Exit the queen. Enter the king, who discovered his beloved's corpse. Inconsolable, he commanded that she be laid to rest in a nunnery, under a mound of her favorite roses.

Well, that's how the legend goes — and like many legends, the threads of fact and fiction are tightly tangled. It would be pleasing to know without a doubt that the flower Henry ordered was the fragrant red-and-white-striped *Rosa mundi*, traditionally known as **'Fair Rosamond's Rose'**, **'Rosamunde'**, **'Rosamonde'**, and other variations on this theme (botanists use the prosaic *R. gallica* **'Versicolor'**). However, the earliest documentary evidence linking this variegated rose with Rosamund Clifford goes back only

ROSA MUNDI, IN A HAND-COLORED ENGRAVING FROM *CURTIS'S BOTANICAL MAGAZINE*, 1816

to the sixteenth century. Furthermore, no historical account solidly confirms that her death, around 1176, was violent or that Eleanor (still under house arrest at the time) played any part in it. Rosamund most likely met her end not at Woodstock, but at Godstow Abbey, a nearby nunnery where she had recently taken refuge from the secular world.

Other episodes of the story, though, are matters of record. The grief-stricken Henry actually did arrange for Rosamund's entombment inside the convent church. His son King John later gave an endowment for the nuns to 'releeve by their prayers the soules of his father, King Henrie, and of Lady Rosamund there interred." Eleanor got her revenge, albeit not by her own hand. Two years after Henry's death, a bishop passing through Godstow voiced his horror that churchgoers venerated the sinful Rosamund's tomb as a shrine; the fallen woman's remains were summarily reinterred in an out-of-the-way graveyard on the abbey grounds.

A Latin inscription on the relocated tomb perpetuated the insult. Even after another King Henry—the one with six wives—had reduced the abbey to ruins during his dissolution of monasteries, this epitaph survived for visitors to ponder: *Hic jacet in tumba Rosa mundi, non Rosa munda; / Non redolet, sed olet, quae redolere solet.* Various authors have penned translations, playing off the pun implicit in Rosamund's name—*Rosa mundi* means "rose of the world" (one reason why the Heritage Rose Foundation chose this Latin title for its journal) and *Rosa munda*, "pure rose." Victorian dictionary compiler E. Cobham Brewer tempered opprobrium with tact: "Here Rose the graced, not Rose the chaste, reposes; / The smell that rises is no smell of roses." His elegant euphemism was a far cry from the bluntness of John Stowe's 1631 doggerel, which included the lines, "Though she were sweete, now foully doth she stinke, / A mirrour good for all men that on her thinke." Fortunately for the gardeners who grow *R. mundi*, this obligingly disease-resistant and shade-tolerant plant comes up smelling like a rose.

FAIR ROSAMUND, BY JOHN WILLIAM WATERHOUSE, 1917

A MOTLEY CREW

During the past two centuries, many multicolored roses have stood out among their monochromatic bedfellows.

'Beauté Inconstante': The name, meaning "inconstant beauty," plays on the double meaning of *inconstant* in affairs of the heart. This fickle tea, introduced in 1892, produces flowers in unpredictable blends of pink, yellow, and coppery red on one bush.

'Bicolore Incomparable': Two shades of pink—dark at the center, light at the rim—distinguish the petals of this gallica.

'Duet': The hybrid tea's blooms are medium pink on top, dark pink on the flip side.

'Joseph's Coat': A climber of many colors, as its Old Testament namesake suggests, this floribunda has red buds opening to flowers that change from yellow and orange to crimson and scarlet.

'Mixed Feelings': Red and white mottled stripes signaled ambivalence to this miniature's Canadian breeder.

'Mixed Marriage': Light and dark rosy stripes account for the floribunda's name (its parent **'Bridal Pink'** must have taken part in the christening).

'Mutabilis': *R. chinensis* 'Mutabilis' acquired the alias **'Butterfly Rose'** because its multicolored blossoms suggest a lepidopterist's dream. Latin *mutabilis*, means "prone to change." As it opens, each flower begins as a creamy white, and then turns coppery pink before ending up a rich red. 'Mutabilis' may have originated in Italy, where it is **'Tipo Ideale'** ("ideal type"), perhaps because it blooms continually.

'Pandemonium': Flashes of orange and yellow all but shout for that overused garden tag "a riot of color."

'Patchwork': This hybrid tea stitches together orange and yellow.

'Tricolore': Since it was bred in 1827, the gallica has lived up to its name by producing near-magenta petals with purple edges and white central stripes.

ROSA RUGOSA

O NE MIGHT CALL *Rosa rugosa* the shar-pei of roses, because of the furrows that quilt its leaves (*rugosa* means "wrinkled" in Latin). And like the dog, it comes from Asia. But the resemblance ends there. As prickly as they come, this is not a plant you'll ever want to pet.

The Swedish botanist Carl Peter Thunberg (as in *Rosa rugosa thunbergii*, this plant's botanical name) was the first Westerner known to set eyes on a rugosa in Japan where the seaside native goes by **'Hama-nasu'** or **'Hama-nashi'**. Thunberg apparently garbled these words into *Ramanas*, the term he used in his illustrated *Flora Japonica* of 1784. *Hama* means "beach." *Nasu* ("eggplant") and *nashi* ("pear") refer to rugosas' large red hips, one of nature's best sources for vitamin C. We lean toward the Western aliases **'Sea Tomato'** and **'Tomato Rose'** only because we're not experts on Asian vegetables and fruits. We readily grasp why in Germany it's called **'Nordische Apfelrose'**, or "northern apple rose." Less obvious is the twentieth-century coinage **'Kreisverkehrrose'**, "traffic circle rose," a result of German landscapers' discovery that roadside rugosas tolerate deicing salt. Sadly, none of these names does justice to the bright pink color and delicious perfume of the plant's large single flowers.

Seemingly impervious to harsh weather and salt spray, rugosa flourishes along our East and West Coasts, in well-kept gardens as well as on dunes

ROSA RUGOSA,
OR THE 'HEDGEHOG ROSE',
AS MARY LAWRANCE LABELED
IT IN THIS 1799 PAINTING

Rosa ferox.
Hedge-hog Rose

in the wild where many North Americans call it **'Beach Rose'**. The bushes thrive in sandy soil, spreading rapidly by sending out suckers that form thick, low clumps. As they mature, their densely prickled stems weave a formidable barrier—thus the British nickname **'Hedgehog Rose'**, which makes painful sense to any gardener reckless enough to prune a rugosa with bare hands. (However calloused they become, veteran rosarians still get scratched, stuck, and stabbed like anybody else.) According to medieval Christians, all roses in the Garden of Eden were innocent of prickles, which emerged only after Adam and Eve fell from grace. German folklore tells that when Satan stealthily tried to climb back into heaven by using the thorns on a briar's vertical stems as footholds, God headed him off by bending the stems sideways.

A quiverful of sharp names not only bears witness to wounds suffered but also demonstrates respect for the weapons that inflict them. The English nurseryman William Paul said this about *R. spinosissima* ("most spiny rose") in 1848: "[T]he spines are as sharp as they are plentiful. They are far more so than they seem to be; and a word of caution here may save the tyro an unpleasant greeting." Another red flag of a label is *R. ferox* ("fierce rose"), whose mean, close-set prickles justify the warning. **'Wingthorn Rose'** is the poetic, abbreviated translation of *R. sericea* subsp. *omeiensis* f. *pteracantha*. Specialists in horticultural arcana prize this Chinese native for the allure of its translucent red thorns: an inch and a quarter wide, they glow when backlit by the sun. Some rosarians speculate that **'Dog Rose'**, *R. canina*, got this name because its large, curved prickles look like canine fangs, or because "dog" evolved from the obsolete *dag*, meaning "stab." Far less menacing is the bristly wichurana hybrid a French breeder named **'Le Poilu'** ("the hairy one").

Thorns provoke philosophizing, such as "no good without paines; no Roses with out prickles" (Michel de Montaigne, in his *Essais*), and "You can complain because roses have thorns, or you can rejoice because thorns have roses" (Ziggy, in Tom Wilson's comic strip). Hedonists' ears prick up when they hear **'Thornless Rose'** (aka **'Zéphirine Drouhin'**, after the wife of a Burgundian amateur horticulturist). The obliging nature of this nearly prickle-free Bourbon climber, bred in 1868, helps to explain why it is often planted near doors, where thorns might snag passersby. The long blooming season of its cerise pink flowers doesn't hurt either.

Some roses beg to be touched. Cuddliest of all are moss rose, *R. muscosa*, and its hybrid offspring, such as **'Old Velvet Moss'** and **'Gloire des Mousseux'** ("glory of the mosses"). The green fuzz on these plants' flower buds, upper stems, and leaflets endeared them to plush-loving Victorians, who also adored their balsamic aroma. As she sniffed her moss-rose tussy mussy, the genteel maiden could reflect on legends of the flower's heavenly genesis. In *Old Garden Roses*,

DOUBLE WHITE MOSS ROSE,
THE BOTANICAL REGISTER, 1816

published in 1936, the English writer E. A. Bunyard gives a sample of the folk-lore: "One day the Angel, who each day brings the dew on her wings, feeling weary, asked the Rose for shelter for the night. On awakening, she asked how this hospitality might be repaid. The Rose answered, 'Make me even more beautiful'. 'What grace', said the Angel, 'can I give to the most beautiful of all flowers?' Meditating on this request, she cast her eyes down to the mossy bed from which the Rose sprang and, gathering some, placed it on the young buds. Thus was born the Moss Rose."

SMOOTHIES

Botanically speaking, all roses are thornless. The correct term for the sharp non-woody protrusion from the epidermis of a rose stem is *prickle*. No rose produces the woody modified stem or branch known as a thorn found on plants such as the shrub *Pyracantha*, or firethorn. As their names proclaim, the following roses are more or less prickle-free:

'Basye's Thornless': This pink-flowered shrub was bred in Texas in 1965 by Robert E. Basye, a specialist in thornless hybrids.

'Drummond's Thornless': The semi-double blooms are carmine pink.

'Smooth Angel': Deep pink, this hybrid tea comes from the same nursery that produced **'Smooth Delight'** (peach) and **'Smooth Prince'** (cerise).

'The Bride's Rose': Also known as **'Madame Plantier'**, the white hybrid China fits comfortably into a wedding bouquet.

'Thornless Beauty': This deep red hybrid tea is intensely perfumed. Its fragrant sport **'Thornless Fringedale'** is pink.

'Thornless Violet': One of the earliest smooth-stemmed hybrids, this purple gallica-China cross predates 1848.

SHIPWRECK ROSE

To the amazement of beachcombers in East Hampton, New York, early one morning in 1842, churning breakers heaved cases of champagne, bolts of bright fabric, and crate-loads of potted trees and bushes onto the sand. As the sun burned through fog and mist, the source of this motley treasure came into view: a tall-masted ship, the clipper *Louis Philippe*, bound from Le Havre to New York City, which had run aground off Long Island's Mecox Beach. The crew had tossed all cargo overboard to lighten the still-seaworthy vessel, in hopes of easing it back into deep water. Amid the flotsam were precious French rose plants, quite possibly ordered by Samuel Parsons, a prominent nurseryman in Flushing, New York. Shipwrecks were all too familiar a hazard in his line of work. As Parsons wrote later, "We have frequently lost in this way two-thirds or three-quarters of an importation, to our great annoyance and expense." He would have taken little comfort from reports that roses off the *Louis Philippe* survived their saltwater swim and found succor in nearby gardens.

The **"Shipwreck Rose,"** passed down by cuttings and transplants through many generations, still grows in dooryards throughout eastern Long Island. In 1953, the regional historian Jeannette Edwards Rattray first identified this fragrant light pink double-flowered plant by the alias **"Louis Philippe,"** echoing a common belief that it came off the ill-starred clipper. One owner of a mature "Louis Philippe" in Sag Harbor traces its ancestry through her grandmother to her great uncle, an East Hampton town employee. Although it is just the sort of European prize that an early-nineteenth-century ship would have transported to New York, it is definitely none of the three pedigreed roses then sold in France as **'Louis Philippe'**, after the reigning monarch — a mauve gallica bred in 1824, a deep crimson China created ten years later, and an 1835 crimson pink hybrid Bourbon. Rosarians have concluded that the Sag Harbor "Louis Philippe" or "Shipwreck Rose" is in fact **'Celsiana'**, a Dutch damask introduced to France before 1732.

Still, historians never know when an old gardener's yarn may contain a thread of truth. "Found" or mystery plants like Long Island's "Shipwreck Rose" / "Louis Philippe" compose a substantial field of horticultural research. Page after page of nursery catalogs list their names, placed between double quotation marks, to distinguish them from "known" varieties with documented botanical genealogy, which are conventionally framed by single quotes. Some found names

'CELSIANA', A "SHIPWRECK ROSE" FOUND IN
LONG ISLAND, NEW YORK

are anecdotal (e.g., **"Burglar Rose,"** a red climber entwining a Louisiana chicken-yard fence that snagged a midnight prowler) or physically descriptive (**"The Heart-Petal Rose,"** with outer petals reminiscent of valentine cutouts). Others acknowledge a gardener who grew a particular plant (**"Mrs. Woods's Lavender-Pink Noisette"**) or the place where it was discovered (**"Corner, Church and Main"**).

Nowadays, when rose enthusiasts come across a rose of uncertain origin, they frequently give it a found name as a provisional label, to be replaced after historical sleuthing has tracked down its true identity. Sometimes, though, the trail goes cold, and a temporary tag ends up a permanent ID. A few European varieties believed to be extinct or lost through neglect have turned up as found roses in America. Perusal of old botanicals, herbals, travelers' diaries, nursery catalogs, and other documents furnishes clues, as does scrutiny of living specimens. In the 1980s, for example, rose experts came across plants in various southern cemeteries that had acquired local aliases: **"Crenshaw Musk,"** **"Temple Musk,"** and **"Burwell School Musk."** Comparative analysis determined that these supposedly different heirlooms were identical. More important, they matched seventeenth-century descriptions of *Rosa moschata*, the ancient musk rose, which may have died out in Europe.

No horticultural lost-and-found in the Western Hemisphere packs greater interest for rose seekers than the twenty-eight square miles of Bermuda. Located along centuries-old trade routes, and blessed with a benign climate, the island chain shelters an extraordinary concentration of vintage roses with enigmatic provenance. It is likely that some Bermuda mystery roses, as they are known universally, have flourished in the archipelago's gardens and cemeteries since the seventeenth century. (A Spaniard shipwrecked on Bermuda in 1639 wrote about the roses he saw English colonists grow.) Thanks to detective work by the Bermuda Rose Society, founded in 1954, some of these genealogical puzzles have been solved. After decades of study, the red **"Belfield"** rose—named after the private garden on Somerset Island where it was discovered in 1953—has been revealed to be **'Slater's Crimson China'**, an Asian hybrid introduced to England in 1790. The pink **"Shell Rose"** has likewise recovered its lost title, **'Duchesse de Brabant'**. What we now know to be **'Niles Cochet'**, an early-twentieth-century tea from California, masqueraded until recently as **"Aunt Jane's Mystery"**—a tough nut of the sort Agatha Christie's Jane Marple likes to crack. Others, however, such as **"St. David's," "Brightside Cream,"** and **"Spice"** remain conundrums.

A venerable shrub rose closely resembling "Spice" grows a few miles from downtown Natchez, Mississippi, in the historic Natchez City Cemetery. (Some rose experts suspect that this mystery plant is actually **'Hume's Blush Tea-scented China'**, one of the long-lost "stud" roses that begat our modern everblooming hybrids.) A seedling of that shrub, propagated and planted by the Natchez Garden Club, now thrives beside a nineteenth-century tombstone inscribed "Louise the Unfortunate." Little is known about Louise, except that she traveled from New Orleans to Natchez as a mail-order bride and, after her husband-to-be rejected her on sight, toiled as a prostitute. Ravaged by disease, Louise died young and penniless. A sympathetic Natchez minister raised enough money for proper burial. The rose that now adorns her grave will remain nameless until Garden Club members settle on an appropriate tribute to a lost soul who lived a spicy life.

North America's lost roses found an early champion in the writer Ethelyn Keays. Her pioneering book *Old Roses*, published in 1935, encouraged fellow gardeners to explore history in their own—and their neighbors'—backyards. This endearing classic chronicles Keays's efforts to collect, catalog, and decipher the legacy she found in her part of Tidewater Maryland. She wrote, "To you who read our little book and go from the highways into the by ways, looking for old roses, we give Godspeed and our best wishes. If what we have learned from collecting and growing old roses, from noting and studying about them, urges you, too, to find and restore and identify more of those enchanting favorites of our elders, the wicket gate shall have served its intention."

At Creek Side, her Calvert County farm above the banks of St. Leonard Creek, Keays converted a former pigpen and chicken and turkey runs into gardens. Within two years of purchasing the farm in 1930, she had amassed more than a hundred old rose varieties. A good number were on the property when she settled in; some she spotted on forays into the countryside; others arrived as orphans brought by friends and household staff. **"St. Leonard's White"** started out as a slip from a white-flowering shrub rose near the St. Leonard post office. Keays's cook passed along **"Faded Pink Monthly,"** the offspring of an antebellum mother plant. The amateur rosarian staked her own claim to **"Mrs. Keays' Pink,"** a small-flowering variety of indeterminate origin. Failing health prompted Keays to sell Creek Side in the late 1940s. Her house and gardens have since disappeared.

LOST AND FOUND

nspired by the work of Ethelyn Keays, gardener Miriam Wilkins of El Cerrito, California, began publishing a one-page newsletter titled *The Old Roser's Digest* in 1974. Her advocacy spearheaded the formation of the Heritage Roses Group, a self-described "fellowship" that now has regional chapters throughout the United States as well as affiliates in the United Kingdom, France, Australia, and New Zealand. Members converge in El Cerrito every May for a daylong "Celebration of Old Roses," to discuss their latest discoveries, purchase vintage gardening books, and swap cuttings of antique rose varieties such as **"Miriam Wilkins,"** a deep pink hybrid perpetual found in a Santa Rosa, California, cemetery in 1981.

That same year saw the organization of another influential group, the Texas Rose Rustlers, under the leadership of Pam Puryear (**"Pam's Pink,"** a China, and **"Lady Pamela,"** a pink climber) and Joe Woodard (**'Joe Woodard'**, a yellow shrub introduced in 2007 and sold as a fund-raiser for the Dallas Area Historic Rose Society). A living icon of the Texan preservation movement is the San Antonio foundling **"Flores Street House Eater."** (Rosarians speculate that the plant may actually be **'Lamarque'**, a sweet-scented 1830 Noisette often trained up porches in the Old South). Anyone who confronts this gargantuan thicket of prickly canes and creamy white flowers—through which walls, a door, and windows are barely visible— suddenly realizes that tales about whole buildings swallowed by rosebushes aren't necessarily fanciful.

When the notorious Noisette blooms in April, rustlers descend on San Antonio. Regrettably, though, a few visitors have broken the cardinal rules of rose rustling: Never take a major chunk of a plant. Always ask the owner's permission before cutting a slip. Do not snoop around after dark. After announcing that he was fed up with chasing rose poachers off his property, the current owner of "Flores Street House Eater" erected a chain-link fence that keeps most of the canes out of reach. But veteran rustlers know that in no time at all the rose will devour the fence.

SINGLE'S BETTER

Harmon Saville—"Harm" to his many friends—proved that everything old is new again when he introduced his latest hybrid, **'Single's Better'**, in 1985. The mossy bud of this miniature rosebush opens to an exquisitely simple flower with only five petals, a form that botanists call "single." Harm had an eye for good roses, and his California nursery, Nor'East Miniature Roses, was legendary for high-quality hybrids. Still, he couldn't help but wonder whether the public would share the controversial opinion stated on his brand-new label.

The most popular mass-market roses of the eighties were voluptuous "doubles," having flowers with at least twenty-five petals each. ("Semi-double" or "semi-plena," as in the old white roses **'Blanche Semi-Double'** and *Rosa* x *alba* **'Semiplena'**, denotes six to twelve petals.) Responding to the expansive mood of the decade when pouf skirts, cabbage rose–festooned curtains, and multiple financing were all the rage, growers strove to produce full-blown varieties flaunting names like **'Double Delight'**, **'Double Star'**, and **'Double Perfection'**. Harm asked himself whether customers would joke that a meager five-petaled mini didn't even look like a rose. Fortunately for him, the answer was a resounding no. Instead of getting laughed off nursery shelves, 'Single's Better' rang up serious profits. When Sean McCann, an international authority on miniature roses, pronounced it "a new rose with an old look," he meant his remark as praise.

Species roses—nature's originals and the oldest roses known to man—are all singles. Many early hybrids are, too. Old garden roses with names such as **'Presque Simple'**, *R. muscosa* **'Simplex'**, and **'Single May Rose'** were popular before the mid-Victorian vogue for newfangled extravaganzas with densely packed petals. Exhibiting these doubles at flower shows and horticultural exhibitions became a fashionable sport for the gardening elite of nineteenth-century Europe and America. Single roses fell out of style, scorned for being unsophisticated and plain.

Nurseries soon deleted singles from their catalogs and gardeners weeded them from their beds to make room for larger, more opulent blooms. Some fancy hybrids incorporated "double" (conveniently the same word in French and English) into their official titles—**'Double Moss Rose'**, **'Double Brique'**, **'Panachée Double'**—to avoid confusion with humble like-named single cousins. It seemed as if hybrid teas, the most sought-after fin-de-siècle roses, couldn't be too rich or too heavy. The weighty blossoms of some doubles bent branches so low that gardeners inserted stakes and props to keep flowers out of the mud.

'SINGLE'S BETTER'

Meanwhile, single roses were banished to outlying shrubberies and semi-wild hedgerows. There, thriving on neglect, these stalwarts displayed their fresh, fragrant blooms, as if waiting patiently for fashion to smile on them again. And, in time, it did.

The same broom that swept excessive ornament from early-twentieth-century art and design also passed through the garden. *Victorian* became a slur. During the decade before the First World War, up-to-date rose catalogs promoted the very latest thing: single-flowered hybrid teas. The English rosarian E. A. Bunyard wrote in 1916, "Singles are God-made, doubles are man-made." This conviction still resonates in the name of a floribunda bred in

A DOUBLE-FLOWERED MOSS ROSE DEPICTED IN 1873

the United States a quarter century later: **'Nearly Wild'**. As a hybrid, the plant by definition resulted from human tinkering. But, being single, it looked as though mother nature had produced it on her own.

By 1920 dozens of novel long-stemmed hybrids with just five petals had won top prizes at prestigious flower exhibitions — and finally gained acceptance in conservative social circles. A founding member of Great Britain's Royal National

Rose Society gladly permitted a five-petaled hybrid tea to bear her name, **'Mrs. Oakley Fisher'**, upon its introduction in 1921. When it came to labeling such plants, however, breeders still shied away from the blunt "single" and "simple," opting for subtler allusions, such as **'Dainty Bess'** (Bess was the wife of English breeder W. E. B. Archer) and **'Innocence'**.

Some observers drew a straight line from single roses to the pared-down aesthetic of the Bauhaus and other modernist design movements. A member of the Royal National Rose Society remarked in 1937: "The single blooming rose, **'Ellen Willmott'** [a hybrid tea with four-to-eight-petaled white flowers], is like the latest block of modern flats, compared to the Viennese baroque palaces of **'George Dickson'** [a 1912 hybrid tea whose crimson blooms flaunted as many as forty petals apiece]."

The singular sensation started in Britain but soon caught on around the world. Most new converts welcomed singles not as harbingers of no-nonsense modernism but as quaint throwbacks to the chaste elegance of pre-Victorian times. This old-fashioned aura made these plants ideal candidates for English-

THE SINGLE-FLOWERED HYBRID TEA 'INNOCENCE'

cottagy herbaceous borders and Colonial Revival formal gardens, the epitome of good taste during most of the twentieth century. Nurseries also seized the opportunity to promote simpler varieties as ideal for flower gardeners who ordinarily steered clear of roses. Some singles masqueraded under the names of other plants, such as **'Clematis'** (a 1924 rambler), or were described as looking like anemones or California poppies — anything but stereotypical Victorian roses.

BEYOND THE FRINGE

Astute hybridizing as well as accidental mutations can alter petal shapes from classically smooth to ragged and pointy. The hybrid rugosa **'Fimbriata'** ("frilled" in Latin) is also known as **'Phoebe's Frilled Pink'** and **'Dianthiflora'** ("carnation flower") because of its petals delicately fringed edges. **'Serratipetala'**, a pink China originally known in France as **'Fimbriata à Pétales Frangés'**, produces petals whose edges are both serrated and fringed (*frangé* in French). Quill-like pointed petals distinguish the nineteenth-century **'Sharp-petalled China Rose'** and **'Cramoisie Picotée'** (the French *cramoisie* means "crimson," and *picoté*, either "pricked with holes" or "pecked at") as well as the modern white and red miniatures **'Picotee'** and **'Zig-Zag'**.

Perhaps the strangest floral formations result from what rosarians call a "vegetative center," the fortuitous emergence of a new stem and flower bud from the center of an open bloom. This bizarre phenomenon — *proliferation* in botanical terminology — occurs in many kinds of flowers. In his *Metamorphose der Pflanzen*, published in 1790, Goethe described proliferation as a significant phase of plant evolution and cataloged examples among anemones, carnations, and roses. Linneaus dismissed such occurrences as "monstrosities," but Redouté, in his third volume (1824) of *Les roses*, illustrated three proliferous roses (characterized in the text as "transient freaks"): *R. damascena Celsiana prolifera*, which produced more vegetation than flowers; *R. gallica Agatha* var. *prolifera*, said to generate a *third* bloom out of the proliferated flower; and *R. centifolia prolifera foliacea*, whose piggybacked flower exhibited foliage entirely different from the parent plant's.

A few specialty nurseries currently sell a variety labeled **'Prolifera de Redouté'**, although it's uncertain which of Redouté's trio this descends from. **'Celsiana'** is still known to proliferate from time to time, and South Carolina rose rustler Ruth Knopf recently discovered a merlot-colored hybrid China with a pointy green vegetative center, now on the market as **"Ruth's Steeple Rose."**

The species *R. monstrosa* (meaning "monstrous rose," aka the **'Green Rose'**) produces a flower composed entirely of sepals, the green leaflike structures that sheathe a rosebud. **'Asepala'** ("without sepals" in Latin), a pink-edged flesh-colored moss rose grown in 1840, acquired that name (**'Sans Sépales'** in its native France) because its buds at first appeared to lack this green covering. In fact, 'Asepala' did have sepals, but they were inconspicuously short. Once sold as a curiosity at the Buist Nursery in Philadelphia, 'Asepala' no longer exists.

SWEETHEART ROSE

B ACK IN THE DAY when people under fifty years of age uttered the word *sweetheart* without an ironic twist, the dainty pink flowers and almost thornless stems of the **'Sweetheart Rose'** made a swell bouquet for a beau to press into his darling's hand. If she blushed as she poked her nose among the petals, to inhale their delicate scent, this might well lead to a different bouquet, the kind that's carried down the aisle. Of course, in an era that greeted roses like **'Gay Heart'** (a 1951 American floribunda) with a straight face, hardly anyone questioned which gender carried, tossed, and caught a wedding bouquet.

Roses have symbolized nuptial bliss since antiquity. Greeks and Romans garlanded a happy couple with roses, in hopes that Hymen, the god of marriage, would smile upon their union. A Roman called his beloved *mea rosa* "my rose." Medieval Christians throughout Europe wove the flowers into a chaplet to crown the bridal veil. A Russian bride circled her brow with red roses, whereas an altar-bound Scottish lass shunned red roses as unlucky—unless her father gave them to her. Armenians decorated the hands of the bride-to-be by laying a rose leaf or petal in each palm and staining the skin around it with henna; the matrimonial toast was drunk in rose syrup. Before her wedding, a Frenchwoman cast petals from her bridal wreath onto a nearby pond or river, with a wish that the bloom of youth would never abandon her. In America, Samuel Parsons noted in 1869, "the toilet of a bride is never considered perfect unless she wears a wreath of roses or other flowers, whose snow-white hue is an emblem of her departing maidenhood."

Today's bride can receive a shower complete with "Sweetheart Rose"–printed paper plates, cups, and napkins; register for "Sweetheart Rose"–pattern china, crystal, and sterling; and order "Sweetheart Roses" online, for her bouquet and the groom's boutonniere. Whether she will actually get the specific flower that horticulturists call 'Sweetheart Rose' is another matter, since — like 'American Beauty' — this name has come to loosely embrace assorted flowers. Now and then, even rosarians bicker about the identity of the true 'Sweetheart Rose.' Most agree, though, that it is a French-bred bush, no taller than three feet, with approximately two-inch blooms that entered horticultural society in 1881 under the formal name **'Mademoiselle Cécile Brunner'**. The French *Journal des Roses* identified the dedicatee as "the charming daughter of the late Ulrich Brunner,

'MADEMOISELLE CÉCILE BRUNNER' FROM THE 1885 FRENCH REVIEW *JOURNAL DES ROSES*

rose-grower at Lausanne." Born in August 1879, this Swiss miss was evidently named after her paternal grandmother, Maria Cécilia, and her father's sister, Cécile. Records in Lausanne's municipal archives indicate that after his nursery business foundered, Ulrich left both city and family behind, apparently never to return. Understandably wary, his daughter waited until she was thirty-eight before marrying and having a child.

Through some stranger-than-fiction coincidence, a 'Mademoiselle Cécile Brunner' bush raised by one Cecil Brunner—a French-born horticulturist living in Riverside, California, during the 1890s—spontaneously put forth a "sport" with longer canes, which eventually came on the market as **'Climbing Cécile Brunner'**. A rumor began to circulate, asserting that the California Brunner had not only created the *parent* bush but named it after his niece. In 1926 this canard came to the attention of another French transplant, the rosarian Jean Henri Nicolas, who shot it down with a stern letter to the editor of *The Flower Grower*. Adieu, false sweetheart.

MODERN ROMANCE

Here's how the love story unfolds:

'Puppy Love': It's an orange and pink miniature.

'Flirtation': Gold on top, pink below, this hybrid tea blooms in flushes all season long.

'First Kiss': The mild-scented pink floribunda is a child of **'Simplicity'**.

'Prom Date': It's a deep blush pink miniature.

'Lovers Lane': 'Red Devil' lurks in this scarlet hybrid tea's genealogy.

'Commitment': This climber blooms a solid dark red.

'Marry Me': It's an enticingly fragrant pink mini.

'Engagement': The pink mini's ancestors include **'Jubilant'** and **'Dearest'**.

'Bridal Shower': Light pink flowers cluster generously on this floribunda.

'June Wedding': An individual plant of this hybrid tea may bloom in various shades of white.

'The Bride': This white tea blushes ever so faintly at the tips of its petals.

'Blushing Groom': One of this white mini's parents is **'Rise 'n' Shine'**.

'Wedding Ring': A golden yellow hybrid tea.

'Honeymoon': The ancestors of this fragrant yellow floribunda include **'Peace'** and **'Rapture'**.

'Pillow Talk': This mauve floribunda resulted from crossing **'Angel Face'** and **'Plain Talk'**.

'The Stork': A pink hybrid tea (no longer available), it was bred from **'The Doctor'**.

'Baby Blanket': This spreading light pink floribunda makes a good ground cover.

'Home Sweet Home': It's a pink hybrid tea with a full damask scent.

'Silver Anniversary': The white flowers of this hybrid tea are exceptionally full.

'Temptation': A carmine large-flowered climber, it blooms continually throughout the season.

'Reconciliation': This sensitive apricot hybrid tea needs to be protected during a harsh winter.

'Together Forever': Sad to say, the Irish orange-pink hybrid tea is unavailable in the United States and Canada.

TEA ROSE

O PEN A TIN OF tea and sniff. You're inhaling the very aroma that enchanted English flower lovers in 1809, when the original tea rose, a Chinese import, first bloomed in the Western world. Fragrance has always played a crucial part in determining the popularity of a rose, and never more so than for this variety and the generation of hybrids it spawned.

The source of the name *tea rose* has certainly stimulated lively theorizing. Some speculate that it reflects the Asian custom of scenting tea by steeping rose petals in the pot. Others propose that similarities between the new growth on tea plants and on rosebushes prompted the link. Still others ascribe the name to the possibility that traders packed Chinese roses in tea crates infused with the odor of their former contents or that large quantities of fresh China tea leaves carried as cargo imparted their subtle bouquet to rose plants in transit on the same clipper ships.

No solid evidence proves any of these hypotheses. All we know for sure is that the earliest tea rose in Europe sailed from Canton to London under the aegis of the East India Tea Company, and that nineteenth-century Western accounts repeatedly mention the tealike perfume of newly opened blooms as the reason for the term *tea rose*. This is more than a matter of folklore. In justifying the scientific name they gave the rose, *Rosa odorata* ("scented rose"), the British botanists H. C. Andrews and Robert Sweetby cited the similarity of the flower's strong scent to that of dried tea leaves—a scent then present in no other rose, including two other recent imports from the Far East, **'Parsons' Pink China'** and **'Slater's Crimson China'**.

The momentous first flowering of *R. odorata* occurred on the Hertfordshire estate of Sir Abraham Hume, a collector of Old Master paintings and rare Chinese plants. The baronet supposedly called his light-pink-petaled acquisition **'Hume's Blush'**, in honor of his wife, Lady Amelia (having named a pale-rose-tinged Chinese camellia 'Lady Hume's Blush' a few years before, he may have wanted to share the credit this time). Despite its unique fragrance and unusual, in that era, ability to rebloom all season long, the rose had serious flaws: weak growth, fragile flowers, and a susceptibility to damage by cold weather. To play down these drawbacks, and emphasize the plant's main asset, a London nursery marketed it as **'Hume's Blush Tea-scented China'**.

This stratagem apparently worked, because the English supplier of Chinese imports to Empress Joséphine of France placed an order for his client. That Great Britain and the French empire were then at war posed only a

REDOUTÉ'S 'TEA-SCENTED CHINA' IS ALSO KNOWN AS 'HUME'S BLUSH TEA-SCENTED CHINA'.

minor obstacle. In 1810 England's prince regent, a great admirer of Joséphine, granted special permission for a cross-Channel plant shipment to breach the naval blockade. Safely in France, 'Hume's Blush Tea-scented China' proved a viable seed producer, yielding nearly two hundred hybrids over the next twenty-five years, all endowed with that distinctive tea fragrance. (The palette expanded beyond pink after another Far Eastern exotic, **'Park's Yellow Tea-scented China'**, hopped from England to France.) A French gardener, one M. LeRouge, wrote of 'Hume's Blush' that "its India Tea scent perfumes the sitting room." Some rosarians contend that LeRouge's application of the phrase *à odeur de thé* ("with the scent of tea") to that rose and its offspring in 1819 marks the true beginning of the rose class we know today as "tea."

Of the small number of tender French hybrids that survived their first winter outside a greenhouse, only a handful went abroad, but that happy few — with names like **'Odoratissima'** and **'Odorata Nouvelle'** — became international sensations. The chic mid-nineteenth-century hostess had a potted tea rose in her conservatory and cut tea roses in her drawing room, to waft what the popular English garden writer Shirley Hibberd called, "a sublime edition of the odour of the first-rate orange-scented Pekoe."

Extensive hybridizing eventually diluted, and sometimes eliminated, that fragrance in many new varieties. To compensate, or avoid charges of false advertising, growers shortened the title of this rose class from "tea-scented" to "tea." Crossing just plain teas with other garden roses yielded a third class, the "hybrid tea." Adding to the confusion are individual varieties with tea-related names. The hybrid tea **'Typhoo Tea'**, for example, has flowers whose red petals match the packaging of its namesake, a well-known British breakfast blend, but whose fruity aroma doesn't smell anything like tea. Although **'Sir Thomas Lipton'** was named after the Scottish tea mogul, it salutes his prowess as a yachtsman not his success as a merchant; moreover it isn't a tea rose but a hybrid rugosa. If you stick your nose into Sir Thomas's large white flowers, you will enjoy one of the "old rose" fragrances that scented the garden before 'Hume's Blush' upset the perfume tray.

TODAY WHEN SOMEBODY SAYS, "Now *that* smells like a rose," chances are he or she has just had a close encounter with a flower that exudes the old-rose scent, even if the plant in question is a recently created hybrid. Louise Beebe Wilder wrote in her 1932 classic *The Fragrant Path*, "The true old rose scent, the scent that has charmed humanity from time immemorial, is assuredly the most exquisite and refreshing of all floral odours — pure, transparent, incomparable — an odour into which we may, so to speak, burrow deeply without finding anything coarse or bitter, in which we may touch bottom without losing our sense of exquisite pleasure." Some nostrils detect essences of fruit, spice, or other flowers as part of the old-rose mix. Roses with R. *wichurana* in their heritage, including numerous climbing roses and shrub roses such as **'Apple Blossom'** and **'Applejack'**, have a trace of green apples in their petals. Several garden varieties that bloom only once a season — a group especially rich in old-rose fragrance — became such staples of the commercial perfumer's art that they acquired "trade" names like **'Rosier des Parfumeurs'** ("rosebush of the perfumers") and **'Rose à Parfum de Grasse'** (referring to the French fragrance-manufacturing center, Grasse). Their flowers have been used for centuries to make rose attar.

As the late-Victorian and Edwardian craze for eye-catching hybrid teas took the spotlight from other types of roses, growers focused on breeding for color and shape, even at the expense of fragrance. Consequently, a vast number of twentieth-century hybrids lack any perceptible scent. Not until the revival of perennial borders, old-fashioned cottage gardens, and old-fashioned flowers during the 1970s did nurserymen begin to heed an oft-repeated plaint: "Roses don't smell anymore!" Hybridizers brought long-neglected antiques down from the garden attic, as an aid to engineering the newest thing: old-rose scent. The hybrid tea **'Fragrant Memory'**, introduced in 1974, blazed a trail for

WORKERS IN A NINETEENTH-CENTURY ROSE-OIL FACTORY IN GRASSE, FRANCE

'**Scentimental**', '**Fragrant Dream**', and '**Pure Perfume**'. After '**Overnight Scentsation**' was launched into outer space in 1998, on board the NASA shuttle *Discovery*, scientists discovered that the tea fragrance its flower exudes on earth changes to an old-rose scent in a gravity-free environment.

HEAVENLY SMELLS CAN BE downright earthy. Musk rose, *R. moschata*, takes its name from a potently odorous substance extracted from an abdominal gland of the male musk deer that has long been an ingredient in perfume. Our word *musk* may be anatomically incorrect, since it possibly derives from the Sanskrit and Persian for "testicle." Although this natural aromatic — or the synthetic substitutes now required by law — is sometimes valued for its own pungent, heavy scent, it is more frequently used to enhance and prolong less assertive fragrances. When Renaissance herbalists and poets praised the musk rose for its spicy sweetness, they had in mind the sort of perfume whose animal magnetism doesn't come on the hoof.

'**Myrrh-scented Rose**', aka '**Splendens**' — the rose of choice for covering arbors and walls in early Victorian gardens — fills the air with a resinous fragrance that the wise men of biblical times deemed a worthy gift for a king. Sometimes, though, it's wiser not to stop and smell the roses. The pretty golden flowers of '**Austrian Yellow**', for instance, can't mask the appropriateness of its botanical name, *R. foetida*: Even people who don't consider this species fetid allow that it smells like linseed oil. Then there's **"Unknown Moth-proof Maude,"** found in a Texas cemetery by rose expert Field Roebuck, who says that its mauve blooms give off "a very pronounced fragrance of an old cedar chest with a hint of turpentine." The booby prize goes to the French

'Le Rire Niais' ("the silly laugh"), alias **'The Stinkbug'**. You've got to respect this rose. Yes, it reeks at close range, but after hanging around for a couple of centuries, it's still going strong.

A BOUQUET OF ROSES

Ever since Pierre-François-Pascal Guerlain launched his perfume Extract of Roses in 1828, the House of Guerlain has relied on French attar distilled from **'Rose de Mai'** ("May rose"), a *Rosa centifolia* hybrid. The formulas for Guerlain scents such as Shalimar (1925), Guerlarose (1930), and Une Rose (1947) all incorporate this natural oil.

Defying the dictates of couturière Coco Chanel—"I want to give women artificial perfume . . . I don't want any rose or lily of the valley"—Ernest Beaux, the fashion designer's professional "nose," surrendered to floral temptation. When Marilyn Monroe told the world that all she wore to bed were a few drops of Chanel No. 5, she was sleeping with essences of 'Rose de Mai' and jasmine.

The hybrid perpetual rose **'Général Jacqueminot'** captured the sweet smell of success for the Coty perfumery. A native of Corsica, allegedly related to Napoléon, François Coty (christened Joseph Marie François Spoturno) learned about fragrance in the rose fields and rose-oil distilleries of Grasse. Unlike all perfumers before him, who sold their products in plain utilitarian bottles, Coty marketed La Rose Jacqueminot, his premier scent, in a stylish Baccarat crystal flask. He jump-started his career in 1905 with what may have been a well-planned accident in an elegant Paris department store. Legend has it that Coty or his wife dropped a sample of La Rose Jacqueminot on the selling floor, shattering it and releasing the fragrance. Enticed by the scent, shoppers clamored to buy it. The store gave Coty a large order, and he became the talk of Paris.

TOURNAMENT OF ROSES

OOTBALL HAD NOTHING TO do with it when residents of Pasadena, California, kicked off the first Tournament of Roses Parade on New Year's Day 1890. Members of a local hunt club had conceived the event as a chance to promote their community's balmy climate to winter-weary easterners and midwesterners. "In New York, people are buried in the snow," one clubman declared. "Here our flowers are blooming and our oranges are about to bear. Let's hold a festival to tell the world about our paradise." They modeled their parade after the Bataille de Fleurs ("Battle of Flowers") in Nice, a winter carnival made famous when the Riviera's elite drove blossom-bedecked carriages through the city. In Pasadena two thousand spectators cheered as the hometown bon ton rolled by in horse-drawn buggies garlanded with freshly picked blooms.

The parade became one of *roses* because these flowers — the pride

'TOURNAMENT OF ROSES'

of Southern California gardens — far outnumbered any other blooms on display. Today about nine hundred thousand flowers decorate the average float. Sturdier varieties are glued to a mesh framework; the stems of less durable blossoms rest in individual water vials. Early promoters called the pageant a "tournament" because the festivities culminated in a chivalric tourney with equestrian lancers vying to spear a series of rings. Even though a storm decimated the floral harvest right before the 1892 parade, nearly causing the occasion to be retitled Tournament of Oranges, the original name survived.

For several decades, tournament organizers varied the postparade show by

ROSE-BEDECKED AUTOMOBILES IN THE 1905 TOURNAMENT OF ROSES PARADE

presenting attractions such as bronco-busting, ostrich races, and a race between an elephant and a camel. A brief fling with football in 1902, pitting the University of Michigan against California's own Stanford, ended disastrously when Michigan's 49–0 victory set off a stampede. Polo replaced football the following year but drew a meager turnout. Crowds returned when the program switched to *Ben-Hur*–inspired chariot races, which continued until 1915, when flagging public interest and exorbitant costs brought these hazardous spectacles to a halt. Pasadena tentatively picked up the pigskin again in 1916, hosting a football game between Brown and Washington State. That event proved successful enough to make the sport a permanent fixture.

In 1961 the horseshoe-shaped tournament stadium, officially named the Rose Bowl in 1923, got its own floral mascot, **'Rose Bowl'**. Appropriately, the scarlet hybrid tea's parents were red-blooded **'Mardi Gras'** (a link to the pre-Lenten carnival tradition of the Bataille de Fleurs) and **'Chrysler Imperial'** (the official car for Tournament of Roses Parade dignitaries since the 1950s). The pink floribunda **'Tournament of Roses'** came out in 1988, ready to celebrate the Tournament's centennial, in 1989. At that Rose Bowl the Michigan Wolverines defeated the University of Southern California Trojans. USC fans did not stampede but swore revenge—which they took at the very next year's bowl game, when the Trojans trounced the Wolverines. Maybe **'Trojan Victory'**, a team-color cardinal red hybrid tea sold at scholarship fund-raisers by the USC Alumni Association, brought them luck.

GOOD SPORTS

W hen ranking these roses for garden performance, look beyond size and team colors. Keep in mind that, like any plant, rose varieties must be handicapped for U.S. Department of Agriculture zone, soil composition, exposure to sun and wind, and other key physical conditions. All-rounders include **'Athlete'**, a red hybrid tea; **'Rookie'**, a white miniature; and **'Olympiad'**, a red hybrid tea named the official rose of the 1984 Summer Olympics. Sorry, basketball fans, the only hoops we've found in the rose garden are for training stems.

BASEBALL

'Babe Ruth': A repeat-blooming orange-pink hybrid tea with a strong fragrance. It was bred in 1950, two years after the Sultan of Swat passed away.

'Connie Mack': Red (a team color) 1952 floribunda marking Mack's half century as manager (and, latterly, part owner) of the Philadelphia Athletics.

'Field of Dreams': Pink-yellow floribunda introduced fourteen years after the 1989 hit movie about a baseball diamond in a cornfield. If you plant it, bees will come.

'Home Run': This is really a double: a 1956 pink hybrid tea and a 2001 red shrub.

BOXING

'Knockout': Stunning red shrub. It is very disease resistant.

'Max Schmeling': Orange-red German floribunda hybridized in 1973, honoring Germany's former World Heavyweight Champion. Famous in the U.S. for his two bouts with Joe Louis, he was less well known for helping Jewish children flee the Nazis.

CRICKET

'I Zingari': This hybrid musk is named after one of England's oldest cricket clubs (founded in 1845) because its scarlet and orange flowers reminded the grower of the club colors.

FOOTBALL

'Pop Warner': Fake pass! White and pink hybrid tea named after Texas rosarian A. J. "Pop" Warner, not the gridiron "Pop," coach Glenn Scobie Warner.

'Touchdown': Red miniature.

GOLF

'Gary Player': This orange hybrid tea was bred in the pro's native South Africa in 1968, the year Player won the British Open for the second time.

'Golf': Golf-ball-white shrub.

'Hole in One': Country-club-pink-striped floribunda.

HORSE RACING

'Jockey': A compact red floribunda.

'Kentucky Derby': This floribunda is red, like the garland of 554 roses presented to each year's winner, a custom that gave the race its nickname, "the Run for the Roses."

'Royal Ascot': Pink hybrid tea. It recalls the flowers on extravagant hats women wear to the English races.

SOCCER

'Middlesborough Football Club': A floribunda in bright red, which is the official color of this pro team in the United Kingdom where soccer is commonly known as "football."

'Pelé': Vigorous white hybrid tea. Named after American rose breeder Frank A. Benardella's dalmatian, it is so called because the dog's black and white markings resembled those of a soccer ball, which in turn evoked Brazilian football star Pelé.

'Wembley Stadium': Pink floribunda. The London stadium is England's national soccer field.

TENNIS

'Centre Court': White hybrid tea edged with pink.

'Chris Evert': Named in 1997 for first player to win one thousand singles matches (in 1984). The grower calls this hybrid tea's orange with red edge a "grand slam" (like **'Grand Slam'**, a red hybrid tea).

XANADU

Y OU COULD CUT THE tension with a budding knife. Dinner is over, the tables have been cleared, and the few brave souls who dare to linger in the banquet hall brace themselves for a challenge: who will win at Rose Alphabet? Although never on the official agenda, a round of this word game provides the raucous climax to many a Heritage Rose Foundation gathering. One tournament, in the mid-1990s, spawned the idea of a rose named **'Xanadu'** (selection of the actual plant, an orange-pink-flowered shrub, came later). For poetry readers, Xanadu conjures up the "stately pleasure-dome" in Coleridge's "Kubla Khan." For movie buffs, it recalls the mansion in *Citizen Kane* and the title of the 1980 Olivia Newton John disco cult classic (replayed on Broadway). But for rose geeks, those three syllables add up to one thing: a winning *X* up your sleeve for Alphabet.

Excitement begins to mount as the letter *A* is announced. All eyes focus on the first player; there's a designated batting order, and each contestant must take his turn or drop out. "**'Adam'**!" shouts player number 1. (*Way too easy.*) "**'Betty Boop'**," chirps player 2. (*Hmm, a modernist.*) "**'Crépuscule'**." (Oh là là—*each vowel enunciated perfectly.*) "**'Duquesa de Peñaranda'**." (*The palatal nasal as smooth as silk. Just enough roll to the* R. *Truly a sophisticated competition.*) But even before the windup for *E*, everyone on deck nervously counts ahead twenty turns. (*Please, please let me not be* X . . .)

Not that Alphabet doesn't set other traps. Take *Q*: There are more than three dozen 'Queen . . .'s to choose from, but for some reason many rookies choke after they've played **'Queen Elizabeth'**. *U* often throws a curve ball—it's so easy to forget **'Uncle Sam'** when a seasoned pro pitches one foreign zinger after another; **'Ulrich Brunner fils'** rattles any greenhorn. *Z* is tough. Few competitors remember the recent influx of patented code names based on breeders' commercial acronyms, even though these legal designations are in bounds. For example, some forty rose names start with "ZIP," the code for grower Herbert Zipper. (**'ZIPtease'**, anyone?) First to go, however, is usually **'Zéphirine Drouhin'** or **'Zeus'**. Only hard-core rosomaniacs speed-pitch arcana like **'Zell'** (a red American mini), **'Zigeunerknabe'** (**'Gypsy Boy'** in German, a major language in pre–World War I Hungary where this purplish Bourbon was bred), and **'Zayed of Abu Dhabi'** (a dark red French shrub introduced in 2006 as a memorial to the first president of the United Arab Emirates).

X marks the sweet spot for aspiring champions. Veterans memorize the *X* page from the latest edition of *Modern Roses* or the *Combined Rose List*. With only a dozen names beginning in *X*, this is a snap—but it won't be for long, if Florida rosarian, amateur hybridizer, and would-be Rose Alphabet champion Malcolm M. Manners has anything to do with it. Having bred 'Xanadu', number twelve in the *X* file, in 2002, he plans to introduce other names with that initial for the sole purpose of acing his rival Rose Foundation members. Hint: lucky number thirteen may relate to Xochimilco, an ancient Aztec lake. Dr. Manners refuses to divulge column *X* on his expanding Chinese scorecard, which extends beyond the Asian standbys **'Xiang Fen Lian'**, **'Xiao Feng Chan Yue'**, and **'Xing Hong Shao Yao'**. Let the games begin!

BLOOPERS

As an entertaining alternative to Rose Alphabet, participants in the 1998 Heritage Rose Foundation conference took turns dreaming up excruciatingly wry parodies of standard rose names. Malcolm Manners jotted down the results, which included 'Aphid Queen', 'Bad Breedin', 'Ill de Bourbon', 'Slugfest', 'Way Too Wild', and 'Xhausted'. These inventions were in wickedly bad taste but no worse than what some real plants have gotten stuck with. Consider the following:

'Angel Dust': When she christened this white miniature in 1978, the American grower was unaware that its name doubled as slang for the controlled substance PCP.

'Aspirin Rose': The disease-resistant white floribunda was introduced in Germany in 1997 to honor the centenary of the pain reliever's formulation by Friedrich Bayer and Company.

'Electric Blanket': Although the floribunda's flowers are a high-voltage salmon pink and the shrubby plant does make a good ground cover, the label should have been mothballed.

'Droopy-leaved Rose': It seems kinder to address this native of India and southeast Asia as *Rosa clinophylla*—and to focus on its sweet-scented white single blooms.

'Dropmore Yellow': Rose gardeners dread the premature fall of yellow foliage caused by insects, disease, and stress. The Canadian who named this hybrid after his hometown, Dropmore, must have perpetrated the pun unwittingly.

'Fanny Bias': A tribute to an early nineteenth-century French ballerina, this light pink gallica has nothing to do with **'Happy Butt'**. The deliberately punning name of that American apricot pink hybrid tea came from a lame joke about a little girl who mispronounced the second syllable of *her* name, "Gladys."

'Flush o' Dawn': The pink-to-white shading of this 1900 hybrid tea evokes an early-morning sky, but gardeners who find the name reminiscent of household plumbing prefer the slightly tweaked variant **'Blush o' Dawn'**.

'Gypsy Moth': Something got lost in translation when the German breeder of this orange-pink floribunda typed its label. The destructive leaf-eating gypsy moth caterpillar horrifies American tree lovers.

'Mutant Charisma': The smoky red floribunda's name conjures up a sinister alien. "Mutant," however, merely records that the cultivar originated as a sport of another rose, **'Charisma'**.

'Pest': Released in Hungary in 1993, this dark red floribunda celebrates the former sister city of Buda.

'Ralph's Creeper': American breeder Ralph S. Moore developed the low spreading shrub with brilliant red and yellow flowers, which is often used as a ground cover. Landscapers have nicknamed it "Creepy."

'DROOPY-LEAVED ROSE' IS MORE FORMALLY KNOWN AS *ROSA CLINOPHYLLA*.

YELLOW ROSE OF TEXAS

W HAT MANY TEXANS CHERISH as their yellow rose hails from the wide open spaces of—hold your hat—New York City. George Folliott Harison, a reclusive lawyer, created this spring bloomer in the early 1830s, either on his family's Manhattan estate, Mount Sinai, in a then semirural area bounded by present-day Eighth and Ninth avenues between Thirtieth and Thirty-first streets, or in the "Amateur's Garden" he established ten blocks north of there around 1833. His property lay in the countryside west of present-day Times Square that was a center for commercial nurseries. In his private greenhouse, Harison bred new varieties of roses as well as other plants, such as *Camellia japonica* var. **'Harrisoni'** [*sic*].

Exactly how Harison (1776–1846) produced his namesake rose is a mystery, for he kept no records of his work. A visitor to his country place in March 1837 describes a haphazard modus operandi: "Mr. Harrison [*sic*] appears to practice hybridization without any regard to the mixing of two particular sorts to produce an intermediate variety; but whenever a flower opens on plants that generally produce seed, the stigmas are impregnated with the pollen of some sort in order to fertilize them." Whatever his technique, he struck gold with the shrub rose that became known as **'Harrison's Yellow'**, the first rose of that color ever created in the United States. Another mystery surrounds the origin of the curious spelling **'Harison's Yellow'**, invariably used now. In all accounts from the 1830s, the names of both the breeder and his rose have a double *r*, although a will filed by Harison's father, Richard, consistently gives his name with a single *r*. This was the spelling handed down in the family since patriarch Francis Harison, an English colonist, settled in New York in 1708.

The rose went on sale in 1835—as 'Harrison's Yellow'—at the Prince Nursery in Flushing, New York, an establishment founded almost a century ear-

lier. William Prince propagated the plants from one of Harison's seedlings, for which he had traded a valuable *Camellia aitoni*. Prince's catalog listed the rose as a "superb double yellow [that] blooms freely and profusely—$2," a high-ticket item, given that most of the firm's other roses then sold for $.50 apiece. The Manhattan nurseryman and florist Thomas Hogg

'HARISON'S YELLOW'

also sold specimens of this variety, which a colleague shipped to England as "Hogg's yellow American rose."

In the United States, 'Harrison's Yellow' soon became the most popular and most traveled hybrid of its day. Homesteaders headed for new territories in the West made room for the shrub in jam-packed Conestoga wagons. Like the pieces of fancy china they tucked into flour barrels, the precious bushes would help to civilize their frontier homes. Many of these transplants ended up in Texas, where settlers' descendants came to believe that the rose they grew up with was a regional native—the same **"Yellow Rose of Texas"** immortalized in the song with that title. Anyone who listens to the words of the song—either nineteenth-century minstrel-show versions or the bowdlerized lyrics of Mitch Miller's 1955 arrangement—realizes that the "rose" it celebrates is a woman, not a flower.

In the same year the Prince Nursery started selling 'Harrison's Yellow', Emily D. West, a freeborn African American, sailed from Connecticut, her home state, to the Mexican colony of Texas. She had contracted with the entrepreneur James Morgan to work as a servant in the town of New Washington, which soon became engulfed in the revolution for Texan independence from Mexico. On April 18, 1836, the Mexican general Antonio López de Santa Anna invaded the settlement, only to find that nearly all of its American-born citizens had fled. Scanty evidence suggests, however, that Emily may have been taken prisoner. All sorts of racy tales have sprung up around her activities during the next few days, but only hearsay supports these legends.

One account relates that the revolutionary leader Sam Houston, spying on the Mexican campsite from a nearby tree on the morning of April 21, spotted a "slave girl" fixing a champagne breakfast for Santa Anna. That afternoon, the story continues, while Texan troops routed the Mexican army, their commander skedaddled off the battlefield wearing nothing but underwear and a pair of slippers. Back in the tent, with the rest of his clothes, was Emily West, who had heroically distracted the general to give her countrymen time to stage a surprise attack.

West departed for New York in 1837, never to be heard of again — except, perhaps, in verse and lyrics. The earliest known title for the folk tune we know as "The Yellow Rose of Texas" appears to have been "Emily, the Maid of Morgan's Point," first published as sheet music in 1858. West has been described as a woman of mixed race, a mulatto, which means she may have had the light complexion known colloquially as yellow. The 1955 reprise muffled racial overtones by deleting a "darky" and decolorizing his beloved as "the sweetest little rosebud, / That Texas ever knew."

Its murky history notwithstanding, a yellow rose remains a token of Texan pride. Hotels, nightclubs, and dance groups flourish the flower in their names or logos. The fraternal order of the Knights of the Yellow Rose, whose members pin yellow rose insignia to their lapels, convenes every April on the site of Santa Anna's camp, to pay tribute to Emily West. In celebration of Texas independence, the Dallas Area Historical Rose Society's newsletter, *The Yellow Rose*, annually features a yellow rose on the cover of its spring issue. Sometimes that flower is 'Harison's Yellow', but, as DAHRS officials explain cheerfully, just about any yellow rose will do.

NEW YORK'S FINEST

Two years after immigrating to New York City from his native Scotland, Thomas Hogg opened one of Manhattan Island's first retail nurseries in 1822. Called the New York Botanic Garden, it stood north of West Twenty-third Street, not far from the Harison homestead. Hogg's nursery became a popular weekend destination for city dwellers, who gaped at the wondrous merchandise: South American orchids, tropical aquatic plants, Asian camellias, and a profusion of imported and domestic roses — including 'Harrison's Yellow', **'Hogg's Straw-colored Rose'** (a seedling Hogg bred from 'Harrison's Yellow'), and another Harison novelty, **'Harrison's White'** (the last two are now extinct).

In 1838, unaware that 'Harrison's Yellow' already had a name, the English editor Robert Sweet illustrated this novelty in his prestigious journal, the *British Flower Garden*, as **'Hogg's Double Briar Yellow'** or *Rosa lutea* var. *Hoggii* with a note that "this variety was brought from New York by Mr James McNab, who received it from Mr Thomas Hogg, Nurseryman, in that city." As soon as Hogg got wind of this — and the embarrassing inference that he had created this plant — he added a note to his catalog stating unequivocally that the rose had been bred by fellow New Yorker George Harison. As New York expanded northward, Hogg relocated his nursery to the vicinity of East Eighty-sixth Street and Third Avenue, where he planted grand herbaceous borders and built greenhouses on twelve acres overlooking the Harlem River.

Roses of local origin appealed to civic pride. During the 1830s, the stylish Greenwich Village shop of nurserymen Michael Floy & Sons stocked the moss rose **'New York Seedling'**, the tea **'New York Odoratissima'**, and the eglantines **'New York Scarlet'** and **'New York White'**, all grown at the firm's distant Harlem outpost. Nevertheless, prestigious foreign roses far outnumbered the handful of Manhattan natives in the Floy catalog, which offered more than two hundred selections.

For true chic—in roses as in fashion and cuisine—status-conscious Knickerbockers looked to Paris. So when the Swiss horticulturist Daniel Boll opened a nursery where West Forty-second Street crossed Bloomingdale Road (now Broadway) in 1836, he advertised his establishment as French. Besides maintaining an open-air garden for the latest European roses trained into elegant treelike "standards," Boll erected a one-hundred-foot-long greenhouse for forcing tea roses, exotic annuals, and florist's blooms. Success enabled Boll to move into larger premises at what is now the northern tip of Times Square and lease land for plant propagation near West Ninety-sixth Street. Gardeners today can still plant two hybrid perpetuals created by Boll's French rose supplier, Joseph Boyau of Angers: carmine pink **'Madame Boll'**, an 1859 introduction honoring Daniel's wife, and **'Souvenir de Monsieur Boll'**, from 1866.

YORK AND LANCASTER

A GARDEN CAN BE A dangerous place. Case in point: Act II of Shakespeare's *Henry VI*, Part I. Two lords from rival branches of England's royal family, the House of York and the House of Lancaster, get into a spat over which side of the family deserves to wear the crown. Instead of drawing a line in the dirt, Richard Plantagenet picks a white rose off a nearby briar and dares every bystander who supports his cause to follow suit. Not to be outdone, his opponent, the Earl of Somerset, plucks a red rose to rally *his* backers. Gentlemen, choose your flowers! Eventually, the family feud escalates into the brutal Wars of the Roses, hostilities that will drag on through four decades—and seven more Shakespeare history plays.

Although followers of the White Rose of York and the Red Rose of Lancaster really did slaughter one another from 1455 to 1487 in a series of battles over royal succession, no evidence suggests that the conflict or its floral symbols originated in a garden squabble. These bellicose flowers had, in fact, entered service as heraldic symbols more than two hundred years earlier. Before appearing on banners, shields, and coats of arms, York's white rose probably started out as a wild variety of *R.* x *alba*, common in Britain and on the Continent. The earliest English king to wear the white rose as his badge was Henry III, who adopted it from his wife, Eleanor of Provence. She had carried her personal floral emblem across the Channel around 1236. (Henry's father had jauntily sprigged his helmet with a broom flower, *planta genesta* in Latin, source of the surname Plantagenet.) Through their son Edward I, the white rose descended to the House of York. But Edward's competitive younger sibling, Edmund, founder of the House of Lancaster, wanted a rose, too. The flower he snagged while on a mission in France—almost certainly *R. gallica* **'Officinalis'**—was just the ticket: a showy crimson bloom with a glamorous background, having reputedly come from exotic Syria.

Nine generations later, after copious bloodshed on both sides, the white rose and the red retracted their thorns for a strategic compromise: the marriage in 1486 of Elizabeth, Duchess of York, to Henry VII, a scion of the House of Lancaster. Henry's politic choice of badge, a stylized flower dubbed "the Tudor Rose" after his surname, paired white and red petals. Early in the reign of Henry's granddaughter Elizabeth I, a bicolor rose came to be known as **'York and Lancaster'**. In 1551 the Spanish physician and botanist Nicolás Monardes wrote a faithful description of the flower still grown today as 'York and Lancaster', or

'YORK AND LANCASTER'

R. x *damascena* **'Versicolor'**, citing "irregularly shaped flowers, that may be pure red or pure white, or part red and part white. Flowers of these different colorings may, and often do, appear on the same bush at the same time." Even now, this plant looks like a fulfillment of the hope voiced by Henry Tudor in Shakespeare's *Richard III*: "We will unite the white rose and the red: / Smile heaven upon this fair conjunction."

COMMEMORATION OF THE COUPLE WHO UNITED YORK AND LANCASTER

THE GAME IS UP

S hakespeare could not have foreseen where or how strife between White Rose and Red Rose loyalists would break out again. It happened in 1906—far from Bosworth Field where Henry Tudor won his decisive victory over Richard III—on a minor-league baseball diamond in Lancaster, Pennsylvania, the Red Rose City (its municipal seal incorporates the flower of its English namesake). In their first game ever against the White Roses of York, Pennsylvania's White Rose City (with seal to match), Lancaster's Red Roses won 9–4. This rivalry lasted until 1961, when the Red Roses stepped up to the plate for the last time. The White Roses faded away six years later. No one ever tried to merge the clubs into a 'York and Lancaster' hybrid with bicolor uniforms, although a Susquehanna Valley rugby-football club with members from both cities was organized in 2000 as the York & Lancaster Roses. The sister team for women plays as the York & Lancaster Thorns.

ACKNOWLEDGMENTS

We are especially grateful to Angela Miller and Kathleen Hackett, without whose guidance this book would never have taken root, and to Andra Miller, whose expert pruning gave it shape and helped it flower. Our thanks also go to the following people and organizations for the advice, assistance, and encouragement they generously provided:

The American Rose Society; Barnsley Gardens; Esty Brodsky; the Brooklyn Botanic Garden Library; Mandy Aftel at Aftelier Perfumes; Etienne Bouret; Tom Carruth at Weeks Roses; Mark E. Dixon; Dr. Jutta Dresch at Badisches Landesmuseum; Fabien Ducher at Roseraie Fabien Ducher; Bob Edberg; Meredith Flynn at Pasadena Tournament of Roses; Amy Gash; Margaret Gillespie; Jean-Pierre Guillot and Pascale Perraud at Roserie Guillot; Charlotte Haring, Betty Vickers, and Marilyn Wellan at the American Rose Center Library; Peter Harkness; the Heritage Rose Foundation; Jeanie Haupt at Greenheart Farms; Steve Hutton at Conard-Pyle Roses; Jeri Jennings at the Heritage Roses Group; Kenyon at imperialclub.com; Margaret Kieckhefer at the Library of Congress; Carolyn Kozo Cole at Los Angeles Public Library; Kent Krugh; Catherine Liles; Henry Liles; Gregg Lowery at Vintage Gardens; Glen MacLeod; Laura Maurer; the LuEsther T. Mertz Library at the New York Botanical Garden; Dr. Malcolm Manners; Phyllis McClintock at the Chrysler Historical Archives; Susan McCoy at Garden Media Group; Denise Otis; Amanda Perez at the Fragrance Foundation; the Schorr Rose Horticulture and Research Library; Elisabeth Scharlatt; Lily Shohan; Mike Shoup at the Antique Rose Emporium; the Speyer Foundation; United Methodist Archives Center at Drew University; Girija Viraragavan; George Wen; Debbie Zary at Jackson & Perkins.

GLOSSARY

AARS: All-America Rose Selections, an association of commercial rose growers who test new varieties in rose gardens throughout the United States

alba: An ancient class of roses that probably resulted from a cross between a damask or a gallica and some form of *Rosa canina* in southern or central Europe

antique rose: See **old garden rose**.

ARS: The American Rose Society, a nonprofit educational organization founded in 1892

attar: Fragrant oil extracted from rose petals

black spot: A fungal disease that causes leaves to develop dark blotches, turn yellow, and fall off

Bourbon: A class of everblooming roses that resulted from a chance cross between 'Autumn Damask' and 'Old Blush China' on the West Indian island formerly known as Ile de Bourbon, now Réunion

budding: A common process of grafting one rose variety onto the **rootstock** of another variety. The budding knife is a tool used for this purpose.

cane: The stem of a rose

centifolia: Short for *Rosa x centifolia* (aka 'Cabbage Rose'). A class of roses with extremely full-petaled rounded flowers that probably originated in sixteenth-century Holland. They bloom once a year.

China rose: A class of repeat-flowering varieties of Asian ancestry, first introduced in the West during the late eighteenth century

climber: A vigorous rosebush with long canes that can be trained against an arbor, trellis, wall, or other support

cross: See **hybridize**.

cultivar: A rose variety developed under cultivation

cutting: A piece, or slip, of a **cane** that can be rooted to develop into a new plant

damask: A class of intensely fragrant varieties that originated in the Middle East as naturally occurring hybrids

deadhead: To remove spent flowers to encourage reblooming

dieback: Sudden death of a **cane** caused by fungal diseases, pests, or damage

double: A rose flower with at least sixteen petals

everblooming: Flowering continually from the start of the season until the dormant period

floribunda: A class of bushy, cluster-flowered roses created in the twentieth century by crossing **polyantha** and **hybrid tea** varieties

florist rose: One of many varieties bred for the cut-flower market that generally thrive only under greenhouse conditions

foetida: A rose species native to the Middle East whose name comes from the Latin for "malodorous," because the flowers of R. *foetida* have a faintly unpleasant scent

found rose: A rose discovered growing in a garden or cemetery that has not yet been identified by its original name

gallica: A class of roses with large fragrant flowers that descends from the ancient species R. *gallica*

grandiflora: A class of large rosebushes with clustered flowers created in the twentieth century by crossing **floribunda** and **hybrid tea** varieties

heirloom rose: A variety that has been in existence for at least half a century

heritage rose: See **heirloom rose**.

hip: The fleshy seed capsule of a rose

hybrid: See **hybridize**.

hybridize: To create a new plant through the exchange of pollen between species or varieties; the result is a **hybrid**. This can occur in the wild through natural pollination of one plant by another. Under cultivation, it usually results from a hybridizer's deliberate transference of the pollen from one variety to the female reproductive part of another. This process is called a **cross**.

hybrid perpetual: A class of rose hybrids first bred in the 1830s to combine the repeat flowering of Chinas with the large flowers of European varieties. Hybrid perpetuals' exact parentage is uncertain, although it may include **Portland**, **Bourbon**, and **damask** stock.

hybrid tea: A class of roses first created during the nineteenth century by crossing a **tea rose** and a **hybrid perpetual**. These are considered the first **modern roses**.

introduce: To announce the commercial availability of a new rose variety

known variety: Any **species** or **cultivar** that has been recorded in botanical literature or in nursery catalogs.

modern rose: A variety in any class introduced from 1867 onward

moss rose: A class descended from **sports** of **centifolia** or **damask** roses that was first recorded in the early eighteenth century. Mosslike green glands cover the buds.

musk rose: The extraordinarily fragrant species *R. moschata*

nematode: A microscopic worm that feeds off rose roots, stunting growth and causing **dieback** or root rot

Noisette: A class of roses first bred in South Carolina around 1802 by crossing the **musk rose** and a **China**

old garden rose: Any rose of a class in existence prior to 1867 (the year when some rosarians claim that the first **hybrid tea** was introduced)

polyantha: A class of **modern roses** with clusters of small flowers originally produced by crossing a **China** with a dwarf strain of the species *R. multiflora*

Portland rose: The earliest class of **everblooming rose** bred from a cross between **China roses** and various European roses

prickle: A superficial growth on a stem, which can easily be detached. The correct term for what is often mistakenly called a rose "thorn." See **thorn.**

rambler: A climbing rose with long supple canes, the majority of which emerge from the base of the plant. Ramblers usually bloom only once a season.

repeat-flowering: Blooming more than once during the growing season

rootstock (understock): A strong, vigorous rose plant onto whose root system the stem of another rose variety is grafted

rosarian: A gardener or horticulturist who specializes in roses

rose rustler: A collector of old garden roses who scouts for neglected and generally forgotten varieties

rugosa: A class of roses with wrinkled leaves descended from the Asian species *R. rugosa*

seedling: A new rose variety cultivated from a seed

semi-double: A rose flower with seven to twenty-four petals

sepal: One of the cluster of leaflike structures that enclose the flower bud

shrub rose: An enormous, loosely defined class of rosebushes with attractive growth habits, whether upright or ground hugging

single: A rose flower with four or five petals

species: A variety that occurs naturally in the wild and remains true to type when grown from seed

sport: A mutation that occurs when one of the branches on a plant differs from the rest of the plant. A plant grown from this genetically altered branch is also termed a sport.

sucker: A new cane that emerges from the root of a rose and forms another plant

tea rose: A class of Asian roses first brought to Europe during the early nineteenth century on clipper ships used in the tea trade. More cold sensitive than a **China rose**.

thorn: A modified branch composed of the same material as the stem of a plant. A thorn is more difficult to remove from a stem than a **prickle**. Roses produce prickles, not thorns.

understock: See **rootstock**.

volunteer: A **seedling** that sprouts unexpectedly and in a random location

wichurana: Either the low-growing Japanese species *R. wichurana* (aka 'Memorial Rose') or a hybrid bred from it

SELECTED BIBLIOGRAPHY

Austin, David. *The Heritage of the Rose.* Easthampton, Mass.: Antique Collectors' Club, 1988.

Beales, Peter. *Classic Roses.* New York: Henry Holt, 1997.

Bermuda Rose Society. *Roses in Bermuda.* Hamilton, Bermuda: Bermudian Publishing Co., 1997.

Breck, Joseph. *The Flower Garden; or, Breck's Book of Flowers.* Boston: Jewett & Company, 1851.

Buist, Robert. *American Flower-Garden Directory.* New York: Orange Judd, 1865.

———. *The Rose Manual.* 1844. Reprint, New York: Coleman, 1978.

Bunyard, Edward A. *Old Garden Roses.* New York: Charles Scribner's Sons, 1937.

Christopher, Thomas. *In Search of Lost Roses.* New York: Summit Books, 1989.

Coats, Peter. *Roses.* London: Weidenfeld & Nicolson, 1970.

Dickerson, Brent C. *The Old Rose Adventurer.* Portland, Ore.: Timber Press, 1999.

———. *The Old Rose Advisor.* Portland, Ore.: Timber Press, 1992.

———. *The Old Rose Informant.* Lincoln, Neb.: Authors Choice Press, 2000.

———. *Roll Call: The Old Rose Breeder.* Lincoln, Neb.: Authors Choice Press, 2000.

Drennan, Georgia Torrey. *Everblooming Roses.* New York: Duffield & Company, 1912.

Ellwanger, H. B. *The Rose.* New York: Dodd, Mead & Co., 1892.

Forestier, Jean C. N. *Bagatelle et ses jardins.* Paris: Maison Rustique, 1910.

Gerard, John. *Gerard's Herball.* 1636. Reprint, London: Spring Books, 1964.

Gordon, Jean. *Immortal Roses.* Woodstock, Vt.: Red Rose Publications, 1959.

————. *Pageant of the Rose.* New York: Studio Publications and Thomas Y. Crowell, 1953.

Gravereaux, Jules. *"La Malmaison." Les roses de l'impératrice Joséphine.* Paris: Editions d'Art et de Littérature, 1912.

Hanbury, William. *A Complete Body of Planting and Gardening.* London, 1770–1771.

Harkness, Peter. *The Rose: An Illustrated History.* Buffalo, N.Y.: Firefly Books, 2003.

Hedrick, Ulysses Prentiss, and Elisabeth Woodburn. *A History of Horticulture in America to 1860 with an Addendum of Books Published from 1861–1920.* Portland, Ore.: Timber Press, 1988.

Hibberd, Shirley. *The Amateur's Rose Book.* London: Groombridge & Sons, 1874.

Hole, Samuel Reynolds. *A Book about Roses: How to Grow and Show Them.* London: William Blackwood & Sons, 1869.

Jekyll, Gertrude, and Edward Mawley. *Roses.* Salem, N.H.: Ayer Co., 1983. Originally published as *Roses for English Gardens.* London: Country Life, 1902.

Joyaux, François. *La rose, une passion française.* Brussels: Editions Complexe, 2001.

————. *Les roses de l'impératrice.* Brussels: Editions Complexe, 2005.

Keays, Ethelyn Emery Keays. *Old Roses.* New York: Macmillan, 1935.

Krussmann, Gerd. *The Complete Book of Roses.* Portland, Ore.: Timber Press, 1981.

Lacy, Allen. *The Glory of Roses.* New York: Stewart, Tabori & Chang, 1990.

Leighton, Ann. *Early American Gardens: "For Meate or Medicine."* Amherst: University of Massachusetts Press, 1986.

Le Rougetel, Hazel. *A Heritage of Roses.* Owings Mills, Md.: Stemmer House, 1988.

McCann, Sean. *The Rose: An Encyclopedia of North American Roses, Rosarians, and Rose Lore.* Mechanicsburg, Pa.: Stackpole Books.

McFarland, J. Horace. *Memoirs of a Rose Man: Tales from Breeze Hill.* Emmaus, Pa.: Rodale Press, 1949.

————. *Roses of the World in Color.* New York: Houghton Mifflin, 1938.

McGredy, Sam, and Seán Jennett. *A Family of Roses.* London: Garden Book Club, 1972.

Miller, Philip. *The Gardeners Dictionary.* London: John and James Rivington, 1754.

Morrison, Ernest. *J. Horace McFarland: A Thorn for Beauty.* Harrisburg: Pennsylvania Historical and Museum Commission, 1995.

Musgrave, Toby, Will Musgrave, and Chris Gardner. *The Plant Hunters*. London: Seven Dials, Cassell & Co., 1999.

Nicolas, J. H. *A Rose Odyssey*. New York: Doubleday, Doran & Co., 1937.

Parkinson, John. *A Garden of Pleasant Flowers*. 1629. Reprint, New York: Dover, 1976.

Parsons, Samuel B. *Parsons on the Rose*. New York: Orange Judd & Co., 1869.

Paul, William. *The Rose Garden*. 1848. Reprint, New York: Coleman, 1978.

Pavord, Anna. *The Naming of Names: The Search for Order in the World of Plants*. New York: Bloomsbury Publishing, 2005.

Pemberton, J. H. *Roses: Their History, Development and Cultivation*. London: Longmans, Green, 1908.

Phillips, Roger, and Martyn Rix. *The Quest for the Rose*. London: BBC Books, 1993.

Prince, William Robert. *Prince's Manual of Roses*. 1846. Reprint, New York: Coleman, 1979.

Redouté, Pierre Joseph. *Les roses*. Paris: Imprimerie de Firmin Didot, 1817–24.

Ridge, Antonia. *For Love of a Rose: Story of the Creation of the Famous Peace Rose*. Boston: Faber Paperbacks, 1979.

Rimmel, Eugene. *The Book of Perfumes*. London: Chapman & Hall, 1865.

Saxton, Charles M. *The American Rose Culturist*. New York: Saxton, 1857.

Scanniello, Stephen, and Tania Bayard. *Climbing Roses*. New York: Prentice Hall, 1994.

———. *Roses of America*. New York: Henry Holt, 1990.

Shepherd, Roy E. *History of the Rose*. New York: Macmillan, 1954.

Shoup, G. Michael. *Roses in the Southern Garden*. Brenham, Tex.: Antique Rose Emporium, 2000.

Stuart, Andrea. *The Rose of Martinique: A Life of Napoleon's Josephine*. New York: Grove Press, 2003.

Thomas, George Clifford. *The Practical Book of Outdoor Rose Growing for the Home Garden*. Philadelphia: J. B. Lippincott, 1914.

Thomas, Graham Stuart. *The Graham Stuart Thomas Rose Book*. Portland, Ore.: Sagapress/ Timber Press, 1994.

Valder, Peter. *The Garden Plants of China*. Portland, Ore.: Timber Press, 1999.

Weber, Bruce, *American Beauty: The Rose in American Art, 1800–1920*. New York: Berry-Hill Galleries, 1997.

Wells, Robert W. *Papa Floribunda: A Biography of Eugene S. Boerner*. Milwaukee: BBG Publishing, 1989.

Wheatcroft, Harry. *In Praise of Roses*. London: Barrie & Jenkins, 1970.

Wilder, Louise Beebe. *The Fragrant Path: A Book about Sweet Scented Flowers and Leaves*. New York: Macmillan, 1936. Reprint, Point Roberts, Wash.: Hartley & Marks, 1966.

Wilson, Helen Van Pelt, and Léonie Bell. *The Fragrant Year*. New York: Bonanza Books, 1968.

Periodicals

The American Rose Annual, 1916– .

American Rose Magazine. 1933– .

The Botanical Magazine. 1787–1800.

Combined Rose List. 2007.

Journal des Roses. 1877–1914.

Modern Roses. 1930– .

Rosa Mundi: Journal of the Heritage Rose Foundation. 2005– .

The Rose Annual of the National Rose Society. 1907–1966.

The Yellow Rose. 1984– .

Web Site

www.HelpMeFind.com/Roses   This site has cataloged more than thirty-one thousand roses with historical references to plant names, breeders, and rose literature.

PICTURE CREDITS

Page 7:   *American Beauty Roses* by Paul de Longpré, 1896.

Page 10:   Photograph of Lillian Russell by W. M. Morrison, c. 1893. Library of Congress, Prints & Photographs Division

Page 16:   'Apothecary's Rose' ('Rose de Provins ordinaire') from *Roses et rosiers* by E. Donnaoud, 1873

Page 18:   Eastman's Wild Rose Extract promotional bookmark, late nineteenth century

Page 21:   'Baltimore Belle' from *Best Michigan Fruits*, late nineteenth century

Page 25:   'Barbra Streisand' © Gene Sasse, courtesy Weeks Roses

Page 27:   Photograph of Greer Garson, c. 1944. Herald-Examiner Collection/Los Angeles Public Library

Page 35:   'Blaze' from Jackson & Perkins Co. wholesale nursery catalog, fall 1932

Page 39:   Borden's Darling Milk label, late nineteenth century

Page 41:   Photograph of Mary Margaret McBride from Jackson & Perkins Co. nursery catalog, 1942

Page 42:   'Cabbage Rose' by Pierre Joseph Redouté, from *Traité des arbres et arbustes que l'on cultive en France en plein terre* by Henri-Louis Duhamel du Monceau, 1801–19. New York Public Library, Digital Collection

Page 47:   *Cherokee Roses on a Purple Velvet Cloth* by Martin Johnson Heade, 1894. Courtesy Berry-Hill Galleries

Page 48:   *The Trail of Tears* by Robert Lindneux, 1942. The Granger Collection

Page 50:   Everblooming ("ever-blowing") China rose from *The Botanical Magazine*, 1794

Page 53:   'Bengal Rose' ('Rosier du Bengale') from *Roses et rosiers* by E. Donnaoud, 1873

Page 57:   Chrysler Imperial advertisement, 1952. Courtesy Chrysler LLC

Page 59:   'Thomas A. Edison' from Conard-Pyle Co. nursery catalog, spring 1932

Page 63:   'Constance Spry' © Kent Krugh

Page 67:   Photograph of Constance Spry. Robertstock.com

Page 71:   Damask rose by Anne-Marie Trechslin, from *Roses* by Eric Bois and Anne-Marie Trechslin, 1962

Page 73:   Woman with rose from *The Book of Perfumes* by Eugene Rimmel, 1865

Page 75:   'Persian Yellow' from *The Rose Garden* by William Paul, 1848

Page 77:   'Dr. Huey' from *Roses of the World in Color* by J. Horace McFarland, 1938

Page 80:   Photograph of Robert Huey from *American Rose Annual*, 1922

Page 83:   Photograph of J. H. Nicolas from *The Rose Manual* by Jean Henri Nicolas, 1934

Page 86:   Double eglantine (*Rosa rubiginosa*, 'Double Red Sweet Brier') by Mary Lawrance, from *A Collection of Roses from Nature* by Mary Lawrance, 1799. New York Public Library, Digital Collection

Page 93:   'Empress Josephine' ('Rosier de Francfort') by Pierre Joseph Redouté, from *Les roses* by Pierre Joseph Redouté and Claude-Antoine Thory, 1817. Library of Congress, Rare Book & Special Collections

Page 94:   Malmaison gardens from *"La Malmaison" les roses de l'imperatrice Joséphine* by Jules Gravereaux, 1912

Page 99:   'The Fairy' © Stephen Scanniello

Page 101:   Rose wreath by Mary Lawrance, from *A Collection of Roses from Nature* by Mary Lawrance, 1799. New York Public Library, Digital Collection

Page 104:   *The Rosy Wreath of June* by Henri Fantin-Latour, 1881. The Granger Collection

Page 111:   'Fashion' from Star Roses nursery catalog, fall 1949

Page 113:   *Rosa centifolia* from *The Flowers Personified* by J. J. Grandville, 1847

Page 114:   'Madame Caroline Testout' from Robert Scott & Son nursery catalog, 1894

Page 117:   'Fortune's Five-colored Rose' ('Rosa indica à cinq couleurs') from *Rosen-Album* by Ferentzel Komlosy, 1868. © Limberlost Roses, 2007

Page 121:   Photograph of Ernest Henry Wilson from *Aristocrats of the Garden* by Ernest Henry Wilson, 1926

Page 125:   'Frau Karl Druschki' from *Roses of the World in Color* by J. Horace McFarland, 1938

Page 126:   'Madame Grégoire Staechelin' from Star Roses nursery catalog, 1932

Page 129:   'Gloire de Dijon' from unknown publication, late nineteenth century

Page 134:   'Gourmet Popcorn' © Gene Sasse, courtesy Weeks Roses

Page 137:   'Double Cinnamon Rose' by Georg Dionysius Ehret, from *Hortvs nitidissimis* by Christoph Jacob Trew, 1768–86. New York Public Library, Digital Collection

Page 139:   'Green Rose' ('Rose Verte') from *Roses et rosiers* by E. Donnaoud, 1873

Page 142:   'Violet Blue' from Miss Ella V. Baines, The Woman Florist, nursery catalog, spring 1910

Page 145:   'Hebe's Lip' from *The Genus Rosa*, vol. 2, by Ellen Willmott, 1914. Courtesy The Phillip and Jeannette Schorr Rose Research Library at the American Rose Center

Page 146:   'Hebe's Cup' ('Coupe d'Hébé') from *The Rose Garden* by William Paul, 1848

Page 149:   Photograph of Helen Keller, c. 1907. Library of Congress, Prints & Photographs Division

Page 150:   'Mademoiselle de Sombreuil' ('Thé Sombreuil'), from *Le journal des roses et des vergers. Revue des jardins*, 4, 1857. Courtesy Bibliothèque Nationale de France

Page 156:   *Rosa sancta* from *The Genus Rosa*, vol. 2, by Ellen Willmott, 1914. Courtesy the Phillip and Jeannette Schorr Rose Research Library at the American Rose Center

Page 161:   'Ayrshire Rose' ('Rosier Ayrshire') from *Roses et rosiers* by E. Donnaoud, 1873

Page 164:   Irish single roses from *Roses of the World in Color* by J. Horace McFarland, 1938

Page 167:   'Jardins de Bagatelle' © Jean Sasse, courtesy Weeks Roses

Page 168:   Bagatelle, 1933, from *The Rose Odyssey* by Jean Henri Nicolas, 1937

Page 171:   'Madame Jules Gravereaux' from *Journal des roses*, 1903. © Limberlost Roses, 2007

Page 177:   *Just Joey Roses* by Karen Armitage. The Bridgeman Art Library

Page 178:   Guillot nursery, early twentieth century. Courtesy Roseraie Guillot

Page 180:   'Félicité Perpétue' from *Revue de l'horticulture Belge et étranger*, date unknown

Page 183:   'Maiden's Blush' ('Rosier blanc Royal') by Pierre Joseph Redouté, from *Les roses* by Pierre Joseph Redouté and Claude-Antoine Thory, 1817. Library of Congress, Rare Book & Special Collections

Page 185:   'Mary Washington' © Kent Krugh

Page 186:   Gardens at Mount Vernon from *The Home of Washington* by Benson J. Lossing, 1870

Page 189:   Advertisement from *Ladies' Home Journal*, March 1896

Page 190:   'Souvenir d'un Ami' from *The Beauties of the Rose*, vol. 2, by Henry Curtis, 1853

Page 195:   'New Dawn' by Anne-Marie Trechslin, from *Roses* by Eric Bois and Anne-Marie Trechslin, 1962

Page 266: Grasse perfume factory, late nineteenth century. The Granger Collection

Page 269: 'Tournament of Roses' © Gene Sasse, courtesy Weeks Roses

Page 270: Rose Parade, 1905. Herald-Examiner Collection/Los Angeles Public Library

Page 277: 'Droopy-leaved Rose' (*Rosa clinophylla*) from *Edwards's Botanical Register*, 1823

Page 279: 'Harison's Yellow' from Taft Nursery catalog, late nineteenth century

Page 285: 'York and Lancaster' from *Roses of the World in Color* by J. Horace McFarland, 1938

Page 286: Portrait of Elizabeth of York and Henry VII from *Memoirs of the Court of Queen Elizabeth*, by Sarah, Countess of Essex, 1825. Private collection/The Stapleton Collection/The Bridgeman Art Library.

FRONT JACKET (clockwise from top left):

'Apple Rose' by Mary Lawrance, from *A Collection of Roses from Nature* by Mary Lawrance, 1799. New York Public Library, Digital Collection

'Hedgehog Rose', ibid.

'Cabbage Rose' by Pierre Joseph Redouté, from *Traité des arbres et arbustes que l'on cultive en France en pleine terre* by Henri-Louis Duhamel du Monceau, 1801–19. New York Public Library, Digital Collection

'Rose des Peintres' from *Choix des plus belles roses*, 1855

'Bengal Rose' from *Roses et rosiers* by E. Donnaoud, 1873

'Souvenir d'un Ami' from *The Beauties of the Rose*, vol. 2, by Henry Curtis, 1853

Damask rose by Anne-Marie Trechslin, from *Roses* by Eric Bois and Anne-Marie Trechslin, 1962

'Apothecary's Rose' from *Roses et rosiers* by E. Donnaoud, 1873

JACKET FLAP

Rosa centifolia 'Pomponia' by Mary Lawrance, from *A Collection of Roses from Nature* by Mary Lawrance, 1799. New York Public Library, Digital Collection

BACK JACKET

'Empress Joséphine' by Pierre Joseph Redouté, from *Les roses* by Pierre Joseph Redouté and Claude-Antoine Thory, 1817. Library of Congress, Rare Book & Special Collections

'Baltimore Belle' from *Best Michigan Fruits,* late nineteenth century

'Rosa mundi' from *Curtis's Botanical Magazine,* 1816

'Maiden's Blush' by Pierre Joseph Redouté, from *Les roses* by Pierre Joseph Redouté and Claude-Antoine Thory, 1817. Library of Congress, Rare Book & Special Collections

INDEX